FAITH, ETHICS AND CHURCH
WRITING IN ENGLAND, 1360–1409

The relationship between versions of the late medieval Church, faith, ethics and the lay powers, as explored in a range of late fourteenth- and early fifteenth-century texts written in England, is the subject of this book. It argues that they disclose strikingly diverse models of Christian discipleship, and examines the sources and consequences of such differences. Issues investigated include whether the Church could shape modern communities and individual identities, and how it could combine its status as a major landlord and trader without being assimilated by the various networks of earthly power and profit. The book begins with Chaucer's treatment of received versions of faith, ethics and the Church, and moves via St Thomas, Ockham, Nicholas Love, Gower, the *Gawain*-poet and Langland to Wyclif's construal of Christian discipleship in relation to his projected reform of the Church. Interdisciplinary in approach, the book will be of interest to all those studying late medieval Christianity and literature.

DAVID AERS is James B. Duke Professor of English and Professor of Historical Theology at Duke University.

FAITH, ETHICS AND CHURCH

WRITING IN ENGLAND, 1360–1409

David Aers

D.S. BREWER

First published 2000
D. S. Brewer, Cambridge

ISBN 0 85991 561 1

D. S. Brewer is an imprint of Boydell & Brewer Ltd
PO Box 9, Woodbridge, Suffolk IP12 3DF, UK
and of Boydell & Brewer Inc.
PO Box 41026, Rochester, NY 14604–4126, USA
website: http://www.boydell.co.uk

A catalogue record of this publication is available
from the British Library

Library of Congress Cataloging-in-Publication data
Aers, David,
    Faith, ethics, and church: writing in England, 1360–1409/David Aers.
        p. cm.
    Includes bibliographical references and index.
    ISBN 0-85991-561-1 (alk. paper)
    1. Christian life – England – History – To 1500. 2. England – Church history – 1066–1485.
3. Christian literature, English (Middle) – History and criticism. I. Title.
BR750 .A34 2000
274.2'05–dc21   99-045714

This publication is printed on acid-free paper

Typeset by Joshua Associates Ltd, Oxford
Printed in Great Britain by
Antony Rowe Ltd.

Contents

Introduction

'What is holy churche, chere frende?' quod y; 'Charite,' he saide;
'Lif in loue and leutee in o byleue and lawe,
A loueknotte of leutee and of lele byleue,
Alle kyne cristene cleuynge on o will,
Withoute gyle and gabbyng gyue and sulle and lene.'
(William Langland, Piers Plowman)[1]

In these lines from the C version of *Piers Plowman* Liberum Arbitrium answers the questioner ("y," or Will). Liberum Arbitrium is not only Christ's creature but kin to Christ, at home in Christ's court where his voice is known and welcomed by all. Not surprisingly then, he knows Conscience and Clergy well (XVII.158–72). A herald of the Good Samaritan, he reminds the wanderer (dreamer and reader) that any search for Charity is bound to the search for Holy Church. The Church unifies human love, faith ("byleue"), and will, shaping the virtues in social practices that are distinctly Christian ("Fayth withouten feet is feblere then nauht/ And as ded as a dore nayl but yf þe dede folowe," I.182–83). Such a vision will not finally sustain any attempt to represent the Christian as an isolated will, an individual whose salvation could be understood in abstraction from the web of relationships, narratives, and sacraments that constitute the Church. It opposes the splitting apart of interiority and practice, of reason, faith, and authority. Being opposed to such splittings does not, of course, mean being blind to their presence and persuasiveness. On the contrary, as *Piers Plowman* demonstrates with remarkable force, it should mean being acutely sensitive to their sources and manifestations. But such discernment cannot be from no place:

> And thenne cam kynde wit Conscience to teche
> And cryede and comaundede alle cristene peple
> To deluen a dich depe aboute vnite
> That holi church stoede in holinesse as hit a pyle were (XXI.360–63).

The need for such a place informs the teaching of Liberum Arbitrium.

Indeed, his statement to Will may seem an unsurprising, if elegant, expression

---

[1] William Langland, *Piers Plowman: The C Version*, ed. George Russell and George Kane (London: Athlone Press, 1997). All quotations in the Introduction are to this version of *Piers Plowman*. Here see C XVII.125–130.

of familiar medieval teaching. Yet its contexts are a passus that follows an especially powerful critique of the contemporary Church and a poem that concludes with a vision of this Church apparently under the domination of Antichrist's forces. So while it remains a memorable expression of familiar instruction, considering it in context, readers have much difficult interpretive work on their hands: how do such expressions of tradition fare in the poem as a whole and in the contemporary Church where the words are written? How does the life of Christian discipleship and virtues relate to the contemporary Church so strenuously analyzed and criticized in the poem? Variants of these questions are considered in chapter 3. Here I wish to draw attention to another aspect of Will's questions: "What is holy churche, chere frende?" The one who asks this is a baptized Christian who had a vision of Holy Church in the first passus, and since then he has traveled sixteen passus towards old age and death. For some readers the fact that the question is asked, let alone that it is asked at this stage of the journey, may seem another obvious sign of Will's inadequacies. This is a rather comfortable judgment, shoring up the reader's superiority to Will – she or he, unlike Will, surely knows the correct answer. But, like so many comfortingly secure judgments in *Piers Plowman*, it is unwarranted. Will has recently been traveling as a pilgrim with Conscience and Patience, eating the bread of Scripture and repentance (XV–XVI), and he will soon receive profoundly illuminating visions of Christ and salvation history, including the gifts of the Holy Spirit in the early Church. His question is taken with utter seriousness by Liberum Arbitrium and, as I have observed, it has actually been provoked by the account of the Church offered in the previous passus – by Liberum Arbitrium himself. The situation is not as dire as the one lamented by a later English poet who renounced his adherence to the Roman Church:

> Show me dear Christ, thy spouse, so bright and clear.
> What, is it she, which on the other shore
> Goes richly painted? Or which robbed and tore
> Laments and mourns in Germany and here?
> Sleeps she a thousand, then peeps up one year?
> Is she self truth and errs? now new, now outwore?[2]

But Langland's own Church had two popes who declared crusades against each other, financed with the help of indulgences, and from the late 1370s was being represented by John Wyclif (and his followers) as under the dominion of Antichrist. (These contexts are addressed in chapter 6.) While such events may tell us little about *Piers Plowman*, they at least remind us of extraordinary and disturbing aspects of the situation within which later-fourteenth-century works were written. Liberum Arbitrium himself, in the version of the poem habitually (but prematurely) assumed to be more "conservative" than its predecessors,

---

[2] John Donne, "Holy Sonnet 18," in *John Donne*, ed. John Carey (Oxford: Oxford University Press, 1990), 288.

proclaims that if "knythoed and kynde wit and þe comune and consience/ Togederes louyen lelelyche" then the Church will be disendowed, thus purging the poison drunk by the Church when "Constantyn of cortesye holy kirke dowede" and providing the necessary "medecyne" for the contemporary Church. Indeed, the peace of Christ now demands that priests should be forced to "lyue by dymes" alone:

> The heuedes of holy churche and tho that ben vnder hem,
> Hit were charite to deschargen hem for holy churches sake,
> And purge hem of þe olde poysen Ar more perel falle
> (See XVII.216–32).

That the urgency in the incitements and their content is a major strand in Wyclif's project of reformation certainly does not entail Langland's convergence with that project (chapter 3 and chapter 6). But it exemplifies something of the common concerns, common discourses, and analysis that this book explores. In the final passus of *Piers Plowman* Conscience cries out that without the help of Clergie he falls "Thorw inparfite prestes and prelates of holy churche" (XXII.238–39). He repeats the call later only to be told by Pees, the gatekeeper, that the Christian people have been so enchanted by their confessors that they "drat no synne" (XXII.375–79). This is a culmination to a vision that "in mannes fourme" Antichrist came to the Church and destroyed "al the crop of treuthe," making "fals sprynge and spede menne nedes" (XXII.51–55). In such circumstances it is certainly not only an inadequate or foolish Will that will ask, "What is holy churche?" Nor is it only those whose commitment to the pursuit of worldly profits leads them to reject justice, conscience, and the eucharist (XXI.383–402) who will wonder what are the relations between ethics ("dowel"), faith, and the actually existing Church (chapters 1–3). On the contrary these questions are among the most generative and agonizing in *Piers Plowman*. Is it possible for the Church to play a prominent role in shaping and maintaining a political order in the fallen world without succumbing to the temptations of earthly power and arrogance which fall under the judgment of God in both Old and New Testaments?

While Langland explores these questions with an intelligence, intensity, and ruthlessness that is itself an act of faith, they are addressed in the work of many later fourteenth- and early-fifteenth-century writers in England. How certain versions of faith, versions of ethics, and versions of the Church are related is the subject of the present book. It sets out with Chaucer and concludes with Wyclif. On the way it goes across genres and brings together aspects of late-medieval culture, and questions in our own culture, that are often compartmentalized within different disciplines of the modern academy. How did Chaucer treat received versions of faith, ethics, and the Church? But how does one begin to address this question seriously without trying to engage with St. Thomas and Ockham, Wyclif, and John Ball? How did Wyclif, Langland's and Chaucer's contemporary, understand Christian discipleship as he sought to reform the Church in which he was priest and theologian? And with what consequences (chapter 6)? How did inherited forms of Christian ethics and politics fare in the face of apparently unprecedented conjunctures in England after the great plague? This question is among those put to Langland and Gower (chapters 3 and 5). How are the specifically courtly forms of Christianity we encounter in the works of the *Gawain*-poet understood in the ecclesiastic, theological, and ethical contexts that concern this book? As this issue is pursued it calls for reflection on the consequences of these courtly forms for the later-medieval Church and its lay elites' model of the virtues (chapters 4 and 5). Some of the questions discussed in this book are ones that Lynn Staley and I examined in *Powers of the Holy*, albeit they are taken here in more explicitly ecclesiological and theological directions; others were not within the scope of that book, but doubtless began to be formulated during that venture as topics I wanted to explore.[3]

In the Introduction to *Powers of the Holy* Lynn Staley and I noted that "it is doubtful that either of us would have written alone what we have written together. This conversation is a testament to how much we scholars need to speak openly with one another; it has brought home the true value of creating scholarly communities held together by . . . a friendship of common goals."[4] Although this is a single-author book, I am very aware that it participates in a range of conversations in the modern academy, ones often being conducted across departments. As Charles Taylor argued in *Sources of the Self*, "a self only exists among other selves"; "My self-definition is understood as an answer to the question Who I am. And this question finds its original sense in the interchange of speakers." This, Taylor remarks, is true of "our languages of moral and spiritual discernment." We learn these "by being brought into an ongoing conversation."[5] One simply cannot be "a self on one's own," not even in an academy where illusions of autonomy and individualism are often assiduously cultivated. "I am a self only in relation to certain interlocutors: in one way in relation to those conversation partners who were essential to my achieving self-definition; in another in relation to those who are now crucial to my continuing grasp of languages of self-understanding . . . A self exists only within what I call 'webs of interlocution.'"[6] So this book, like any other,

---

[3] Aers and Staley, *The Powers of the Holy: Religion, Politics, and Gender in Late Medieval English Culture* (University Park: Pennsylvania State University Press, 1996).

[4] Aers and Staley, *The Powers of the Holy*, 11.

[5] Charles Taylor, *Sources of the Self: The Making of Modern Identity* (Cambridge, Mass.: Harvard University Press, 1989), 35. Although Taylor himself does not do so, writing as a philosopher and not a theologian, these formulations, for anyone within Christian traditions, will call out for theological reflections on the creating and redeeming Word, perhaps along lines suggested by Robert W. Jenson, *Systematic Theology*, vol. 1 (New York: Oxford University Press, 1997), chaps. 5–6 and vol. 2 (New York: Oxford University Press, 1999), chapters 17–18.

[6] Taylor, *Sources of the Self*, 36.

participates in "webs of interlocution" that include present contexts together with past ones. Thus, for example, chapters 1 and 2 include arguments directed against certain ways in which faith and ethics are currently construed in Chaucer studies. Such arguments bear witness to the existence of scholarly communities in which articulation and exploration of differences is part of the way such communities are held together; we hope, and often find, that as sharp oppositions are addressed there will emerge "a friendship of common goals." That this is probably less likely to be recognized in a postmodern academy than in a medieval university gives me no reason for abandoning the model to which such language belongs. Furthermore, the "webs of interlocution" I am conscious of in writing this book include ones going beyond medieval studies and beyond departments of English. This will probably be most obvious in chapter 6, but has been true of a considerable amount of the book's work. They also include, however notoriously problematic the claim, the dead. Certainly those about whom I write, and especially those who have shaped and enabled the traditions out of which I write: to them, gratitude.

Gratitude also to those who have helped me do the thinking and questioning that shape this book. Most frequent and present of my interlocutors has been Sarah Beckwith. Our conversations about medieval and modern Christianity, literature, theory, and history go back to 1982 and have been greatly facilitated by working in the same university since 1995. I reckon that all the arguments in this book have been tried out at some point with her – which is not to shuffle off responsibility for the outcome. Lynn Staley and Stanley Hauerwas have been important interlocutors throughout this project; I can only hope that I have learnt something from their intellectual generosity, knowledge, and wisdom. Alasdair MacIntyre read an early version of chapter 1 and his work (which I began reading in graduate school) has been a continuing presence, challenge, and inspiration. By now, the voice of my teacher Derek Pearsall has become an internalized questioner. With Elizabeth Salter he directed my doctoral dissertation and gave me a model of the ways in which teaching can become friendship. Others whom I wish to thank for reading or discussing parts of this book are Allen Frantzen, Katherine Little, Lee Patterson, Paul Strohm, Winthrop Wetherbee, Bob Yeager, and Nicky Zeeman. I also thank the admirable graduate students in medieval studies with whom I have worked at Duke University. Their intelligence, commitment to a theoretically informed historicism, and ability to engage seriously with religious discourses, together with their ability to create a mutually supportive community, have been delightful. I would especially like to thank Katie Little who has been an ideal research assistant while completing an outstanding thesis on religious conflict in late-medieval England; my debts to her are very great.* Finally, I thank my closest friend, Christine Derham, who is also my wife.

* I would also like to thank Rebekah Long who greatly helped with the final stages of the project.

    The earliest piece of writing in this book is chapter 3, now revised from its original appearance in a collection of essays on *The Work of Work* (Glasgow: Cruithne Press, 1994). Earlier versions of chapters 1 and 5 appeared in 1998 and 1999, while the first section of chapter 4 appeared in *A Companion to the "Gawain"-Poet* (Cambridge: Brewer, 1997). Scattered as the publication of these essays have been, they are part of the project that is this book, one that points towards further explorations of the Church and Christianity in late-medieval England. I thank the following for permission to use materials: *Journal of Medieval and Early Modern Studies* (for material in chapters 1 and 2), Cruithne Press (for material in chapter 3), Boydell & Brewer Ltd (for material in chapter 4), and Pegasus Press (for material in chapter 5).

1

Faith, Ethics, and Communities

Be three things man stondith in this life, be which three God is worshippid
and we be spedid, kept, and savid. The first is use of manys reason naturall.
The second is commen teching of Holy Church. The thred is inward, gracious
werkyng of the Holy Gost. And these three ben all of one God: God is the
ground of our kindly reason, and God, the teaching of Holy Church, and God
is the Holy Gost.   (Julian of Norwich, *The Shewings*)[1]

In the epigraph to this chapter Julian of Norwich reflects on the worship of God
and the salvation of humans. She determines that the divine gifts necessary for
salvation include reason, faith as taught by Holy Church, and the inward
processes of sanctification which are the Holy Spirit's working. In the
continuation of this passage, she observes that these gifts may now only yield
a little knowing. But faith *is* a "knowing" and that knowing, however little, is
enough. Nearing the end of her great visionary and theological work, she affirms
that all these gifts in us are Christ's agency (chapter 80). Humans need all three
to be kept and saved. For Julian, the contrast is between the "little knowing" we
have here and the "fullhede in hevyn"; it is not between reason and faith, nor
between the faith taught in the visible Catholic Church and the visionary's
individual leap across the river, the leap attempted by the dreamer towards the
end of the contemporary poem *Pearl*. Could Julian's position be sustained in
late-fourteenth-century England outside her own extraordinary, subtle, and
distinctive theological work?[2] In many ways, Julian's questions and explorations
inform the questions that are pursued in this book, however different the modes
of inquiry and however alien the context.

I have chosen to set out from within the field of Chaucer studies, currently
dominating medieval literary studies. There it dominates the undergraduate
curriculum, graduate studies, and current publications. As such, it is a good
indication of common assumptions in the field, including ones about Christian
faith and ethics in late medieval England, my own concerns here. This chapter
examines some of these assumptions, juxtaposing them with texts from the
medieval Christianity they claim to represent. Through the juxtaposition I open

---

[1] Ed. G. R. Crampton (Kalamazoo, 1993), chap. 80, p. 149.
[2] Aers and Staley, *The Powers of the Holy: Religion, Politics and Gender in Late Medieval Culture*
(University Park: Pennsylvania State University Press, 1996), chaps. 3 and 4.

out considerations of faith and ethics in Chaucer's writing to be pursued in the second chapter. This moves rather against the grain of Chaucer studies at the time I write. It seems that since the demise of Robertsonianism in the later 1970s and early 1980s the most influential and intellectually searching works on Chaucer have not been greatly interested in what is specifically Christian about the poetry, its culture, and its questions. Prevalent critical paradigms, including those that are historicizing, have tended to sideline (not simply ignore) distinctively Christian practices, ideas, and difficulties. In works of great critical force, from a variety of ideological dispositions, Christianity has been either marginalized or briskly subjected to the master discourse of psychoanalysis, usually in some version of Lacan.[3] While I believe this to be an accurate characterization of the work that has dominated Chaucerian studies over the last decade or so, Robertsonianism's space has not remained vacant – the field, after all, abhors a vacuum. There are certainly Chaucerians for whom Christian doctrine, devotion, and spirituality are of paramount concern. The form such criticism currently takes can be represented by a book published in 1990 and now widely referred to by those who discuss the relations between Chaucer's writing and late medieval Christianity. The volume is entitled *Chaucer's Religious Tales*, edited by C. David Benson and Elizabeth Robertson.[4] My own project leads me to put some questions to this and like-minded studies: What is the version of Christian faith that this work composes? And what are the ethical and political implications of this composition? Does it represent late-medieval Christianity as adequately as it claims to do? Does it represent the relations

---

[3] The works I have in mind are the following: Susan Crane, *Gender and Romance in Chaucer's Canterbury Tales* (Princeton: Princeton University Press, 1993); Carolyn Dinshaw, *Chaucer's Sexual Poetics* (Madison: University of Wisconsin Press, 1989); Elaine Tuttle Hansen, *Chaucer and the Fictions of Gender* (Berkeley: University of California Press, 1992); H. Marshall Leicester, *The Disenchanted Self: Representing the Subject in the "Canterbury Tales"* (Berkeley: University of California Press, 1990); Lee Patterson, *Chaucer and the Subject of History* (Madison: University of Wisconsin Press, 1991); Paul Strohm, *Social Chaucer* (Cambridge, Mass.: Harvard University Press, 1989); Strohm, *Hochon's Arrow: The Social Imagination of Fourteenth-Century Texts* (Princeton: Princeton University Press, 1992); David Wallace, *Chaucerian Polity: Absolutist Lineages and Associational Forms in England and Italy* (Stanford: Stanford University Press, 1997). For an excellent characterization of "Robertsonianism," see Lee Patterson, *Negotiating the Past: The Historical Understanding of Medieval Literature* (Madison: University of Wisconsin Press, 1987), 20–39; also see the trenchant essay by Derek Pearsall, "Chaucer's Poetry and its Modern Commentators," chap. 7 in *Medieval Literature: Criticism, Ideology, and History*, ed. David Aers (New York: St. Martin's Press, 1986).
[4] *Chaucer's Religious Tales*, ed. C. David Benson and Elizabeth Robertson (Cambridge: Brewer, 1990). There are many and assorted fellow-travelers, ranging from the sometimes subtle close readings of Jill Mann, *Geoffrey Chaucer* (Hemel Hempstead: Harvester, 1991) to pious readings which lack serious engagement with Chaucer's texts and late-medieval theology, a genre exemplified by Robert Boenig, *Chaucer and the Mystics: The "Canterbury Tales" and the Genre of Devotional Prose* (Lewisburg, Pa.: Bucknell University Press, 1995). Also relevant to these reflections are Roger Ellis, *Patterns of Religious Narrative in the "Canterbury Tales"* (Totowa: Barnes and Noble, 1986) and John M. Hill, *Chaucerian Belief* (New Haven: Yale University Press, 1991).

of Chaucer's work to contemporary Christianity as adequately as its often strikingly confident claims suggest?

In the introduction to *Chaucer's Religious Tales* David Benson asserts that while "virtually all" the *Canterbury Tales* could be called "religious," four tales are most especially "religious tales." These are the *Clerk's Tale*, the *Man of Law's Tale*, the *Prioress's Tale* and the *Second Nun's Tale*. What makes these works particularly "religious"? Benson's answer is reassuringly simple: "Because they celebrate an otherworldly spirituality instead of a more practical morality." They are "tales of transcendence," a term that for him, as later in the volume for Barbara Nolan, poses no epistemological questions at all.[5] How could this be so? The answer seems to reside in the claim that they are "the tales of faith and spirituality in the *Canterbury Tales*." They can be confidently classified as such because they allegedly affirm "unquestioning faith, obedience, passivity in the face of oppression and the acceptance of supernatural mystery."[6] And they do so, apparently, without a moment of critical reflection on this position. Such, Benson insists, is the authentic image of Christian spirituality in the Middle Ages. If readers wish to understand Chaucer's poetry in all its Christian depth, and in its historical otherness, they will accept Benson's claims about faith in the Middle Ages and use these as the grid through which to read Chaucer, now freed from the distortions of various anachronistic modernisms.

This line is supported by many of the contributors.[7] I will focus here on one who has since published an elaboration of her approach, Linda Georgianna. She presents herself as fighting a battle to free Chaucer from over three-and-a-half centuries of what she calls "Protestant" misreading. Those who illustrate this deviation included John Foxe, Lounsbury, Donaldson, Robertson, Fleming, and possibly Pearsall. The virus of misreading reaches what she calls "its most virulent form" in Aers, so we can take her diagnosis of his writing to indicate her own norms, norms she assumes to be Chaucer's and those of all his Christian contemporaries. She believes that because Aers has a commitment to what she calls "rational belief" he "simply dismisses faith."[8] In her paradigms "rational belief" and "faith" are apparently antithetical, incompatible. She also believes that "rational belief" must belong to Protestantism and Marxism while it is simply alien to medieval Christians who, so she seems to imagine, all lived in

[5] *Chaucer's Religious Tales*, 1; see too Barbara Nolan's essay in the same volume, "Chaucer's Tales of Transcendence: Rhyme Royal and Christian Prayer in the *Canterbury Tales*," 21–37.
[6] Benson and Robertson, eds., 2, 5.
[7] For observations on ways in which the essays in this volume are less unitary in approach than the editor's introduction suggests, see H. Marshall Leicester, "Piety and Resistance," in *The Endless Knot: Essays on Old and Middle English in Honor of Marie Boroff*, ed. M. T. Tavormina and R. F. Yeager (Cambridge: Brewer, 1995), 151–60. One of the more striking contrasts overlooked in the introduction to the volume is that between Morse's view on the *Clerk's Tale* ("I would not call the *Clerk's Tale* a 'religious tale,'" 71) and the line taken by Benson, Georgianna, Kirk, and Nolan.
[8] Linda Georgianna, "The Protestant Chaucer," Benson and Robertson, eds., *Chaucer's Religious Tales*, 65.

3

unified, homogeneous communities where critical reflections, divisions, and rational disputations over matters of Christian practice and doctrine were impossible. Furthermore, she rather bizarrely assumes that only Protestants and Marxists could talk about what she calls "the repressive agenda of the fourteenth century church" (62) and that only they would see "a controlling, inquisitorial church" in the later Middle Ages (55–56; see too 63). For *medieval* Christians there was apparently a "gulf separating critical inquiring minds" from faith since Christian faith was seen to entail "irrationality" and "arbitrariness" (67). Chaucer most firmly celebrates this in the *Clerk's Tale* which "rubs our noses in the discomfort, the irrationality, the arbitrariness of faith's demands" (67). In 1995 this scholar developed these ideas in *Speculum* where it is argued that the *Clerk's Tale* "is designed" to show "the radical demands of Christian faith."[9] As in her earlier contribution to the Benson and Robertson volume, she claims that faith makes Christians "transcend the political and moral context" in which they live (801; similarly 805). Once more we are being taught that in the Middle Ages faith and spirituality were divorced from practical reason and ethics, divorced, that is, from the tasks of building communities which could at least make human flourishing possible. Perfect Christian faith is allegedly exemplified by a woman whose uncritical obedience of her secular sovereign leads her to hand her children over to be murdered by the secular power, one as absolute as any projected by John Wyclif (addressed in the final chapter). To Linda Georgianna this is Chaucer's exquisite illustration of the way that "moral grounds" and "justice or the natural law" are irrelevant to authentic Christian faith (809) – at least before Protestantism and Marxism. As in 1990, she unequivocally affirms that "medieval Christian belief" (810) is a "nonrational affective recognition of mystery" (815).

A remarkable feature of the version of Christian faith sponsored by the literary scholarship under discussion is that the Church, the community of the faithful, seems absent. The act of faith seems to owe nothing to human polities, even to the Church militant. But such an approach to faith is seriously mistaken. For faith, including the most intimately experienced faith, involves and involved collective *praxis* in determinate historical communities. As the Dominican theologian Edward Schillebeeckx writes in his recent work, *The Church*, Christian faith "is not a separate sector, for example, of human inwardness, but embraces the whole of the reality in which we live and of which we ourselves are also part."[10] Faith, even "very abstract confessions of faith can have a very specific social significance and political function. And here the question is always *Cui bono?* Who profits from these particular concepts of God? And who are their victims?"[11] While such perspectives have emerged among theologians belonging

---

[9] Linda Georgianna, "The Clerk's Tale and the Grammar of Assent," *Speculum* 70 (1995): 793–821: here the quoted phrase appears on p. 794 and is repeated on p. 818. References to this essay appear in the text.
[10] Edward Schillebeeckx, *The Church* (New York: Crossroads, 1993), 70.
[11] Schillebeeckx, *The Church*, 58.

to different strands of Christianity,[12] they are quite alien to the Chaucerians with whom I began. But here I can imagine an objector's voice, along lines such as these: "you may quote or cite as many modern theologians from as many Christian traditions as you like, but characteristically you forget that they are modern and in doing so you reveal the anachronistic nature of your approach." This very familiar voice, a compound ghost indeed, has accompanied the generation of my present project, and here I offer the outlines of a brief response. A good place for such a summary to begin is from within late-medieval theology.

In the treatise on faith in the *Summa Theologiae*, St. Thomas observed that Christian faith is handed on (*traditur*) in the person of the whole Church bound together by living faith and sanctified by the Holy Spirit.[13] This perspective pervades the treatment of the sacraments in part three of the *Summa* where St. Thomas makes clear that a life of faith is communicated to humans in a specific community of faith (the Church), through bodily media (the sacraments). Human beings need these, he argues, because they only come to know the spiritual through the bodily world perceived with the senses. The sacraments of the Church are signs that sanctify and incorporate the human creature into the body of Christ.[14] And the body of Christ is that mystical body, the Church, the one ark outside of which, he writes, there is no salvation.[15] In part one of the *Summa* he had observed that the conditions of faith include preaching (Romans 10.17) and now, in part three, it is emphasized that the Church's baptism is foundational to all the sacraments necessary to salvation.[16] In summary, St. Thomas stresses the embodied and social nature of humans: our spiritual life,

---

[12] Beside the work of Schillebeeckx already cited, see the following: Stanley Hauerwas, *The Peaceable Kingdom: A Primer in Christian Ethics* (Notre Dame: University of Notre Dame Press, 1983); Hauerwas, *In Good Company: The Church as Polis* (Notre Dame: University of Notre Dame Press, 1995); J. W. McClendon, *Systematic Theology: Ethics* (Nashville: Abingdon Press, 1986); Gustavo Gutierrez, *A Theology of Liberation* (Maryknoll: Orbis, 1973); Juan Luis Segundo, *Liberation of Theology* (Maryknoll: Orbis, 1979); Segundo, *Jesus of Nazareth Yesterday and Today*, vol. 1 (Maryknoll: Orbis, 1984); John Howard Yoder, *The Politics of Jesus*, 2nd edn. (Grand Rapids, Mich.: Eerdmans, 1994); Nicholas Lash, *A Matter of Hope: A Theologian's Reflections on the Thought of Karl Marx* (London: Darton, Longman and Todd, 1981); Herbert McCabe's early work on ethics is still illuminating: *What is Ethics About?* (Washington, D.C.: Corpus Books, 1969).

[13] *ST* II–II.1.9 *ad* 3. For the *Summa Theologiae* I have used the Blackfriars edition (London: Blackfriars, 1964–80) together with *Summa Theologica* [*sic*], 4 vols. in 6 (Rome: Forzanus, 1894). Hereafter the *Summa* is cited as *ST* in the text.

[14] *ST* III.60.2, III.62.1, III.62.5, III.73.3.

[15] *ST* III.73.3. This is of course standard dogma: besides *Unam Sanctam* (trans. in Henry Bettenson, ed., *Documents of the Christian Church*, 2nd edn. [Oxford: Oxford University Press, 1963], 159–61), see the Florence-Ferrara Council of 1442, in Schillebeeckx, *The Church*, xvii and 247 n. 1.

[16] See *ST* I.111.1 *ad* 1, *ST* III.67, *ST* III.68.5, III.69.3, III.73.3. Faith is a *habitus* of the mind by which eternal life begins in us now: *ST* II–II.4.1. See also the use of Romans 10.17 in the related context in *Summa Contra Gentiles*, IV.1.7, trans. Charles J. O'Neil, *Summa Contra Gentiles Book Four: Salvation* (Notre Dame: University of Notre Dame Press, 1975).

according to him and his tradition, can only develop insofar as we are members of a whole community in which we live as the social creatures we are.[17] We find the same spiritual anthropology in his sermon commentary on the Apostles' Creed. Faith is bound up with baptism into the community of the faithful.[18] Here too he emphasizes that just as there was no one saved outside Noah's ark, so humans need to be members of the community of the faithful if they are to develop the virtue of saving faith.[19]

The difference between this understanding of Christian faith and the one propagated by literary medievalists such as Georgianna and Benson is immense. For St. Thomas people become faithful followers of Christ not as abstract individuals but as members of a specific community where faith, ethics, Christology, and ecclesiology are bound together. Faith means becoming incorporated in a specific, social body rooted in the life, death, and resurrection of Jesus, a visible community dependent on the Holy Spirit. It is here that Christianity's shaping narratives and saving sacraments are encountered. As Thomas Netter informed Wycliffites in his monumental *Doctrinale Fidei Catholicae*, the withering away of the visible community, which they held in contempt, would lead to the withering away of Scripture's authority and the Christian faith they wished to proclaim.[20] Faith and ethics respond to the narratives of Jesus within determinate historical communities, themselves part of the world the narratives challenge as they reflect and call for an alternative society centered on the kingdom preached, practiced, and promised by Jesus. Christian belief, in St. Thomas's account, takes place in the ecclesial context, as it does for Julian of Norwich. There is no assumption of a necessary dichotomy between the individual (inner, spiritual) and the collective (outward, public). Neither body nor polity is a mere husk to be cast aside or ignored as the individual becomes spiritually awake. On the contrary, human teleology, in this tradition, was guided by the resurrection of the body, and, in the words of St. Augustine, "the view that the life of the wise man should be social" is to be supported:

---

[17] *ST* III.65.1; see James M. Blythe, *Ideal Government and Mixed Constitution in the Middle Ages* (Princeton: Princeton University Press, 1992), chap. 3. See St. Thomas's part of *De Regimine Principum* in *On the Government of Rulers: "De Regimine Principum": Ptolemy of Lucca with Portions Attributed to Thomas Aquinas*, trans. James M. Blythe (Philadelphia: University of Pennsylvania Press, 1997), I.1.

[18] *The Sermon-Conferences of St. Thomas Aquinas on the Apostles' Creed*, trans. and ed. Nicholas Ayo (Notre Dame: Notre Dame University Press, 1988), 18/19, 124/125.

[19] *Sermon-Conferences*, 126/127. On St. Thomas's understanding of the virtues, see *ST* I–II.49–67; and Alasdair MacIntyre, *Whose Justice? Which Rationality?* (London: Duckworth, 1988), chaps. 10–11.

[20] Thomas Netter, *Thomae Waldensis Doctrinale Antiquitatum Fidei Catholicae Ecclesiae*, ed. B. Blanciotti (Venice 1757–59, reprint Farnborough: Gregg, 1967). Here see II.22.11–II.23.2 (vol. 1: 360–62), and II.18.5 (vol. 1:332–33).

For here we are, with the nineteenth book in hand on the subject of the City of God; and how could that City have made its first start, how could it have advanced along its course, how could it attain its appointed goal, if the life of the saints were not social?

[Quod autem socialem vitam volunt esse sapientes, nos multo amplius adprobamus. Nam unde ista Dei civitas, de qua huius operis ecce iam undevicensimum librum versamus in manibus, vel inchoaretur exortu vel progrederetur excursu vel adprehenderet debitos fines, si non esset socialis vita sanctorum?][21]

When Georgianna asserts that Christian holiness involves being a "whole self" independent of "the supposed exterior shadow of a self," involves being an "autonomous individual," she reveals a set of assumptions far removed from those of St. Thomas and the traditions to which he belonged and revised.[22]

Another profoundly important area of difference between St. Thomas and literary scholars such as those I have been considering is the understanding of the relations between faith and reason. This is a substantial issue, and here I only draw attention to a few of the relevant points. In the *Summa Theologiae* St. Thomas presents reason as the "subject" of faith and faith as a specific ordering of the mind to God in regard to understanding (*secundum intellectum*).[23] Faith is midway between science and opinion, a *cognitio* which is presupposed by the gift that turns humans to God.[24] As Brian Davies shows in *The Thought of Thomas Aquinas*, it is absolutely clear that "Aquinas does not think that those with faith must lack reason for believing as they do."[25] From this it does not follow that faith can be demonstrated – like most medieval theologians St. Thomas explicitly denies this. But the idea of "a separation between intellect

---

[21] St. Augustine, *City of God*, XIX.5, trans. Henry Bettenson (London: Penguin, 1984), 858; Latin text from *De Civitate Dei*, ed. Bernard Dombart and Alphonse Kalb, 2 vols. (Stuttgart: Teubner, 1981 and 1993), 2:362–63. See also Augustine, *De Utilitate Credendi*, 10.24: "God is only with those who, seeking him, have also a care for human society," in *Earlier Works of St. Augustine*, trans. J. H. S. Burleigh (Philadelphia: Westminster Press, 1953).

[22] Georgianna, "The Clerk's Tale," 805 and n. 29. The Catholic theologian Nicholas Lash represents the medieval traditions toward which I am pointing in his *Theology on the Way to Emmaus* (London: SCM Press, 1986), 192; see too his comments in *The Beginning and the End of "Religion"* (Cambridge: Cambridge University Press, 1996), chap. 9. Ironically, Georgianna's assumptions seem to belong to what Lash calls "the imagination of modern Western culture" with its belief that "spiritual" life is concerned with changing one's mind rather than the wider conditions of human existence (*Theology on the Way*, 192).

[23] See *ST* I–II.56.3 *resp.*, and I–II.113.1–2.

[24] See *ST* I–II.113.4 *ad* 2 and *ad* 3; see also I–II.6.1. Once again, much of the whole treatise on faith is relevant here, II–II.1–10.

[25] Brian Davies, *The Thought of Thomas Aquinas* (Oxford: Clarendon, 1992), 281; and see 274–85. See too Peter Geach, *The Virtues* (Cambridge: Cambridge University Press, 1977), chap. 2 and Karl Rahner, "Faith between Rationality and Emotions," in *Theological Investigations*, trans. D. Morland (New York: Crossroads, 1979), chap. 5, especially 62.

7

and will . . . is foreign to him. He holds that will and intellect are always bound up with each other."[26] As hope and charity perfect the will which moves us, so faith perfects the mind.[27] And faith is, contrary to Georgianna's assertions, but akin to William Langland's, "a thinking accompanied by searching [intellectus quae est cum quadam inquisitione]."[28] Faith issues from both will and intellect, and its object is Truth.[29] St. Thomas treats the light of reason as God's light, as the image of divine reason that made it. This is why it is a light that can disclose the eternal law which is also disclosed by supernatural revelation.[30] Believing is an act of the intellect (*actus intellectus*) assenting to divine truth in obedience to the will moved by God through grace.[31] God infuses the light of grace whereby the human creature is "perfected for the exercise of virtue, both as regards knowledge, inasmuch as man's mind is elevated by this light to the knowledge of truths surpassing reason, and as regards action and affection, inasmuch as man's affective power is raised by this light above all created things to the love of God, to hope in Him, and to the performance of acts that such love imposes." So St. Thomas writes in his *Compendium of Theology*.[32]

But here another question is likely: "what about 'skeptical fideism,' what about Ockham and late medieval 'nominalism?'" Isn't this the source of Chaucer's theology? It is certainly true that many Chaucerians have asserted this over the last thirty years. The standard claim is that late-medieval theology, under the influence of Ockham, involved a fusion of radical epistemological skepticism and "fideism," a fusion shaping Chaucer's writing.[33] The volume of essays from which I set out contains an example of this line in a chapter entitled "Nominalism and the Dynamics of the *Clerk's Tale*." Here Elizabeth Kirk

---

[26] Davies, *The Thought of Thomas Aquinas*, 284–85, citing *ST* I–II.17.1 and I.81.3; see too Blythe, *Ideal Government*, 39.

[27] *ST* II–II.1.3 *ad* 1; see on this also I–II.62.4 *resp.*, and I–II.65.4.

[28] *ST* I–II.2.2; see too II–II.2.9.

[29] *ST* II–II.4.2.

[30] See the treatise on happiness, *ST* I–II.1–21. Here I refer to I–II.19.4 *resp* and *ad* 3; see also I–II.18–6 and I–II.19.1 *ad* 3.

[31] This is from the treatise on faith: II–II.2.9 *resp*. See also the treatment of the relations between truths of faith surpassing reason and the truths known naturally by reason in *Summa Contra Gentiles*: I.7.1; I.7.5–6; I.8 and IV.1.10. For Wyclif's view, see *Trialogus cum Supplemento Trialogi*, ed. G. Lechler (Oxford: Clarendon Press, 1869), I.6, 55–56. This goes against those who maintain that the "light of faith" contradicts the "light of nature."

[32] St. Thomas Aquinas, *Compendium of Theology*, trans. Cyril Vollert (St. Louis: Herder, 1948), 153.

[33] For characteristic examples of this approach to Chaucer and the alleged "skeptical fideism" of late-medieval theology, see the following: Sheila Delany, *Chaucer's House of Fame: The Poetics of Skeptical Fideism* (Chicago: University of Chicago Press, 1972); Delany, *The Naked Text: Chaucer's Legend of Good Women* (Berkeley: University of California Press, 1994), for example, 96, chap. 1; Russell A. Peck, "Chaucer and the Nominalist Questions," *Speculum* 53 (1978): 745–60. See too R. J. Utz, ed., *Literary Nominalism* (Lewiston, Pa.: Edwin Mellen, 1995).

maintains that Ockham and late-medieval nominalism sponsored a radical new split between faith and reason, one in which God now "recedes into unknowability." This "unknowability," however, seems to be knowable as "radically unconditioned will." Now, so it is alleged, theology projects a "more frightening" image of human relations to God and "the ethics of a William of Ockham are sheerly arbitrary in the sense that they reflect God's radically unconditioned will."[34] Such claims about late-medieval theology are familiar as glosses on Chaucer's poetry and as guides as to how we should read his understanding of Christian faith. Yet there is a rather striking feature about Kirk's essay. At no point does it engage with any text by any so-called nominalist theologian. This absence seems oddly characteristic of a great deal of the Chaucerian scholarship claiming the special relevance of late-medieval "nominalist" theology to Chaucer's work.[35]

If we turn to Ockham's *Quodlibetal Questions*, we meet a philosophical theologian whose approaches seem to have remarkably little in common with that ascribed to him by many lettrists. Logical and grammatical arguments, often of a thoroughly specialized kind formulated within the terms of scholastic Aristotelianism together with questions about issues of change, motion, and timing, have a prominence in Ockham that one would not have expected from his use in the work of literary scholars.[36] Human knowledge is gained through

---

[34] Elizabeth Kirk, "Nominalism and the Dynamics of the *Clerk's Tale*," 111–20, in Benson and Robertson, eds., *Chaucer's Religious Tales*. It is interesting to note that Kirk both acknowledges and sidelines David Steinmetz's emphasis on the reliability of God's *potentia ordinata* (115), a matter I return to later in this essay. For Steinmetz's essay, see "Late Medieval Nominalism and the *Clerk's Tale*," *Chaucer Review* 12 (1977–78): 38–54. For a still more recent repetition of Kirk's line, see Elizabeth Keiser, *Courtly Desire and Medieval Homophobia: The Legitimation of Sexual Pleasure in "Cleanness" and its Contexts* (New Haven: Yale University Press, 1997), 105–106. More nuanced, but in this tradition still, are the comments of Frederick Bauerschmidt, *Julian of Norwich and the Mystical Body Politic of Christ* (Notre Dame: University of Notre Dame Press, 1998), 25–31. He also addresses the *Quodlibetal Questions*.

[35] It is also often combined with a tendency to ignore recent work that has contradicted this picture of "nominalist theology." Jesse Gellrich's recent study, *Discourse and Dominion in the Fourteenth Century: Oral Contexts of Writing in Philosophy, Politics, and Poetry* (Princeton: Princeton University Press, 1995), is an exception to the tendency I have noted – and he does not present Ockham as a "skeptical fideist."

[36] For Ockham's *Quodlibetal Questions* I use the English translation by Alfred J. Freddoso and Francis E. Kelley, 2 vols. (New Haven: Yale University Press, 1991); and the Latin text of *Quodlibeta Septem*, ed. J. C. Wey, vol. 9 of Ockham's *Opera Philosophica et Theologica* (St. Bonaventure, New York: Franciscan Institute, 1980). References to pages in the Latin text will be preceded by *QS*; all other references are to the English translation. For an example of the perspectives I have mentioned, consult Ockham's treatment of the Eucharist in *Quodlibetal Questions*, IV.13.30–34, VI.3, VII.19, and in his treatise on the sacrament, *The "De sacramento altaris" of William of Ockham*, ed. T. Bruce Birch (Burlington, Iowa: Lutheran Literary Board, 1930). I have found especially helpful here: Marilyn McCord Adams, *William Ockham*, 2 vols. (Notre Dame: University of Notre Dame Press, 1987), esp. chaps. 10–14, 21–26; and Katherine H. Tachau, *Vision and Certitude in the Age of Ockham* (Leiden: Brill, 1988), chapter 5.

the rigorous analysis of propositions. But even if we set aside this problem of genre, we encounter positions that Chaucerian scholars have not led us to expect. I will mention a few relevant ones:

1. God "is an absolutely perfect being and consequently he moves things intelligently and rationally [*est ens perfectissimum, et per consequens movet intellectualiter et rationabiliter*]."[37]

2. "Nor should the distinction [between God's ordained and absolute power] be understood to mean that God is able to do certain things ordinately and certain things absolutely and not ordinately. For God cannot do anything inordinately [*Nec sic est intelligenda quod aliqua potest Deus ordinate facere, et aliqua potest absolute et non ordinate, quia Deus nihil facere inordinate*]".[38]

3. Right reason as a basic criterion is strongly emphasized in Ockham's understanding of ethics.[39] He states the following explicitly: that the criterion of right reason is central in determining a virtuous act; that one's act is not morally good unless either *accompanied by* an act of willing to follow right reason or *caused* by such an act.[40]

4. Ockham maintains that non-positive moral science is a demonstrative science. This is so because a cognition that deduces conclusions syllogistically from principles known *per se* or by *experience* is demonstrative. (An example of a principle known *per se* is that my will should conform to right reason.) Ockham states that moral science is more certain than many sciences, very subtle and useful. [*Et ultra dico quod ista scientia ("moralis scientia") est certior multis*

---

[37] See *Quodlibetal Questions*, II.2, reply to problem 1 (98–99).

[38] See *Quodlibetal Questions*, VI.1, first article. On this, and the relevant contexts, see W. J. Courtenay, "The Dialectic of Divine Omnipotence," chap. 4 in *Covenant and Causality in Medieval Thought* (London: Variorum Reprints, 1984), 14–15. See also Courtenay, *Schools and Scholars in Fourteenth-Century England* (Princeton: Princeton University Press, 1987), 211–13. In a very different genre, note Ockham's characteristic invocation of "ratio recta fundata in scripturis autenticis" and of "scriptura sacra et ratio recta": *An Princeps . . .*, in *Opera Politica*, vol. 1, ed. H. S. Offler, 2nd edn. (Manchester: Manchester University Press, 1974), chap. 6, 251. See also part 3, tract 2 of his *Dialogus*, in *A Letter to the Friars Minor and Other Writings*, ed. Arthur Stephen McGrade and John Kilcullen, trans. Kilcullen (Cambridge: Cambridge University Press, 1995).

[39] On the role of right reason in Ockham's ethical reflections see the following: D. E. Luscombe, "Natural Morality and Natural Law," chap. 37 in *The Cambridge History of Later Medieval Philosophy*, ed. Norman Kretzmann, Anthony Kenny, and Jan Pinborg (Cambridge: Cambridge University Press, 1982), esp. 714–15; D. W. Clark, "Voluntarism and Rationalism in the Ethics of Ockham," *Franciscan Studies* 31 (1971): 72–87; Lucan Freppert, *The Basis of Morality According to William Ockham* (Chicago: Franciscan Herald, 1988), esp. chaps. 3, 5, and 6. Especially helpful is Marilyn McCord Adams, "The Structure of Ockham's Moral Theory," *Franciscan Studies* 46 (1986): 1–35.

[40] *Quodlibetal Questions*, II.15 and III.15 (*QS* 180 and 260). The response to the first problem reads as follows: "Similiter nullus actus est moraliter bonus vel virtuosus, nisi sibi assistat actus volendi sequi rectam rationem, vel quia causatur a tali velle." Compare St. Thomas's approach to happiness and the role of right reason in begetting virtuous acts: *ST* I–II: 18.5 and 6; 18.9 *resp*; 19.1 *ad* 3; 19.3; 19.4.

aliis, pro quanto quilibet potest habere maiorem experientiam de actibus suis quam de aliis. Ex quo patet quod ista scientia est multum subtilis, utilis, et evidens][41]

5. As for faith: In the fourth of the *Quodlibetal Questions* Ockham maintains what is a thoroughly traditional position, namely that an act of faith involves an act of will – that is, in faith the will, presupposing a dictate of right reason, commands assent virtuously in order that the intellect adhere to the articles of faith [*Et concedo quod illa volitio virtuosa praesupposit rectam rationem quod sic est imperandum, licet non praesupponat rectam rationem evidentem quocumque modo. Tamen scienter imperat, quia percipit se sic dictare*]."[42]

This seems the place to make an observation about the specialist literature on Ockham. We need to note the decisive discrediting of earlier-twentieth-century claims that Ockham and the *via moderna* produced a theology characterized by skepticism, voluntarism, fideism, and a version of God as utterly arbitrary, utterly unreliable.[43] As long ago as 1963, in a work widely cited by lettrists, Heiko Oberman showed that for Ockham and the *via moderna* "Faith is not irrational or contrary to natural reason, but rather ungraspable by natural reason," while the acceptance of the Church's authority and tradition need not mean the negation of reason or a blind jump. Among the bridges between faith and reason is the Thomistic argument that "the will cannot love an unknown object: the act of cognition has to precede."[44] Since Oberman's *Harvest* such themes have been confirmed and elaborated.[45] But some literary scholars may wish to object that these arguments overlook Ockham's use of God's *potentia absoluta*: isn't this a radical rupture with tradition, especially with

---

[41] Ibid., II.14.3 (149; see 148–50; *QS* 178). Perhaps the remoteness of this from anything akin to "skeptical fideism" is worth remarking.

[42] Ibid., IV.6, reply to objection 1 (*QS* 325, and see 322–27). Also helpful here is the treatment of penance in his commentary on the *Sentences*, IV.11, in *Opera Philosophica et Theologica, Opera Theologica*, vol. 7, ed. R. Wood and G. Gal (St. Bonaventure, New York: St. Bonaventure University, 1984), 214.

[43] The discrediting of early-twentieth-century claims that the *via moderna* entailed skepticism, individualism, voluntarism, and an unreliable God has been extensive: perhaps a good place to begin is William J. Courtenay, "Nominalism and Late Medieval Religion," in *The Pursuit of Holiness in Late Medieval and Renaissance Religion*, ed. Charles Trinkaus and Heiko A. Oberman (Leiden: Brill, 1974), 26–59, together with Courtenay, "Nominalism and Late Medieval Thought: A Bibliographical Essay," *Theological Studies* 33 (1973): 716–34; and Courtenay, "Covenant and Causality in Pierre d'Ailly," *Speculum* 46 (1971): 94–119. It should have been clear to literary historians from Courtenay's "Bibliographical Essay" of 1972 alone that the earlier-twentieth-century characterization of Ockham and the late-medieval *via moderna* was unsustainable. Since then research has confirmed and enriched the evidence of Courtenay and scholars to whose work he was attending. For two major examples, see the following: Gordon Leff, *William of Ockham: The Metamorphosis of Scholastic Discourse* (Manchester: Manchester University Press, 1975); and Adams, *William Ockham*, vol. 2, chap. 28. Also invaluable is Courtenay, *Schools and Scholars*, chap. 7, 11–12.

[44] Heiko A. Oberman, *The Harvest of Medieval Theology* (Cambridge, Mass.: Harvard University Press, 1963), 42, 80, 242; see too 52, 67–69, 224–26, 241–48, chap. 2.

[45] See n. 43 and the work of M. McCord Adams cited in n. 36 and n. 39.

St. Thomas's understanding of God? As the statements about God already quoted from Ockham's *Quodlibetal Questions* make clear, Ockham maintains that God orders the creation intelligently and reliably. True enough, God could have arranged things otherwise. For example, in Question III.10 Ockham affirms the orthodox view that original sin is removed only by created grace. He then observes that through God's *potentia absoluta* God could have arranged for original sin to be removed in some other way – *but God didn't*, and our *knowledge* that God didn't is warranted by the authority of *our community of faith*, the Catholic Church and its traditions.[46] Similarly, when he addresses the question as to whether humans can be saved without the gift of created charity, he notes the distinction between what God *could* have arranged and *has* arranged, the distinction between *potentia absoluta* and *potentia ordinata*. Through the former God *could* have given eternal grace to those lacking grace or created charity; but *in reality* God ordained that no human will be saved without created grace and that no act be meritorious without such grace. This *we know*, in the appropriate way, through the community to which we adhere, the Church and its traditions.[47] I emphasize "in the appropriate way" to suggest a fact that contemporary medievalists often seem to occlude. Namely, that forms of human knowledge are inextricably bound up with determinate human institutions and traditions: this, contrary to certain enlightenment dogmas, does not make them "unknowledge."[48] And in the case of the Church those who belonged to this community believed that in and through this institution, which was also the mystical body of Christ, God disclosed knowledge about reality that could not be discovered by natural reason unillumined by grace, a position represented earlier in this essay from St. Thomas's *Compendium*.

The distinction between God's *potentia absoluta* and God's *potentia ordinata* articulates the traditional Christian belief that God is the creator who is free from chance and necessity. It would be salutary for those mesmerized by the term *potentia absoluta* to recollect that in the first part of the *Summa Theologiae* St. Thomas himself stressed that God's wisdom and creativity are not bound by any particular set of arrangements. He affirmed that God, *de potentia absoluta*, could do anything noncontradictory. However, he observed, God has ordained his power to realize the actual order we inhabit.[49] He had also shown, at the

---

[46] *Quodlibetal Questions*, III.10 (*QS* 240–43, esp. 240–41); see similarly IV.29, thesis 1 (*QS* 446–47 [conclusio 1]).

[47] Ibid., VI.1; similarly, VI.2 and VI.4. The theological virtues "are infused by divine agency in accordance with the sacramental system of the Church" (Adams, "The Structure of Ockham's Moral Theory," 14; take this with the commentary on 22–23, 26–27, 34–35: all gold!). See also Adams, *William Ockham*, 2:1009–10. Compare St. Thomas, *ST* I–II.5.7 *resp*, an example of Aquinas's envisaging how God could bypass the forms he had ordained. I return to St. Thomas in the next paragraph of the text.

[48] On these issues and the relevant history see the following by Alasdair MacIntyre: *Whose Justice? Which Rationality?* (London: Duckworth, 1988) and *Three Rival Versions of Moral Enquiry* (London: Duckworth, 1990), esp. chaps. 3–7.

[49] *ST* I.25.5. See Courtenay, "Dialectic of Divine Omnipotence," 9–10, 27–28 (n. 28) and

opening of the *Summa*, how inadequate must be our language and knowledge of God, rooted as they are in the created world, *a knowledge perhaps more truly about what God is not.*[50] In no way does the deployment of the distinction entail "skepticism," "fideism," or "skeptical fideism."

I have now indicated serious problems in the account of medieval Christian faith offered by those Chaucerians for whom this is a major concern. In doing so I have suggested some of the kinds of correctives needed, correctives that will be theological, ecclesiological, social, and political. Only when such inquiries are elaborated will it be possible to address questions concerning the relations between literary works, including Chaucer's, and faith and ethics in fourteenth-century Christianity. I will now exemplify the materials and issues currently occluded by the versions of faith I have criticized. My aim is to suggest just how such occluded materials are relevant both to understanding late-medieval Christianity in England and to understanding the relations of Chaucer's writing to that Christianity.

If Christian faith is the life of faith in a determinate community; if, to reiterate St. Augustine's contention, the life of the saints is necessarily social; and if, in St. Augustine's much quoted remark, here taken from Duns Scotus's *Quodlibetal Questions*, "I would not believe in the Gospel, did not the authority of the Catholic Church compel me";[51] then our explorations of Christian faith in the Middle Ages had best abandon the liberal individualism which, rather ironically, shapes the literary scholarship I have invoked. Instead we will need to approach particular articulations of faith as voices in a complex conversation. Just as a "self" only emerges in "webs of interlocution," just as human identity only emerges with "reference to a defining community," so medieval versions (plural) of faith belong to particular webs of interlocution that assume particular communities and particular historical circumstances with their own sometimes unprecedented challenges.[52] We will only have even a chance of understanding what it meant to have produced a particular articulation of Christian faith and ethics when we read it in relation to other articulations, both similar and different, only when we begin to grasp the pressures, the questions, the alternatives addressed, ones often addressed implicitly, indirectly.[53] In late-fourteenth-century England the relevant pressures included new

M. McCord Adams, *William Ockham*, vol. 2, chap. 28. On St. Thomas here, see Courtenay, *Schools and Scholars*, 361–62.

[50] See *ST* I.13. On this, see Brian Davies, *The Thought of Thomas Aquinas*, chap. 4; also David Burrell, *Aquinas, God, and Action* (London: Routledge, 1979), 18–69.

[51] John Duns Scotus, *God and Creatures: The Quodlibetal Questions*, trans. Felix Alluntis and Allen B. Wolter (Princeton: Princeton University Press, 1975), 14.21 (320). Augustine commented, "Ego vero Evangelio non crederem, nisi me catholicae Ecclesiae commoveret auctoritas" (*Contra Epistolam Manichaei*, I.5.6; *Patrologia Latina*, 42:176).

[52] Quotations are from Taylor, *Sources of the Self*, 1–2. On the challenges here see Aers, *Community, Gender, and Individual Identity in English Writing 1360–1430* (London: Routledge, 1988), intro.

[53] Here my basic models remain those developed by Quentin Skinner and M. M. Bakhtin:

conflicts that were political, economic, and religious. As forms of dissent became classified as heresy (a contingent historical development, not some doctrinal and "transcendent" necessity), as heresy became classified and dealt with as sedition (through parliamentary acts and the secular power), the ways in which the languages and practices of religion were inextricably bound up with the languages and practices of governance and politics became especially transparent.[54] In *English Preaching in the Late Middle Ages*, H. Leith Spencer argues that sermons and the English language itself became politicized as the hierarchy sought to combat the challenges of Lollardy and its emphasis on the vernacular. She observes that "disputes over what the lay people should be taught to believe ended inexorably in suspicion of even the basics of Christian faith in English form."[55] Faith, this should remind us, was (and still is) inextricably bound up with language, institutions, and politics.

This fact, together with some of its implications, is richly unfolded in a myriad of fascinating ways by a long vernacular poem written by one of Chaucer's contemporaries. Langland's *Piers Plowman* is both a sustained exploration of faith and itself an act of faith in what the poet experienced as a time of especial trouble in all domains of English communities, including the Church. Near the beginning of the poem the wandering, searching visionary meets a figure who descends from the castle representing heaven, a figure who had taught him "the feith."[56] She is Holi Chirche. Using a variety of literary strategies, she instructs the dreamer on a wide range of doctrinal, ethical, and political issues. The questing dreamer

---

Aers, *Community, Gender, and Individual Identity*, 2–5; and Aers, ed., *Culture and History: 1350–1600* (Hemel Hempstead: Harvester, 1992), 1–3.

[54] On religion and politics in this period, basic to the present concerns are the following works: Margaret Aston, *Lollards and Reformers: Images and Literacy in Late Medieval Religion* (London: Hambledon, 1984), esp. chaps. 1–6; Anne Hudson, *The Premature Reformation: Wycliffite Texts and Lollard History* (Oxford: Oxford University Press, 1988); Sarah Beckwith, *Christ's Body: Identity, Culture, and Society in Late Medieval Writings* (London: Routledge, 1993); Peter Heath, *Church and Realm, 1272–1461: Conflict and Collaboration in an Age of Crisis* (London: Fontana, 1988), chaps. 3–8; Peter McNiven, *Heresy and Politics in the Reign of Henry IV: The Burning of John Badby* (Woodbridge: Boydell & Brewer, 1987); Aers and Staley, *Powers of the Holy*; H. Leith Spencer, *English Preaching in the Late Middle Ages* (Oxford: Clarendon Press, 1993); Nicholas Watson, "Censorship and Cultural Change in Late Medieval England," *Speculum* 70 (1995): 822–64; Fiona Somerset, *Clerical Discourse and Lay Audience in Late Medieval England* (Cambridge: Cambridge University Press, 1998), chap. 6; also relevant is Paul Strohm, "Chaucer's Lollard Joke: History and the Textual Unconscious," *Studies in the Age of Chaucer* 17 (1995): 23–42, and his *England's Empty Throne* (New Haven: Yale University Press, 1998), chapters 2 and 5.

[55] Spencer, *English Preaching*, 5; see too 5–9, 14–17, 47–49, 163–68, 377–78. Relevant here are the works by Hudson and Watson cited in n. 54. For Arundel's Constitutions see *Concilia Magnae Britanniae et Hiberniae*, ed. David Wilkins, 3 vols. (London, 1737), 3:314–19.

[56] The text of Langland's works used here is *Piers Plowman: A Parallel-Text Edition of the A, B, C and Z Versions*, ed. A. V. C. Schmidt (London: Longman, 1995). Unless otherwise stated all references are to the B version. It will become clear that I see no force in James Simpson's assertions about the inadequacy of Holy Church as a teacher: see his *Piers Plowman: An Introduction to the B-text* (London: Longman, 1990), 14–45.

asks her to turn from the just ordering of resources in God's creation to teach him to have faith in Christ. He wants to have this "kyndely," and he wants to know how he may save his soul (I.81–84). While her responses include a beautiful and complex lyric on the self-gift, the self-diffusion of God in creation and the Incarnation (the enigmatic answer to the dreamer's question which the whole poem will unfold), she resists his attempt to split off individual faith and salvation from matters of social practice (I.85–209). She insists that the way God's love was poured out in the Incarnation has clear entailments for present practices in Christian communities (I.148–84). She emphasizes that faith without the social works she describes is less than nothing, "as deed as a doornail" (I.185–87). Faith, that is, must be formed by charity, enabled through Christ's works, and realized as a *praxis* within the community to which the faithful belong. Holi Chirche resists any attempt to think of faith as an individualistic leap into the abyss, as an inner, privatized movement as free from determinate social consequences as it is from the perfection of intellect. Her approach to faith is sustained by the teachers encountered in the tenth passus. Studie locates faith within the community that is the Church, as an act with ethical, practical consequences (X.121–23). Clergie joins faith with "Dowel and Dobet and Dobest," similarly emphasizing its location in the Church community while adding a legitimization of the role of rational disputation in discovering the limits of reason (X.230–50). This passus concludes with a brilliantly staged and moving critique of fideism. Scripture has insisted that wealth and power are impediments to salvation (a theme that dominates Passus XIV) and that salvation will not be through faith alone. As Holi Chirche had done, Scripture maintains that faithful love must be practiced "in dede," in acts of kindness, a perspective unequivocally confirmed by Christ himself (X.331–63; XVII.204–350). But Will rejects the fusion of faith and ethics, rejects the demand that Christian faith be a *praxis* within a given historical community, and makes a striking move in doing so. He projects an arbitrary and inscrutable deity about whom the less we think or know or see the better: before this deity salvation will be from a "pure bileue" to which the practice of the virtues in a human community seem quite beside the point. While this bears no relation to the incarnate God figured forth by Holi Chirche and to be encountered from Passus XVI to XVIII, it may represent an orientation rather close to the one we have seen Georgianna ascribe to the "medieval" Christian, and to Chaucer in particular. For Langland, however, it is a product of Will's reluctance to accept that faith demands *praxis*, demands an ethic of active love involving the cardinal virtues. Furthermore, Langland shows that fideism cannot withstand the challenge of Scripture who diagnoses its causes in massive self-ignorance (XI.1–3). The consequence of such fideism, according to this poet, is that its subject will yield up moral questions in despair, yield up any recognizably Christian *praxis* and collapse into a hedonistic life in "the lond of longynge" (XI.1–60).

Here I do not intend to follow the way Will is delivered from this state, nor to offer a commentary on the poet's elaboration of his Christocentric and committedly ethical understanding of faith through the rest of this work, but it remains necessary to recollect this process. First, when Langland brings Faith into the poem he does so as Abraham immersed in both liturgy and history, pursuing, following, and mediating Christ (XVI.172–269; XVII.48–59, 88–94; XVIII.1–109). Secondly, human salvation needs the sacraments flowing from Christ's work and entrusted to the community of the faithful, the Church (XVII.91–133). Thirdly, Christ himself is given a long, powerful oration in which he makes absolutely clear that Christian faith is not a blind leap beyond the subject's community and received ethical imperatives, but a *praxis* rooted in kindness, in love of neighbor as Christ the Samaritan has just enacted it – that is, a love, a quality of life that makes, finds, and cherishes neighbors. What will lead to final catastrophe, he stresses, is *unkindness* (for example, XVII.251–66). And fourthly, from XIX.385 to the poem's conclusion Langland shows, time and again, that without a commitment to the virtue of justice, a virtue that includes the will to restore what one owes to others in the community and to God in the repentance God calls for, the eucharist is inaccessible and the contemporary Church itself likely to become not an ark of salvation or a house built on the rock ("*Petrus id est Christus,*" XV.212) but rather the home of Antichrist.[57] Perhaps, in such a catastrophe, "*sola fides sufficit*": that was what Anima suggested earlier when describing the contemporary Church as the root of "alle yueles" (XV.92–141, 318–54, 485–90) and noting that when "folk of Holy Kirke" cannot even read the liturgy adequately, then, for the "lewed peple" (but not the "clerkes"), *sola fides sufficit* (XV.384–88). ·Here Anima deals with what is presented as a disastrous situation by deploying the traditional distinction between implicit and explicit faith,[58] and by invoking a Wycliffite program of clerical disendowment under lay control (XV.550–68). By the poem's end this turns out to be no answer. It is, in summary, clear that for this poet, faith could not be treated as a purely inner and private matter separate from a network of interrelated practices and institutions in the historical communities he inhabited. Langland may well turn out to be a better guide to our understanding of "faith," "ethics," and their relations in this period than many of the devotedly historicist Chaucerians from whom we set out, ones so admirably seeking to rescue their poet from the ravages of the beast Marxism and the beast Protestantism.

Piers Plowman has moved us from scholastic writings to the late fourteenth-century vernacular, and I shall now illustrate the specific webs of interlocution obscured by the contemporary version of faith from which we set out. For the present occasion I have chosen two texts produced within a decade of Chaucer's death. The first, by Nicholas Love, prior of Mount Grace, represents

[57] On these issues, see Aers, *Chaucer, Langland, and the Creative Imagination* (London: Routledge, 1980), chap. 2; and Simpson, *Piers Plowman*, 240–51; and see chap. 3 of the present book.
[58] See *ST* II–II.2.5–8. On the history of this material, see John van Engen, "Faith as a Concept of Order in Medieval Christendom," in *Belief in History: Innovative Approaches to European and American Religion*, ed. Thomas Kselman (Notre Dame: University of Notre Dame Press, 1991), 19–67.

Christian devotion within the emerging orthodoxy of late-fourteenth and early-fifteenth-century England, one formulated in Arundel's Constitutions. Indeed, Arundel himself approved Love's work.[59] Here I will take one passage from his treatise on the sacrament of the altar, a text that circulated with *The Mirror of the Blessed Life of Jesus Christ*.[60]

Love maintains that any dissent from the Church's current definitions of Christian faith, including its attempts to describe the presence of Christ in the eucharist with neo-Aristotelian scholastic terms, is necessarily opposition to God. Near the work's beginning he instructs his readers that when they are told anything that goes beyond "kyndly reson" they must "trowe soþfastly þat is soþ as holy chirch techeþ & go no ferþer" (22). At the same time he totally identifies obedience to "oure Lord Jesus" with obedience to all clergy, assumed to be speaking with one voice:

> do þat he oure lord Jesus biddeþ in the gospel & þe lawe & þe prophetes, & also þat he biddeþ by his ministres, & be buxom to hes vikeres, þat bene in holy chirch þi souereyns, not only gude & wele lyuyng bot also schrewes & yuel lyuyng . . . (24)

In the margin is written, *contra lollardos*, reminding the reader, in case she or he imagined otherwise, that spiritual exercises and current battles over authority in the Church were not in autonomous realms.[61] So while we seem to be encountering the kind of relations between reason and faith assumed by Chaucerians such as Georgianna, a matter to which I shall return, we should note a striking difference. Namely, faith is not approached through individualistic or inward categories, but as an institutionally determined and organized act of obedience, including obedience to those admitted to be "schrewes & yuel lyuyng." Opposition to the priests and orders of the Roman Catholic Church is defined as opposition to God, a doomed lack of faith, produced, so Love maintains, by trust in "bodily wittes & kyndely reson" (227). If, he insists, "þei byleue not as god himself & holi chirch haþ tauht" concerning

---

[59] The edition of Nicholas Love used here is the *Mirror of the Blessed Life of Jesus Christ*, ed. Michael G. Sargent (New York: Garland, 1992). References to this edition will hereafter appear in the text. Still invaluable is Elizabeth Salter, *Nicholas Love's "Myrrour of the Blessed Lyf of Jesu Christ"* (Salzburg: Analecta Cartusiana, 1974). On the ideological context, see especially Beckwith, *Christ's Body*, 63–77; and Hudson, *Premature Reformation*, 437–40. On the hermeneutic contexts, see K. Ghosh, "'Authority' and 'Interpretation' in Wycliffite, Anti-Wycliffite, and Related Texts, c. 1375–c. 1430" (Ph. D. diss., Cambridge University, 1995), this Ph. D. is due to be published by Cambridge University Press; and Katherine Little "Reading for Christ: Interpretation and Instruction in Late Medieval England" (Ph. D. diss., Duke University, 1998).

[60] See Sargent's introduction in *Mirror*, lxxvi and liii–vi, esp. liii on evidence of Love's intentions of "concluding his *Mirror* with the 'Treatise on the Sacrament.'" For description of the manuscripts, see lxxii–lxxxv.

[61] For a good introduction to the systematically polemical aspects of Love's work see Sargent, *Mirror*, xliv–lviii, together with the work of Salter, Beckwith, and Hudson cited n.59.

transubstantiation, Christians are for "dampnacion" – "*contra lollardos*" in the margin (153), and in the text, against "þe lewede lollardes þat medlen hem of hem aȝeynus þe feiþ falsly" (154). This faith is the "feiþ of holi chirch" taught by its doctors and clerks, "confermede by many maneres of myracles as we redene in many bokes & heren alday prechede & tauht" (154). Love notes a problem here: these extra-Scriptural but ecclesiastically approved sources hold no independent authority for Wycliffites. The Lollards, he says, scorn the Church's "allegance of seche myracles, haldyng hem bot as maggetales & feyned illusions" (154). For Love, representing orthodoxy in his Church, refusal to grant the status of canonical Scripture to ecclesiastically approved stories about miracles that confirm the current definition of transubstantiation demonstrates a lack of faith (153–54). He judges such lack to be "more reprouable as in þat part þan Judas" (153). Turning from definition and argument to the felt "experience" he writes of the "delectable paradise" given in the "blessede bodily presence" of the eucharist, through which the orthodox "feleþ him sensibly with unspekable ioy as he were ioyneded body to body" (154). In this "myraculouse wirching" Jesus shows "sensibly his blessede delectable bodily presence" (155). In obedient faith to the Church's current account of transubstantiation, the receiving subject may experience "felyng aboue comune kynd," one in which, "alle þe membres of þe body bene enflaumede of so deletable & ioyful a hete þat him þenkeþ sensibly alle þe body as it were meltyng for ioy as waxe doþ anentes þe hote fire" (154). This thoroughly individual "experience" is the potential reward of an ecclesiastically formed and obedient faith, one that dismisses Wycliffite attempts to gather Christian communities focusing on the narratives of Scripture. For Nicholas Love faith and reason are simply antithetical, a simplicity that, to him, seems free of problems. Unlike St. Thomas, Love proceeds as though there are no questions concerning the relations between language and the God of faith. Since language is rather obviously bound up with "kyndely reson" and "bodily wittes," Love's apparent confidence in this procedure is startling. It becomes positively bizarre when one considers the contexts of his work, contexts made explicit both in his own introduction to his *Mirror* and on many occasions both in the text and, as we have noted, in margins. Namely, contexts in which the struggles between Wycliffites and orthodox Catholics made the language of faith, the language of Scripture and liturgy, a thoroughly contested domain.

However, the pressures of the historical moment, other voices in the webs of interlocution, cannot be kept in the margins. Love introduces a hypothesis generated in response to these very pressures: what if the Catholic Church maintains as Christian faith that which is false, "not soþe" (228)? Specifically, what if the current definition of transubstantiation, in defense of which the Catholic Church was prepared to flog, imprison, and kill, should be false? Love's answer to his own hypothesis illuminates his version of Christian faith and ethics, one, we recall, circulating under the warrant of Archbishop Arundel himself. He maintains that even if the Church teaches falsity, it is safer "to byleue as holy chirch techeþ with a buxom drede" (228). Such faith given to admittedly false doctrine is perfectly safe, Love argues, because it involves the abandonment of reason ("in þat we leuyn oure kyndely reson"), together with unquestioning obedience to the Church God has allegedly ordered us to obey unconditionally (228). Love assures his readers that this abandonment of reason and truth, "soþe," combined with faith in what are said to be falsities, will gain the Christian reward ("mede") from God (228). At no point is Love troubled by what might seem strong counter-statements in the Gospels, such as Jesus's proclamation that in faithful discipleship "you will know the truth: and the truth shall make you free" (John 8.32; see too John 4.3, 14.6, and 18.37). Nor is he bothered by Paul's fusion of truth and charity (1 Cor. 13.6; see too 2 Cor. 13.8, Eph. 4.15, 25, 6.14, and Col. 3.9). We are in a very different universe from Langland's: there God is named "truþe" and Satan the source of "falshede," while Holi Chirch herself teaches that "Whan alle tresors arn tried . . . treuþe is þe beste."[62] Love insists that however untrue contemporary doctrine concerning transubstantiation might be, anyone who concludes that this makes current forms of devotion to the host inappropriate, let alone idolatrous, should be judged a "fals heretyke." False because the heretic's faith, whatever its sources in Christian traditions or Scripture or God's own judgment, is a faith that resists the current determinations of the Church. And as Love well knew, from 1401 the penalty for being a convicted heretic in England was death by burning. This sacralization of violence, one which St. Thomas wholeheartedly defends in his treatise on faith, exemplifies the fusion of Church and secular power to which we will return in the next chapter and in the final chapter of this book.[63] As I noted above, despite Love's very different emphasis on the Church's authority, there may still be some similarities between Love's version of faith and that ascribed to all medieval Christians by Georgianna and like-minded Chaucerians. In both reason is assumed to be antithetical to faith and is aligned with heresy. Perhaps Chaucer's Griselda figures forth this particular version of Christian faith? The prevalent account of Griselda in Chaucer scholarship seems congruent with such a view.

However, if it were to be shown that Griselda does figure forth the version of faith propagated by Nicholas Love and his fellow-travelers, the *meanings* of such

---

[62] See *Piers Plowman* I.12–16, 61–64, 85–86.

[63] See *ST* II–II.11.3; I return to this in chap. 2. On the relevant history in the Church, see especially R. I. Moore, *The Formation of a Persecuting Society* (Oxford: Blackwell, 1987). For a specifically English history, see McNiven, *Heresy and Politics in the Reign of Henry IV* and Margaret Aston, *Faith and Fire: Popular and Unpopular Religion, 1350–1600* (London: Hambledon, 1993) and *Lollards and Reformers*. Also extremely informative are the forced abjurations and punishments recorded in *Heresy Trials in the Diocese of Norwich 1428–31*, ed. Norman P. Tanner (London: Camden Fourth Series, vol. 20, Royal Historical Society, 1977) and *Kent Heresy Proceedings 1511–12*, ed. Tanner (Maidstone: Kent Archaeological Society, 1997).

a figuration would only become clear once the figuration had been understood within the contemporary webs of interlocution where it was made and received. That is to say, such a Griselda would only be adequately understood when she was read not as some "transcendent" model of a supposedly homogeneous pre-Reformation faith but rather in relation to different late-medieval versions of faith and ethics, differences within whose terms her own identity would have been made and within which the poet would have her do her own theological, ethical, and political work. A Love-ian Griselda in the 1390s would not be the bearer of an apolitical and transcendent Christian faith. Rather she would be a partisan in a conflict of versions of faith.

At this stage I am not either affirming or denying that Chaucer's Griselda is some kind of Love-ian figuration. But I do wish to emphasize one of the major differences between Nicholas Love's version of faith and that ascribed to medieval Christians by Benson and not a few other Chaucerians. Love envisages faith as a thoroughly collective practice involving unconditional adherence to the formulations of the actually existing ecclesiastical hierarchy. Obedience is similarly envisaged as an act of submission to the rulings and agents of the visible Church, "þi souereyns," as Love calls them (24). To reiterate, there is no trace here of faith as belonging to a desocialized interiority or to that "numinous" sublime of the "holy" which Georgianna, invoking the Lutheran theologian Rudolf Otto, and doing so without irony, ascribes to Griselda, the representative of perfect pre-Protestant faith.[64]

The second text I have chosen to exemplify the webs of interlocution relevant to understanding late-medieval faith in England is a Wycliffite work presenting an encounter between Archbishop Arundel and his prisoner, William Thorpe.[65] For Arundel, as for Nicholas Love, the issue of due authority is paramount: did not St. Paul tell priests to obey their ecclesiastical "souereyns?" And did not St. Paul make the rule that all "sogetis owe to be obedient to her

---

[64] For Georgianna's use of Otto's work, see "The Clerk's Tale," 805–6. It is worth moving from Georgianna's oddly uncritical use of Otto to Karl Barth's passing comments in *Church Dogmatics*, I/1 (Edinburgh: T. & T. Clark, 1975). In this section on the Word of God as the speech of God, and as a "rational" event, Barth notes that, "Whatever 'the holy' of Rudolf Otto may be, it certainly cannot be understood as the Word of God, for it is the numinous, and the numinous is irrational, and the irrational can no longer be differentiated from an absolutized natural force. But everything depends on the differentiation if we are to understand the concept of the Word of God" (135; see too 136–38, 142–43, 152–53, 156). It seems to me that Otto's idea of "the holy" has more to do with the legacy of vestigially protestant Romanticism than with late-medieval theology, ethics, and literature.

[65] I use the edition of Thorpe's Testimony in *Two Wycliffite Texts*, ed. Anne Hudson, EETS o.s. 301 (Oxford: Oxford University Press, 1993): references given in the text are to pages in this volume. Important work on Thorpe since Hudson's edition includes the following: Rita Copeland, "William Thorpe and His Lollard Community," in *Bodies and Disciplines: Intersections of Literature and History*, ed. Barbara Hanawalt and David Wallace (Minneapolis: University of Minnesota Press, 1996), 199–221; Fiona Somerset, *Clerical Discourse and Lay Audience*, chap. 6; Katherine Little, "Reading for Christ," chap. 2.

souereyns, and not oonli sogettis owen to be obedient to good soucreyns and
vertues but also to trowantis þat ben vicious men" (46)? This, we have seen, was
the position announced by Nicholas Love.[66] But for Thorpe the position is
more complex than it seems to the orthodox authorities. Is not Thorpe a priest,
and are not priests committed to proclaiming the Gospel, "bounden bi dyuerse
witnessingis of Goddis lawe and of greet doctours" to do so, "wiþouten any
mencioun makynge of bischopis lettres" (46–47)? In this perspective Scripture,
many doctors of the Church, and the "witnesse of seintis" provide an overwhelming "autorite," one that must be obeyed against the orders of a particular
bishop or hierarchy seeking to license and limit priests' evangelical proclamation. Most decisive of all, of course, is the obligation to imitate Christ, the
"ensaumple of his holi lyuynge and techynge" (47). Thorpe agrees that Paul
"biddeþ sogettis to obeien to her souereynes" (48). But this statement has to be
interpreted: it does not necessarily or exclusively carry the meaning Arundel
assumes.[67] Thorpe introduces a distinction as he explores the forms of Christian
faith and obedience. There are, he argues, two kinds of sovereigns: "vertues
souereynes and vicious tirauntis" (48). Christians should obey the former.
Translating Hebrews 13.7, he defines these as sovereigns who speak the word
of God and whose "conuersacioun ȝe knowen to be vertuous." They are ones
devoted to the individual and collective pursuit of Christian virtues in a form
which fuses faith, ethics, and politics. Christian faith does not owe obedience to
sovereigns whose practice is immoral and outside the law: "sogettis owen not to
be obedient to trowauntis, whiche ben vicious tirauntis, siþe her willes, her
counseilis, her heestis and her werkis ben so vicious þat þei owen to be hatid
and left" (48). Faith here involves a discipleship which may lead to open
confrontation with the ruling powers, secular or religious. This may be as
unimaginable a version of Christian faith to certain modern scholars as it was to
Nicholas Love, but it is, nevertheless, as "medieval" as Love's or Arundel's.

The Archbishop is not satisfied with Thorpe's understanding of faith and
presents a hypothesis: "If a souereyne bidde his soget do þat þing þat is vicious,
þis souereyn herinne is to blame, but þe soget for his obedience deserueþ mede
of God, for obedience plesiþ more God þan ony sacrafice" (49). Just as

---

[66] The issue of obeying "souereyns" who are "schrewes," to quote Love again (24), had of
course been given a sharply political turn by Wycliffites and the opposition they
encountered. For the scholastic context, see A. J. Minnis, "Chaucer's Pardoner and the
Office of a Preacher," in *Intellectuals and Writers in Fourteenth-Century Europe*, ed. Piero
Boitani and Anna Torti (Cambridge: Brewer, 1986), 88–119. In fact, the position held by
Love and Arundel was also held by Wyclif with regards to *lay* sovereigns, albeit with some
rather absurd inconsistency. I come to Wyclif's own views on dominion, which were by no
means the views followed by all Lollards, in chap. 6 below. Wyclif's view on obedience to
lay sovereigns, who are the vicars of God, is illustrated in his *Tractatus De Officio Regis*, ed. A.
W. Pollard and C. Sayle (London: Wyclif Society, 1887), 8, 13–19, 21–22, 118–22. Consult
Anne Hudson, *Premature Reformation*, 362–67.

[67] For characteristically informative comments on relevant texts and contexts see Hudson's
notes in *Two Wycliffite Texts*, 114–15 (notes to 707ff., 742–46, 751ff., 795ff.).

Nicholas Love promises divine "mede" to Christians whose obedience to sovereigns leads them to pursue false doctrine, so Arundel promises divine "mede" to those whose obedience to sovereigns (lay or ecclesiastic) leads them to "vicious" acts. The Wycliffite text thus presents the Archbishop as propounding a split between Christian faith and Christian ethics not dissimilar to what we find in numerous commentators on Chaucer's *Clerk's Tale*. Christian faith so defined demands obedience to duly constituted governors even if they command torture, massacre, or genocide: it was exemplified in the way the mainstream German Lutheran Church accepted the Nazi practices of their sovereigns.[68] Thorpe's response is that Samuel, David, St. Paul, and St. Gregory all agree that "not oonli þei þat don yuele ben worþi deeþ or dampnacioun, but also þei þat consenten to yuele doeres" (25). And he then makes an observation which should at least be put into some contact with the *Clerk's Tale*: "And, ser, þe lawe of holi churche techiþ in decrees þat no seruaunt to his lord, neiþer child to his fadir ne to modir, neiþer wiif to her housebonde, ne monke to his abbot owiþ to obeie, no but in leeful þingis and lawful" (49).[69] So here Christian faith is committed to disobedience in the face of illicit commands, even if these commands are given by a lord to his servant, or by a husband to a wife. Neither Thorpe nor any medieval reader would expect such disobedience to be without punitive and severe consequences for the subject, a fact we should recall when addressing Chaucer's *Clerk's Tale* in the next chapter.

Later in the text, Thorpe returns to the issue, asking Arundel whether a subject should obey a prelate who commands what is "vnlaweful" (75). Arundel reiterates his position, Nicholas Love's position. The subject should simply believe that the superior would not order what is "vnlaweful." If the superior's command is indeed "vnleeful," the Christian who enacts it need have no ethical or spiritual anxiety because she or he "tristiþ," acts in faithful obedience to the prelate, shows faith. Thorpe's response is as eloquent as it is terse: "Sere, I triste not herto" (75). Thorpe's understanding of the limits to obedience seems to me quite as congruent with the teaching of St. Thomas as it is with Ockham's defenses of his disobedience to the Pope. In the *Summa Theologiae* St. Thomas argues that insofar as human law deviates from right reason it becomes a perversion of the law: lacking the reason of law, *lex tyrannica* ceases to be law. Tyrannic laws are against the good of humans, their communities, and divine

---

[68] It would be interesting to explore the following in connection with the issues discussed in the present chapter: one of the models of what Georgianna presents as authentically Christian faith (and therefore Chaucer's and "medieval" faith) is Rudolf Otto's. Otto was a Lutheran whose obedience to his sovereigns was such that he, like most Lutherans, refused to support Lutherans like Bonhoeffer (who resisted the Nazification of church and society and the consequent genocide). See Otto, *The Idea of the Holy* (Oxford: Oxford University Press, 1923, rep. 1973), xi. For Georgianna's use of Otto, see "The Clerk's Tale," 805–806. A relevant introduction to Bonhoeffer and literature on his work is in McClendon, *Systematic Theology: Ethics*, chap. 7.

[69] Hudson, *Two Wycliffite Texts*, 116 n. 835, cites the relevant passage from the "decrees."

law and are emphatically not to be obeyed (citing Acts 5.29). Indeed, to the extent that law is not directed to the common good it lacks the force and reason of law, and to the extent it falls short of this it does not oblige us to obey.[70] St. Thomas makes it clear that an inferior should not obey a superior when he commands something that contradicts God's law or when he commands something he has no right to command. He illustrates this (in *ST* II-II.104.5) by noting that slaves do not have to obey masters, or children parents, if they are commanded to marry or to remain as a virgin, an argument and illustration we might do well to ponder when Walter commands Griselda to hand her children over to be murdered. Furthermore, we might recall that in his commentary on Aristotle's *Politics*, St. Thomas makes it clear that a husband does not have plenary power over his wife any more than does a rector over the city he must rule according to its laws and statutes.[71]

Thorpe cannot trust Love's or Arundel's version of faith because his own faith, whatever the habitually unacknowledged hermeneutic problems, seeks its decisive models in the stories of Jesus's life related in the Gospels, the very text Love's *Mirror* aims to mediate, control, and displace.[72] This characteristic Wycliffite move entails an understanding of faith, authority, and Church which is very different from Nicholas Love's and the one emerging as orthodoxy in late-fourteenth- and early-fifteenth-century England. Yet it should be remembered that Wycliffite teaching emerged within late-medieval Catholic Christianity and illustrates the differences in available models of faith. This, in turn, should remind us that we should not approach texts of this period as though no Christian had any choices to make in the construal of faith and the virtues. The comparison between Thorpe and Love helps us recollect that models of faith were bound up with models of ethics and politics. We have no good reason to project onto late medieval Christianity a version of faith that splits off its interiority from the institutions and practices that cultivate that interiority, a version that forgets that faith included believing the Church, in whatever way the Christian took the relevant article of the Creed: *Credo ... unam sanctam catholicam et apostolicam Ecclesiam*. Only scholars projecting some such split will seek to persuade us that faith and devotion existed in some interior or transcendent realm beyond or above ethics and politics. Finally, this chapter, with its concluding comparison of Thorpe and Love, has shown that even fideistic and affective piety is not as apolitical and transcendent as some scholars imagine. In the eighty-third chapter of her *Revelation of Love*, Julian of Norwich writes that reason is the highest gift we have received and that it is grounded in "kinde" (both God and our God-given nature). It is perfectly congruent with

---

[70] See *ST* I–II.92.1 *ad* 4; I–II.93.3 *ad* 2; I–II.96.4 *resp.*; I–II.96.6 *resp.* See too his part of *De Regimine Principum*, in *On the Government of Rulers*, esp. I.4; I.11–6–7.

[71] St. Thomas Aquinas, *In Libris Politicorum Aristotelis Expositio*, ed. R. M. Spiazzi (Rome, 1966), I.10, 152–53.

[72] On relations between Love's text and the Gospels, see his comments, *Mirror*, 9–11; on Thorpe and the Gospels, see Aers and Staley, *Powers of the Holy*, 49–52.

faith, also a light from God in which Christ (our mother) and the Holy Spirit lead us, in the night we now inhabit. From this perspective, fideism would never be seen simply as Christian "faith" but a particular version, historically, culturally, and politically determinate, one that split apart and distorted what Julian, like St. Thomas, took to be the gifts of God:

> I beheld with reverent drede, and heyly mervelyng in the syte and in the feling of the swet accord, that our reason is in God, understondyng that it is the heyest gifte that we have receivid, and it is groundid in kinde. Our feith is a light kindly command of our endles day that is our fader, God, in which light our Moder, Criste, and our good lord, the Holy Gost, leidith us in this passand life.[73]

---

[73] *The Shewings*, chap. 83, 153. See n. 1.

2

Faith, Ethics, and Chaucer

> May no medicyne vnder mone þe man to heele brynge,
> Neiþer Feiþ ne fyn hope, so festred be hise woundes,
> Wiþouten þe blood of a barn born of a mayde.
> And he be baþed in þat blood, baptised as it were,
> And þanne plastred wiþ penaunce and passion of þat baby,
> He sholde stonde and steppe; ac stalworþe worþe he neuere
> Til he haue eten al þe barn and his blood ydronke.
>
> (William Langland, *Piers Plowman*)[1]

Beginning with some reflections from Julian of Norwich, the first chapter looked at versions of faith propagated as "medieval" by certain scholars especially interested in Chaucer's Christianity and juxtaposed this with a range of medieval works. In doing this I sought to develop an inquiry that would remain open to the complex web of interlocutions in which Christian traditions of faith, ethics, and politics were being made, webs within which particular texts were written to be received. Keeping the arguments and evidence of the first chapter in mind, I now address some of Chaucer's later work. The aim is to explore models of Christian faith and ethics in the *Canterbury Tales*, to explore the forms of Christianity emerging in this extraordinary book and to see how these are a dialogue with other voices, events, and pressures in late fourteenth-century England. Coverage of these issues in the *Canterbury Tales*, in whatever sense "coverage" might be construed, is not an ambition. My interests in Chaucer's fictions belong to broader questions about the history of the Church, a history that includes theological, ethical, and political dimensions, inseparably bound together. But such interests are not alien to the maker of the *Canterbury Tales*, however oblique and polysemous the modes he favored in pursuing them.

In the Chaucerian scholarship considered in chapter one, the *Clerk's Tale* was taken as an example of the distinctively Christian and devotional in Chaucer's stories, and I shall now address this work. My contention is that Chaucer's poem belongs to the webs of interlocution I have been describing, ones out of which

---

[1] *Piers Plowman: The B-version*, ed. George Kane and E. Talbot Donaldson (London: Athlone, 1988), XVII.94–100. All references will be to this edition unless otherwise stated. For the C-version, see *Piers Plowman: An Edition of the C-text*, ed. Derek Pearsall (London: Arnold, 1978), and *Piers Plowman: The C Version*, ed. George Russell and George Kane (London: Athlone Press, 1997).

the texts of Love and Thorpe were soon to emerge.[2] Let us recall how some scholars believe that the *Clerk's Tale* "rubs our noses in the discomfort, irrationality, the arbitrariness of faith's demands" while Griselda's obedience to Walter is "the mark of Chaucer's highest religious values."[3] In Jill Mann's words, this obedience is to be read "as a surrender of the self to divine providence . . . a leap in the dark, an act of faith." The poem shows "the depths of trust needed to have faith in the benignity of the divine will." Griselda herself is "an image of human suffering" who is also "figuring forth the divine," one who "images" Christ.[4] I hope that the first chapter has made clear that if this was indeed the way Chaucer's story constituted Christian faith then he was making a set of choices within complex but to some extent identifiable webs of interlocution and contested practices. But what is the nature of his choices in this context?[5]

One area of the *Clerk's Tale* seems especially relevant to the hypothesis put forward by Nicholas Love and Archbishop Arundel in the two texts I have considered. What should faithful Christians do when the sovereign commands that an unequivocally false doctrine should be followed or an unequivocally evil act committed? Chaucer's version of this hypothesis is the sovereign's apparent intention to murder two children and his demand that his subject, Griselda, assent to his will and cooperate in the event. For Linda Georgianna the poem's response to this hypothesis is that "politics" and "morality" are utterly irrelevant to matters of faith, as befits "medieval Christian belief." Indeed, like many other commentators, she maintains that in assenting to the sovereign's wickedness (which Chaucer's narrator rightly calls "his crueel purpos" and his "wikke usage") Griselda "becomes a type of Christ himself, whose suffering and sympathy are not only exemplary but redemptive."[6]

---

[2] For an earlier attempt to sketch some of the relationships here, see Aers, *Chaucer, Langland and the Creative Imagination* (London: Routledge, 1980), 169–73. Since then much that has been written on the *Clerk's Tale* engages seriously with such issues. See Lynn Staley in *Powers of the Holy: Religion, Politics and Culture in Late Medieval English Culture* (University Park: Pennsylvania State University Press, 1996), 233–59 and her references to the scholarship on this tale. For readings concentrating on sexual politics, see especially Carolyn Dinshaw, *Chaucer's Sexual Poetics* (Madison: University of Wisconsin Press, 1989), 132–55 and Elaine Tuttle Hansen, *Chaucer and the Fictions of Gender* (Berkeley: University of California Press, 1992), 188–207.

[3] Linda Georgianna, "The Protestant Chaucer," in *Chaucer's Religious Tales*, ed. C. David Benson and Elizabeth Robertson (Cambridge: D. S. Brewer, 1990), 67–68; see similarly Georgianna, "The Clerk's Tale and the Grammar of Assent," *Speculum* 70 (1995), 794, 805, 818; also Barbara Nolan, "Chaucer's Tales of Transcendence: Rhyme Royal and Christian Prayer in the *Canterbury Tales*," in *Chaucer's Religious Tales*, 28, 30.

[4] Jill Mann, *Geoffrey Chaucer* (Hemel Hempstead: Harvester, 1991), 148, 156–57, 158, 159.

[5] For related but sometimes rather different answers to these questions, see Staley in *Powers of the Holy*, chap. 5.

[6] Georgianna, "The Clerk's Tale," 808–809, 810, 817; Mann, *Chaucer*, 160. All quotations from Chaucer come from *The Riverside Chaucer*, ed. Larry D. Benson (Boston: Houghton Mifflin, 1987); here see IV.734 and 785. All references to the *Canterbury Tales* are to fragment and line number.

However, we have seen that this is only one possible version of faith, the version most congenial to those in the role of sovereigns seeking to cultivate subjects who will sacralize the sovereigns' powers and commands. It is the version most congenial to sovereigns seeking unconditional obedience to arbitrary powers, precisely those Thorpe called tyrants. As observed in chapter one, he pointed out that tyrants could take the form of husbands as well as of lords.[7] The Christian faith ascribed to Chaucer by Georgianna is not only far removed from Thorpe's but also from St. Thomas's understanding of the due relations between faith, reason, and ethics. St. Thomas, let us recall, argues that sovereigns who make tyrannical decrees have no legitimate claim to the subjects' obedience. This is so because tyrannical orders only serve private interests, harm others, and establish practices that are at odds with the true end of communities, the life of the virtues in accord with reason, a life moving us toward our supernatural goal.[8] If Chaucer is doing what Georgianna, Mann, and others claim he is doing, then he is making choices to set aside those strands of Christian tradition which provided powerful resources for resisting tyranny and evil commands, ones retained by William of Ockham.[9] And he would be doing so in the years following the great rising and its suppression, the years which saw the emergence of Lollardy and the hierarchy's attempts to suppress it, the years in which Richard II sought to establish a more absolute sovereignty allowing him to sideline all opposition and settle scores with the magnates who had overwhelmed him from 1386 to 1388.[10] If he was making such choices in these

[7] "The Testimony of William Thorpe," in *Two Wycliffite Texts*, ed. Anne Hudson, EETS 301 (Oxford: Oxford University Press, 1993), 49. For an illuminating study of marital and jurisprudential discourses in Langland which are plainly relevant to the *Clerk's Tale*, see Elizabeth Fowler, "Civil Death and the Maiden: Agency and the Conditions of Contract in *Piers Plowman*," *Speculum* 70 (1995): 760–92. For a reading of the *Clerk's Tale* as an affirmation of lay authority and absolute monarchy, but with no mention of Wyclif, see Larry Scanlon, *Narrative, Authority, and Power: The Medieval Exemplum and the Chaucerian Tradition* (Cambridge: Cambridge University Press, 1994), 175–91.

[8] See *Summa Theologiae* (London: Blackfriars, 1964–80), I–II.92.1, II–II.42.2, especially *ad* 3; *De Regimine Principum*, trans. James M. Blythe, *On the Government of Rulers: De Regimine Principum: Ptolemy of Lucca with Portions Attributed to Thomas Aquinas* (Philadelphia: University of Pennsylvania Press, 1997), I.1, I.4.3.

[9] For Ockham himself on the limits of due authority and licit resistance to sovereigns, see the following: William of Ockham, *A Letter to the Friars Minor and Other Writings*, ed. Arthur Stephen McGrade and John Kilcullen, trans. Kilcullen (Cambridge: Cambridge University Press, 1995), 8, 209, 312–13, 318; *A Short Discourse on Tyrannical Government*, ed. Stephen McGrade, trans. John Kilcullen (Cambridge: Cambridge University Press, 1992), III.3, 79–80; *Octo Quaestiones de Potestate Papae*, in *Opera Politica*, vol. 1, ed. J. G. Sikas (Manchester: Manchester University Press, 1940), 203–4; and still invaluable here is McGrade, *The Political Thought of William of Ockham* (Cambridge: Cambridge University Press, 1974). John of Salisbury's defense of tyrannicide should also be recalled in this context; see Cary J. Nederman, "A Duty to Kill: John of Salisbury's Theory of Tyrannicide," *Review of Politics* 50 (1988): 365–89, reprinted in his *Medieval Aristotelianism and its Limits* (Aldershot: Variorum, 1997). In that collection, also relevant is "Conciliarism and Constitutionalism: John Gerson and Medieval Political Thought," chap. 16.

[10] On the relevant contexts of the *Clerk's Tale* see Staley, *Powers of the Holy*, chap. 5, an

contexts then, plainly enough, his version of faith and his art was doing quite determinate political work, not simply reproducing an apolitical and uniformly "medieval" version of Christian obedience.

Specifically Christian obedience, it may be recalled, is envisaged as obedience to God in the light of the life, death, and resurrection of Jesus. It entails a distinctively Christian discipleship lived within a specific community, the Church, and should not be confused with a generalized obedience to secular powers. Alongside St. Paul's instructions that Roman Christians should not resist their pagan rulers (Romans 13.1–8) is set St. Peter's insistence that "We ought to obey God rather than men" (Acts 5.29). In his Rule of 1221, St. Francis determined that even a friar vowed to obedience "is not bound to obey if a minister commands anything that is contrary to our life or his own conscience, because there can be no obligations to obey if it means committing sin." In chapter 10 of the 1223 Rule, he reminds friars that they have "renounced their own wills for God's sake," commanding obedience to ministers as a manifestation of this renunciation. Once more he makes the qualification that such obedience is "in everything that they promised to God and is not against their conscience and their rule."[11] However, there undoubtedly were tendencies within Chaucer's culture to represent the lay sovereign as the vicar of God with powers unprecedented in the feudal and Catholic Europe of the previous two-hundred-and-fifty years, tendencies considered in this book's final chapter. If Chaucer was defending unconditional obedience to absolute lay sovereignty, encapsulated in Walter's dominion over Griselda, then his work would, in this respect, be contributing to a project whose consequences involved a massive transformation of the role of the Catholic Church in Christian lives and communities. Was his work doing anything like this?[12] The *Clerk's Tale* includes strands related to these issues, approached with characteristic obliqueness. If we are to investigate them we have to consider his figuration of Griselda.

Here it is necessary to address the extremely widespread claim that Griselda is "a type of Christ himself," "a figure . . . of Christ himself . . . obedient even unto death."[13] During the exchanges in which Griselda agrees to hand over her children to her tyrannical and compulsive sovereign so that he can murder them,

---

exceptionally detailed and careful contextualization of Chaucer's *Canterbury Tales*. Since that book was written, Nigel Saul has published a major study of Richard II: *Richard II* (New Haven: Yale University Press, 1997), esp. chaps. 9–16.

[11] *St. Francis of Assisi: Writings and Early Biographies*, trans. R. Brown et al., ed. M. A. Habig (Quincy, Ill.: Franciscan Press, 1991), 35 and 63. I have found work by Stanley Hauerwas and Charles Pinches especially helpful in my attempt to understand the issues here: *Christians Among the Virtues* (Notre Dame: University of Notre Dame Press, 1997), 133, 137, 140–42, 145–48, 204 (n. 13 and n. 16).

[12] Larry Scanlon, whose perspectives exclude Wycliffism and the ecclesiological issues that concern me, answers in the affirmative: *Narrative, Authority, and Power*, 175–91.

[13] For Georgianna here, see "The Clerk's Tale," 817 and in Benson and Robertson, *Chaucer's Religious Tales*, 142; similarly, Mann, *Chaucer*, 158–160 and Ann W. Astell, *Chaucer and the Universe of Learning* (Ithaca: Cornell University Press, 1996), 169.

as the mother unequivocally believes (IV.519–74), the language in which she describes herself and them is revealing. She turns those who according to traditional Christian doctrine are God's creatures made in the image of God into the secular sovereign's "owene thyng." She also affirms that this earthly sovereign cannot do anything, including the present evil (murdering a child) which could "displese" her. All her desire, she says, is for this man; her sole fear is to lose him (IV.498–511). Her sole fear is *not*, we should note, to cut herself off from God. She reiterates the language of reification when she hands over the second child:

> Ye been oure lord; dooth with youre owene thyng
> Right as yow list . . .   (IV.652–3)

With this reification she reaffirms her unconditional obedience to his thoroughly secular and thoroughly arbitrary power (IV.652–65). I can find no theological, let alone Christocentric, focus in these utterances. What Griselda says to one of the children she hands over to be killed deserves far more attention than it is usually given: "this nyght shaltow dyen for my sake" (IV.560).[14] Here she explicitly puts the *child* in the role of victim sacrificed to save herself, the mother. Griselda, by her own account, is willing to let her child be killed for her sake. This statement should have proved another decisive block to scholarly assertions that *throughout the poem* Griselda herself remains a figure for Christ. Furthermore, anyone who wants to make Griselda the figure of Abraham sacrificing Isaac to God should recollect that Griselda is apparently a Christian living under the new covenant made by Christ's life and work. Christian allegory points toward and is enabled by Christ; it draws Christians toward Christ and the new creation, not back towards the old covenant and law.[15] Also worth recollecting here is Augustine's comment in the *City of God*: "if anyone decides to sacrifice his son to God, his action is not free from crime just because Abraham did this and was praised for doing it."[16] Walter himself is a tyrannical lord, an epistemophiliac driven "to knowe" his wife's heart. He is so addicted to this impossible quest that "he ne myghte out of his herte throwe/ This merveillous desir" (IV.451–55), a man likened to someone "bounden" to a stake (IV.701–7).[17] Griselda never maintains that she is obeying this man

---

[14] This line, IV.560, is rarely discussed: for an exception, see Elizabeth Kirk, "Nominalism and the Dynamics of the *Clerk's Tale*," in *Chaucer's Religious Tales*, 113. In lines added by Chaucer, Griselda makes the sign of the Cross over the daughter who is to be murdered, but she seems to think that God the Father died on the Cross. She does not mention Jesus Christ (IV.555–60). Does Chaucer *want* us to observe this strange move? If not, why is it introduced? If he does want us to note it, to what purpose? Are we to take it as a sign that Griselda is less shaped by orthodox Christian teaching even here than most critics have assumed?

[15] The best introduction to these matters remains the wonderfully rich work of Henri de Lubac, *Exégèse Médiévale*, 4 vols. (Paris: Aubier, 1959–64). For Langland's treatment of the relations between Abraham (Faith) and Christ (Samaritan) see XVI.252–XVII.98.

[16] *City of God*, I.26.

[17] This was emphasized by Aers, together with a characterization of Walter as one driven by

because she loves Christ and wishes to pursue her supernatural end. On the contrary she maintains that she obeys Walter because she said she would and because she dreads the loss of nothing but Walter (IV.645–58, 508).[18]

We have seen that many strands of Christian tradition provided resources that would have legitimized Griselda's refusal to assent to her ruler's sins against both old and new law. Her choice not to draw on these resources is a choice that is not necessitated by the tradition to which they belong. Indeed, Griselda herself, as I have observed, never claims that her actions are shaped by the love of Christ and commitment to obedient discipleship. If Griselda was an exemplar of specifically Christian virtues, what might that Catholic tradition lead readers to expect from her?

One might reasonably expect that she would see herself in terms of specifically Christian narratives and practices. These narratives (Gospels, Acts, Apocalypse) and practices (liturgical, sacramental) were enacted in a specific community that saw itself as the body of Christ, the Church that gave its members the resources of the new creation (2 Corinthians 5:14–19; 1 Corinthians 12). This was the Creedal Church, both the object of faith and the enabler of faith's practices necessary to salvation.[19] In the light of this community and its founding narratives, the claims of secular power could be seen as folly, often demonic folly.

But Griselda does not apparently see herself as part of this community. Nor does the *Clerk's Tale* show her as living within the liturgy and sacraments of the Church. I cannot find signs that her children were baptized, let alone that this sacrament was given anyone's attention. Nor are there any signs that Griselda embraced the sacrament of penance or the sacrament of the altar, no sign that she received or desired the eucharist, let alone that she felt the orthodox and fervent desire we found in Nicholas Love's *Mirror*. True enough, she is married,

---

the lust for dominion (understood in an Augustinian framework) in *Chaucer, Langland, and the Creative Imagination*, 170–71. See, for the relevant Augustinian framework, *City of God*, XV.7, XIV.28, XIX.15; Satan's preference for imperial rule in XIV.11 is also relevant. For a different reading of both Augustine and Chaucer here, see Scanlon, *Narrative, Authority, and Power*, 179–84. On Walter and tyrants of Lombardy, see David Wallace, *Chaucerian Polity* (Stanford: Stanford University Press, 1997), chap. 10.

[18] If someone is tempted to maintain that Griselda's oath binds her, as much as Arveragus assumes his wife's gamesome and immediate 'promise' in the *Franklin's Tale* obligates her to have sexual intercourse against her will and her marital fidelity, then he or she simply forgets Jeptha and the standard medieval teaching that acting out a morally mistaken oath makes matters far worse than breaking it. This is made clear in *Melibee*, VII.1064–66. On this issue, see Alan Gaylord, "The Promise in *The Franklin's Tale*," *English Literary History* 31 (1964): 331–65.

[19] On the confession of faith in the whole Church united by faith, see St. Thomas, *ST* II–II.1.9, esp. *ad* 3. For an excellent introduction to the relevant patristic, medieval, and reformation literature here, see Henri de Lubac, *The Christian Faith: An Essay on the Structure of the Apostles' Creed*, trans. R. Arnandez (San Francisco: Ignatius Press, 1986), chaps. 5–7; on no salvation outside the Church, see pp. 213–16, 199–200. I have been greatly helped here by Edward Schillebeeckx, *The Church* (New York: Crossroads, 1993).

and marriage, as both the *Merchant's Tale* and the *Parson's Tale*, observe is "a ful greet sacrement" (IV.1319 and X.918). The Parson observes that God made it in paradise, "wolde hymself be born in mariage," sanctified it at Cana (John 2.1–11) and through it "replynesseth hooly chirche of good lynage" (X.918–20). The epistle to the Ephesians presents marriage as a great sacrament ("sacramentum hoc magnum est," 5.32). Through it Christ's love for the Church is figured, as is the unity of Christians in Christ's body (5:25–30). The Parson also invokes this passage: "mariage is figured bitwixe Crist and holy chirche" (X.922). Yet, even though we are shown Griselda marrying Walter, reiterating her subordination to him and her love of him, there are no indications that she sees her marriage in these sacramental and specifically Catholic terms. Given the absence of the other sacraments to which I have pointed, this is worth pausing over. First, the marriage ceremony itself seems exclusively secular and courtly. The ruler has her dressed up to match his status, gives her a ring, sets her on a snow-white horse, takes her to his palace and spends the day in revel "til the sonne gan descende" (IV.365–92). There are no signs of the Church or a priest, let alone of the customary mass.[20] Second, Griselda at no point suggests to Walter that their marriage should be understood as more and other than a secular contract between them, as more and other than a political arrangement for begetting heirs in the service of the worldly security of himself and his people (see IV.470–511, 624–67, 791–889). She never suggests to him that it must be understood as a sacrament figuring the union "bitwixe Crist and holy chirche" and, as such, a union through which the spouses "may not be departed in al hir lyf" (X.922, 917). Third, as already noted, she reifies their child and herself as Walter's "owene thyng" (IV.501, 504), whereas Catholic teaching, dutifully reproduced in the *Parson's Tale*, saw children as one of the ends of marriage, as God's creatures to be nourished in the Church, "to the service of God" and to fill "hooly chirche" (X.883, 919). She represents a conspicuous *lack* of any such Christian vision. She accepts, without question, Walter's claims to absolute possession of the children, accepting that they are his to dispose of as he wills, his to kill for the conveniences of worldly dominion. Fourth, when Walter tells Griselda he intends to set her aside and take another wife, for an avowedly

---

[20] Contrast the conventional form followed by Januarie and May in the *Merchant's Tale*, IV.1700–14, 1819. On marriage in the Middle Ages, the literature is voluminous, but a good place to start is St. Augustine, *On the Good of Marriage [De Bono Conjugali]*, in *Seventeen Short Treatises of St. Augustine*, trans. by members of the English Church (Oxford: Parker, 1847), 275–307 with *Piers Plowman* IX.110–201. For a rich scholastic discussion of marriage, see John Duns Scotus, *Ordinatio* IV, d 33, q 3, trans. by A. B. Wolter in *Duns Scotus on the Will and Morality*, ed. Wolter and A. B. Frank (Washington D.C.: Catholic University Press, 1997), 212–19. Still extremely useful is Henry A. Kelly, *Love and Marriage in the Age of Chaucer* (Ithaca: Cornell University Press, 1975). For one of the rare critical responses to Griselda's understanding of parental obligation, see Saul N. Brody, "Chaucer's Rhyme Royal Tales and the Secularization of the Saint," *Chaucer Review* 20 (1985): 113–31, esp. 121–27. Also relevant here, Aers, *Chaucer* (Brighton: Harvester, 1986), 34. The essential essay on the *Clerk's Tale* remains Elizabeth Salter, *Chaucer: The Knight's Tale and the Clerk's Tale* (London: Arnold, 1962), 37–70.

secular reason (a prophetic type of Henry VIII), she gives no word to suggest that she sees the action in terms of Catholic teaching, as a perilous breach of sacramental union (IV.790–847).

So: no sign of the sacrament of baptism, no sign of the sacrament of penance, no sign of the sacrament of the altar (or of desire for this), no understanding of marriage as a sacrament, no signs of liturgical practice and the presence of the Church in her life. We are shown the married Griselda in palace and at court, exercising the greatest skills of just political governance, in her sovereign's absence, and of "wyfly hoomlinesse" (IV.428–441). But we are never shown her presence in the Church or her desire for any such presence. There are no indications that she ever communicates with a priest at all. Her virtues before and in marriage are emphatically *extra ecclesiam.* Her lack of commitment to the visible Church, her lack of awareness that it has a divinely given role in her and her family's pilgrimage to their supernatural end, her unquestioning, absolute obedience to the secular, murderous ruler, none of these traits belongs to an orthodox Catholic Christianity in the later Middle Ages.

Before asking what they *do* belong to, it should be noted that her sovereign's ethical and religious practices are also remarkably indifferent to the Church, its sacraments, its central narratives, and its authority. One might expect this in a figure represented as a tyrannical epistemophiliac driven by the lust for dominion so memorably analyzed in Augustine's *City of God*.[21] Still, unlike Griselda, he does show momentary awareness of the Church. Pursuing his compulsive will to know and control Griselda, he goes to the Catholic Church for help in securing permission to set aside the wife with whom he has had two children, allegedly for the sake of peace between him and his people (IV.736–49). Turning to the head of the ecclesiastical hierarchy, he is apparently able to command the Roman Curia to make bulls, "As to his crueel purpos may suffyse." These declare, "that the pope, as for his peples reste,/ Bad hym to wedde another, if hym leste" (IV.736–42). The next stanza states that Walter ordered the Curia to "countrefete/ The popes bulles" to this effect (IV.743–49).[22] This episode shows that Walter's awareness of the Church is limited to seeing it as a useful instrument of his thoroughly secular power and obsessions. But it also suggests something about the Roman Curia and the Church it leads: the Church acts as a subordinate political authority. It is prepared to place its sacred authority and powers in the service of secular power and its "crueel purpos" (IV.740). The episode thus represents the Church abandoning its vocation as bride of Christ, as new creation, as alternative community to the worldly structures of cruel injustice and domination. It accepts a role as the instrument of secular power and its "wikke usage" (IV.785). The sequence thus raises extremely sharp questions about the Church, just the kind of questions

---

[21] See the references to Augustine in n. 17.

[22] On this episode see Staley in *Powers of the Holy,* 252; her study of the *Clerk's Tale* is on pp. 233–59. It is a study with which my writing here is in close conversation. See also Scanlon, *Narrative, Authority, and Power,* 188.

put by Langland, Wyclif, and Wycliffites, the kind of questions the Church was seeking to silence with the help of the secular power, a search moving to the burning of heretics from 1401, Arundel's Constitutions of 1409, and the anti-Wycliffite legislation of 1414 in the Leicester parliament.[23] The questions the episode raises are related to the other representations of the Church in the *Canterbury Tales*, to which we shall come. But the *Clerk's Tale* refuses to elaborate them or explore them. Noting this refusal, I will return to Griselda.

Despite the evidence presented above about Griselda's extraordinary lack of concern with the Catholic Church and its sacramental life, about the ways in which her ethical and religious practices do not belong to a specifically Catholic Christianity, it is possible that some readers may still want to affirm the dominant view that Griselda is "a type of Christ."[24] A "type of Christ" so detached from the Church is not an orthodox Catholic type of Christ in Chaucer's period, which is the issue here, but instead of pursuing this objection any further I will offer some comments of the version of Christ assumed by scholars such as Jill Mann, Linda Georgianna, and David Benson, a version defined by the patient suffering of boundless cruelty, by the crucifixion. In *Powers of the Holy*, I showed that while this version was certainly pervasive in late medieval culture, it must be understood *as produced* and analyzed *as produced*. It involved making extremely important choices in its representations of Scriptural narratives and their liturgical forms. Nor, I argued, should its pervasiveness be allowed to occlude alternative versions of Christ's humanity. I do not need to go over the complex ground I sought to explore in that book, ground that is theological, political, and ideological, but a few related observations are appropriate in the present context.[25] The Gospels' stories about Jesus give us an active, mobile prophet and healer, who proclaims a new community he calls the kingdom of God (Luke 4.18, 21; Matthew 11.3–6). Faith, ethics, and the formation of this new community are fused in his proclamation and practice. Jesus was not crucified for submitting obediently, silently, and unconditionally to the Walters of this world. Nor did he marry them, have children with them in palaces, enjoy aristocratic feasts of great "costage," live in courtly "heigh prosperitee" and reproduce a family of worldly princes (IV.1121–38). His form of life, the food he offered, and the community he created belonged to a very different teleology. Here an objector might acknowledge this but state that because Griselda had suffered greatly, she is a "type" of Jesus who suffered

---

[23] On this history, consult the following: Margaret Aston, "Lollardy and Sedition, 1381–1431," *Past and Present* 17 (1960): 1–44, reprinted in her *Lollards and Reformers: Images and Literacy in Late Medieval Religion* (London: Hambledon, 1984), chap. 1; Peter McNiven, *Heresy and Politics in the Reign of Henry IV: The Burning of John Badby* (Woodbridge: Boydell, 1987); on some of its consequences in English Christianity, see the illuminating study by H. Leith Spencer, *English Preaching in the Late Middle Ages* (Oxford: Clarendon Press, 1993).

[24] See above, n. 13. For an original and unusually nuanced version of this traditional allegorizing, see Staley in *Powers of the Holy*, 237–40.

[25] See Aers and Staley, *Powers of the Holy*, chaps. 1–3.

cruelly and was crucified. My response is that Jesus suffered in a particular way as the consequence of a particular kind of life devoted to proclaiming and embodying the kingdom of God. He endured a political execution. The cross, as has been amply demonstrated, was the standard punishment for insurrection against Caesar, "a political punishment."[26] It was the violence of the world against the kingdom of God, against the one who disclosed and obeyed its demands. In no way, as we have seen, is Griselda's suffering the product of following the path of Jesus, of discipleship. In no way is it the product of her religious or secular sovereigns finding her life a danger to their power. Not all human suffering, however grim, necessarily involves a figuration, let alone an imitation, of Jesus's suffering and life.[27] Once this is recognized, it will be possible to understand that the construal of Christ's life and death as a generalized, extra-ecclesial, and apolitical suffering is itself an occlusion of major components of the Gospels' narratives and involves a thoroughly political set of determinants. This will be so whether the occlusions are medieval or modern.[28]

The evidence we have worked through thus far shows that Griselda is not a figure of Christ, that she does not participate in the sacramental life of the Catholic Church and that specifically Christian traditions do not shape her life. They do not motivate her form of obedience, which, we have seen, was to "a mortal man" addicted to "wikke usage" (IV.1149–50, 785). We need now to reconsider her patience in this light. It is a patience dedicated to obeying Walter and his projects. She tells him that although her children have been killed, "At youre comandement," he should continue doing whatever he wills while she herself will do whatever he wants: "I wol youre lust obeye" (IV.647–57). This is the motive and teleology of her patience, as of her obedience. And as with the latter, her form of patience seems rather less specifically Christian than many Chaucerians have maintained.

It is of course possible to follow the Clerk and say that one can take such patient obedience to the vicious ruler as an analogy of the patient obedience due to God (IV.1142–62). Such analogizing, pervasive in medieval homilies and sermons, remains extrinsic to Griselda's form of patience and its teleology as these have been unfolded in the *Clerk's Tale*. It can tell us nothing about Griselda in that story: just as analogizing David's murder of Uriah (in pursuit of adultery) to Christ's redemption of humanity can tell us nothing about David's treatment of Uriah or Bethsabee [Bathsheeba] and his motives (2 Kings [Samuel] 11 and 12).[29] Furthermore, such analogizing of the *Clerk's Tale* encourages a misunderstanding of the virtues. It encourages the assumption that ends and means are separable, that the teleology of the virtues (their end in

[26] John Howard Yoder, *The Politics of Jesus* (2nd ed. [Grand Rapids, MI: Eerdmans, 1994]), 125.

[27] See, for example, Yoder, *Politics of Jesus*, 95–97.

[28] Edward Schillebeeckx, *Christ* (New York: Crossroad, 1990), 699; see also 694–700, 724–30, 734–839.

[29] On the allegorizing of David here, see de Lubac, *Exégèse Médiévale*, I, part 2, 458–63.

God) is separable from their immediate practice. But as St. Thomas's treatment of theological and cardinal virtues (*ST,* II–II) makes clear, the ends towards which virtues direct us are immanent within the means they lead us to choose: this relationship is constitutive of Christian virtues.[30]

St. Thomas's treatment of patience in the *Summa Theologiae* brings out the relevant issues. It comes in his consideration of cardinal virtues, under fortitude, and we should remember that this has been preceded by his analysis of the theological virtues.[31] The third article on patience investigates whether it is possible to have patience without grace (II–II.166.3). It may seem that this is possible because people can endure hardships and sorrows in the pursuit of evil or good without grace (II–II.136.3 *obj* 1 and 2). However, distinctively Christian patience is from God (quoting from Psalm 61.6, "But be thou, O my soul, subject to God: for from him is my patience"). And its practice belongs to *charity,* which loves God above all else. Hence patience, if it is to be a Christian virtue, is *caused by charity.* St. Thomas quotes St. Paul: "Charity is patient" (1 Corinthians 13.4). He then observes that it is impossible to have charity without grace, quoting Romans 5.5: "the charity of God is poured forth in our hearts, by the Holy Ghost who is given to us." It follows, therefore, that it is impossible to have patience without the help of grace (II–II.136.3 *contra* and *resp*). St. Thomas makes clear the distinctiveness of a Christian understanding of patience and its practice. It is not the individual strength of will and detachment, the individual's self-sustaining ability to achieve firmness and rationality in the face of sorrows and fears.[32] As Augustine had argued in the *City of God,* the Christian understanding is not to be confused with Stoic versions emerging in the cultivation of *apatheia* or *inpassibilitas.*[33] St. Thomas's emphasis on the priority of the theological virtues, especially charity, and on the

---

[30] For my understanding of these areas of St. Thomas's *Summa Theologiae,* I am indebted to Alasdair MacIntyre's recent work: *Whose Justice? Which Rationality?* (London: Duckworth, 1988), 164–207, and *Three Rival Versions of Moral Enquiry* (London: Duckworth, 1990), chaps. 3 and 6. Also particularly relevant here is Stanley Hauerwas and Charles Pinches, *Christians Among the Virtues* and John Milbank, *Theology and Social Theory* (Oxford: Blackwell, 1990), 160–61.

[31] On patience, see *ST* II–II.136. The theological virtues were treated in II–II.1–46. For all quotations from the Bible I have used the Douai–Rheims translation of the Vulgate, *The Holy Bible* (London: Burns and Oates, 1964). On patience, the Middle English poem of that title and relevant secondary literature, see chap. 4 below, section 3.

[32] On charity, see *ST* II–II.23–46.

[33] See Augustine, *City of God,* IX.4, IX.5, XIV.9, and XIX.4. Here I paraphrase from XIV.9. St. Thomas makes use of Augustine's *De Patientia,* trans. in *Seventeen Short Treatises of Saint Augustine,* 543–62. For a representative fourteenth-century preacher's treatment of patience, see *Fasciculus Morum: A Fourteenth Century Preacher's Handbook,* ed. and trans. Siegfried Wenzel (University Park: Pennsylvania State University Press, 1989), II.5–7, 134–47. Here, as in Chaucer's *Parson's Tale,* patience is treated as a remedy for wrath. For the centrality of Christ in the treatment of patience in *Fasciculus Morum,* see II.7 (lines 36–62). For Chaucer's *Parson's Tale, Canterbury Tales,* X.659–76. Christ is at the core here, but the text invokes "olde payens" without making the careful distinctions of Augustine and St. Thomas. For the texts of Augustine's *City of God* used here, see p. 7, n. 21 above.

presence of the supernatural end in the activity of patience, through grace, sets the virtue within the Church, which is the divinely given mediator of sacramental grace and the gifts of the Holy Spirit. *Extra ecclesiam, nulla salus*, as we have noticed. The contrast with Griselda's form of patience and its teleology is striking, a contrast that matches the remarkable absence of the Church, its priesthood, and its sacraments.

Having identified these absences, one further question may be put. Why did Chaucer produce them, and produce them in combination with an uncondi-tional, uncritical obedience to a tyrannical sovereign who persuades Griselda to collude with murder (twice) and with a divorce that would have been illicit in the terms of Catholic Christianity?[34] Such questions are notoriously tricky. If they are designed to sponsor some quest for a writer's psychological intention, they are mistaken about what is possible. But if they invite consideration of a textual and cultural intentionality, they are reasonable. It is in this second way that I shall proceed, as an inquiry into what kind of work might be done by such choices in a determinate network of conversations and actions. I will summarize my answers before taking leave of the *Clerk's Tale*.

The story contributes to political conversations in the later 1380s and 1390s. Here the role of Walter is central, particularly his lust for dominion, his demand for absolute, unquestioning obedience from Griselda, and his use of the Catholic Church to further his own thoroughly secular interests. In 1980 I sketched out, rather briskly, suggestions about the story's political work and its uses of conventional gender and marital ideology. Chaucer's poem was viewed as a critical examination of tendencies to absolutism in the later stages of the reign of Richard II. It was seen as a defense of current theories of "*limited monarchy*" and of the "*desacralization* of secular power." The reading was linked to the Articles of Deposition (1399) and the "Complaint of Chaucer to his Purse," a link intended to evoke the political discourses to which the tale belonged: the Clerk was warning modern Walters not to expect their subjects to be wives like Griselda (IV.1162–69).[35] Since 1980 there have been a number of richly informative studies of the tale's political bearings and its uses of gender.[36] In the light of this scholarship, especially Lynn Staley's, I have come to see the

[34] It is noteworthy that Griselda *never* seeks advice from a confessor or a priest on either of these issues. I drew attention long ago to the relevance of the medieval commonplace in which wife and husband figure people and ruler: *Chaucer, Langland, and the Creative Imagination* (London: Routledge, 1980), 172–73. See also Lynn Staley Johnson, "The Prince and his People: A Study of Two Covenants in the *Clerk's Tale*," *Chaucer Review* 10 (1975): 17–20; and now, Staley in *Powers of the Holy*, 233–59.

[35] Aers, *Chaucer, Langland, and the Creative Imagination*, 169–73. On medieval traditions of constitutional history see the recent study by James M. Blythe, *Ideal Government and the Mixed Constitution in the Middle Ages* (Princeton: Princeton University Press, 1992).

[36] See especially David Wallace, "'When She Translated Was': A Chaucerian Critique of the Petrarchan Academy," in *Literary Practice and Social Change in Britain, 1380–1530*, ed. Lee Patterson (Berkeley: University of California Press, 1990), 156–215. See also his *Chaucerian Polity*, chap. 10; Staley, *Powers of the Holy*, 233–59; Stephen Knight, *Chaucer* (Oxford: Blackwell, 1986), 108–12.

political implications as far more bleak and more complex than I had realized. Staley shows how the *Clerk's Tale* belongs to "Chaucer's participation in an elaborate literary conversation about tyrannical power."[37] But while it does offer a devastating critique of such power, it also undermines assumptions that there are subjects who could participate in a limited monarchy, let alone offer principled resistance to a ruler with "autocratic" aims, a ruler such as Richard II may have been from May 1389.[38] The story tells its audience, "the subjects of Richard II," that there are no guarantees that the sovereign will not continue to follow his "wikke usage" (IV.785): Walter "does not promise not to do it again."[39] It also implies that there are no alternatives to Walter or to the unprincipled "people" whom he rules. Griseldas have all gone (IV.1163–68). In this respect the poem is in dialogue with the subject of the present book's final chapter, John Wyclif:

> the *Clerk's Tale* "answers" another Oxford scholar who argued for a strongly king-centered state as the prerequisite for reformation. To Wyclif and all others who looked for a new world, Chaucer offers this one, which is described in the idealized language of Solomon's marriage song but, in fact, is held together by the coin of the realm . . . mostly brass.[40]

So the poem works not only as a critical meditation on aspirations of Richard II to a more Walter-like power, but also on the hopes Wyclif placed in the expansion of the sovereign's powers, perhaps a mocking response to *De Officio Regis*. If the *Clerk's Tale* represents this political vision, it entails not only abandoning the prophetic and eschatological resources of Christianity but also the understanding of the virtues and their relation to a good community articulated within the Christian transformation of Aristotle's *Ethics* and *Politics*. For what? Rather than address this question, Chaucer has the Clerk retreat from his "ernestful matere" through rings of irony and "song" that are part of an exchange with the Wife of Bath (IV.1175–1212). Such a retreat enacts the abandonment just described. Not, of course, that this "song" is the last word of the *Canterbury Tales*.

I have now delivered part of my answer to the question as to why Chaucer would produce a work combining the absences, discussed above, with a depiction of uncritical obedience to tyrannical secular power. But, as we have observed, the absences go to the heart of Catholic Christianity in the Middle Ages, and the remainder of the answer needs to address this more directly. Here Wyclif's version of Christian reformation is relevant. As we shall see in the final chapter, this involved not only the exorbitant increase in secular power just mentioned, but also a massive transformation in the nature of the Catholic Church, depriving it of both its saving sacramental role and its divine authority.

[37] Staley, *Powers of the Holy*, 235, 241–43, 246; also Wallace, cited in n. 36.
[38] Staley, *Powers of the Holy*, 236–37, 243–45, 247; on "Richard II from May 1389," 247–52.
[39] Staley, *Powers of the Holy*, 255–57.
[40] Staley, *Powers of the Holy*, 259; alluding to *CT*, IV.1166–72. See Staley, *Powers of the Holy*, 256–57.

This transformation would, as we shall see, bring the reformed (and greatly diminished) clergy under secular control, a control perhaps shadowed in Walter's use of the Roman Curia. If Staley is right in seeing the *Clerk's Tale* in dialogue with arguments of Wyclif, among whose questioners and followers Chaucer had friends,[41] Chaucer's fiction imagines a world where such a withering away of the Catholic Church's presence has taken place. The absences identified above would be products of this as yet hypothetical situation: so would Griselda herself. Absence begets absence: no priests, no confession, no eucharist, no nuptial mass, no baptism. This is certainly *not* to suggest that Chaucer's interest is in imagining an achieved Wycliffite reformation. There are no signs of mobile preachers like Thorpe, no signs of Wycliffite schools gathering to hear scripture in English, or Wycliffite tracts, no signs of a Hawisia Mone or Margery Baxter in Griselda's village nor a Sir John Clanvowe or Sir John Oldcastle at Walter's court, nor any signs that Walter has taken *De Officio Regis* as his guidebook. Chaucer has imagined absences, imagined the consequences for Christianity of a certain withering away of the traditional Church, without feeling obliged to imagine a Wycliffite alternative.

One consequence of this situation not discussed above is Griselda's individualistic mode of being, individualistic in the sense that it transcends all communities (peasant village, court, Church). She is able to rule justly in her husband's absence, to fulfill "wyfly hoomlinesse" (IV.428–41), to be a perfect courtly servant and domestic organizer (IV.953–80), and to be a perfect peasant laborer sustaining the lord's poorest serf, her father (IV.204–31). But wherever she is and whatever virtues she practices, she remains markedly detached from any community. She seems as independent and isolated in her home village as in the palace. Whatever else this autonomy may be, it is among the consequence of the withering away of the Church's presence. Catholic tradition taught that in the Church, "we being many, are one bread, one body: all that partake of one bread" (1 Corinthians 10.17); it taught that Church and eucharist are sacraments of unity in Christ. It taught that spiritual life, like bodily life, needs to be strengthened: this applied to individuals, who are necessarily members of a specifiable community in which we live as naturally social creatures.[42] Griselda's autonomy represents the absence of all this. She becomes an exemplar of the possible consequences of a Wycliffite ecclesiological and political reformation, an exemplar of Christianity transformed beyond the traditions of Catholic Christianity, *extra ecclesiam*. Here we can see a path opening out from Christianity to a Stoicism that is only, if at all, vestigially Christian. This would certainly be a

[41] See Anne Hudson, *The Premature Reformation: Wycliffite Texts and Lollard History* (Oxford: Clarendon Press, 1988), 390–94; Paul Strohm, "Chaucer's Lollard Joke: History and the Textual Unconscious," *Studies in the Age of Chaucer* 17 (1995), 23–42; K. B. McFarlane, *Lancastrian Kings and Lollard Knights* (Oxford: Clarendon Press, 1972), 139–226. On McFarlane, see Strohm's cautionary note in "Chaucer's Lollard Joke," 33, n. 43.

[42] These are all commonplaces of traditional teaching, but on the union of the faithful and Christ in the sacraments of the Church I have in mind particularly St. Thomas, *ST* III.65.1, III.80.20, III.22.6, and III.73.3.

rather ironic outcome for any Christian reformation, but especially for one as purportedly Scriptural as Wyclif's. Be that as it may, the versions of patience and constancy figured forth in the *Clerk's Tale* belong to a form of individual identity which has more in common with Stoic aspirations to autonomy and fixed self-sameness, fixed self-consistency, than to specifically Christian accounts of the subject's utterly dependent creatureliness, sinfulness, need for endless forgiveness, need for Christ and the Church. However, the disparity here has not prevented the rival tradition of Stoicism from proving extremely attractive to Christians in various cultural contexts and difficulties. There may perhaps be some reasons, as I have suggested elsewhere, to wonder whether Chaucer himself might have been one of these Christians, a question to which I return at the end of this chapter.[43] With this observation I conclude my discussion of the exploration of faith and ethics in the *Clerk's Tale*. The discussion has included an account of what it might have meant in the later 1380s and 1390s to produce the absences that have been identified and to combine them with the central subject's devoted service to tyrannical secular power.

The issues under consideration emerge in many of the *Canterbury Tales*, but I wish to juxtapose the *Second Nun's Tale* with the commentary just offered on the *Clerk's Tale*. The latter imagines the Roman Church dissolving into absences and colluding with a tyrannical secular power; the former imagines the Church in its early evangelical days under persecution from tyrannical secular power. From the churchless, isolated heroine of the *Clerk's Tale*, paying unconditional obedience to her ruler (even in murder), we move to a heroine in the Church, one who opposes such power, preaches against it, converts others from its obedience, and resists its demands, to death. The contrasts between the two works are sharp. For the *Second Nun's Tale*, Chaucer chose a devotional genre that belonged to practices and beliefs central to late medieval Catholicism, the cult of saints.[44] At the time Chaucer was writing the *Canterbury Tales*, this cult and

---

[43] See Aers, *Chaucer*, 59–61.

[44] On saints' legends and cults there is abundant helpful material. In the present contexts the following may be especially relevant: Eamon Duffy, *The Stripping of the Altars* (New Haven: Yale University Press, 1992), chap. 5; Thomas J. Heffernan, *Sacred Biography: Saints and their Biographers in the Middle Ages* (New York: Oxford University Press, 1988); Michael E. Goodich, *Violence and Miracle in the Fourteenth Century* (Chicago: University of Chicago Press, 1995); André Vauchez, *La Sainteté en Occident aux Derniers Siècles du Moyen Age* (Rome: École Française de Rome, 1981); Sherry L. Reames, *The Legenda Aurea* (Madison: University of Wisconsin Press, 1985); Renate Blumenfeld-Kosinski and Timea Szell, *Images of Sainthood in Medieval Europe* (Ithaca: Cornell University Press, 1991), which includes an essay by Gail B. Sherman on Chaucer's *Second Nun's Tale*, "Saints, Nuns, and Speech in the *Canterbury Tales*," 136–60. The essential work on the sources of Chaucer's *Second Nun's Tale*, together with the significance of his selection and composing of different versions of the legend of St. Cecilia, has been done in a sequence of major studies by Sherry Reames: "The Sources of Chaucer's 'Second Nun's Tale'," *Modern Philology* 76 (1978–79): 111–35; "The Cecilia Legend as Chaucer Inherited It and Retold It," *Speculum* 55 (1980): 38–57; "A Recent Discovery Concerning the Sources of Chaucer's *Second Nun's Tale*," *Modern Philology* 87 (1990): 337–61; "Artistry, Decorum, and Purpose in

its literary forms had come under attack from Wycliffites appealing to the practices of the early Church and its founding narratives, the Gospels.[45] Introducing a saint's legend, about a saint intransigently resisting secular power, and ascribing it to a pilgrim on the way to the shrine of St. Thomas Becket, a saint murdered by the sovereign for resisting secular power over the church, was an inventive and characteristically complex way to develop the explorations of faith and ethics in the *Canterbury Tales*.

The directions in which Chaucer revised his sources in making the *Second Nun's Tale* have been recently investigated by Sherry Reames and Lynn Staley in very different but converging ways.[46] It emerges from their research that the poem's representations of the early Church are crucial to the poem's contemporary force:

> The *Second Nun's Tale* offers a picture of the primitive church as a group joined by love for Christ and belief in the Gospels, shepherded by Urban, to whose sacramental powers Cecilia sends her "children," her husband, and her brother-in-law. Chaucer depicts a church that, in fact, serves a new society, the codes and relationships of which reverse those of pagan society.[47]

The Church actually *is* the "new society." It has apparently taken seriously Jesus's command to his disciples about secular dominion: "You know that the princes of the Gentiles lord it over them and they that are the greater exercise power upon them. It shall not be so among you: but whoever wilt be the greater among you, let him be your minister" (Matthew 20.25–26; see also Luke 22.25–25). The pope in this Church is "Pope Urban" and, unlike his current successor of that name, lives among "the povre folkes" in "halkes [hiding places]," criminalized by the secular powers and under perpetual sentence of death by burning (VIII.305, 174, 309–18). The relations fostered in this Church are well described in the passage just quoted from Lynn Staley's study, and the poem foregrounds the role of preaching, conversion and baptism in the making of Christians (for example, VIII.319–53, 372–90, 537–39). Faith is profoundly social. People do not take isolated leaps in the dark that keep them in some private world of spirituality: they are converted in dialogue with others, called to become members of a particular Church and then, only then, experience the visionary fruits of faith (VIII.218–41 follows 162–217; VIII.354–57 follows 319–52). Faith unites its members in a confessing community centered on the sacrament of baptism, the word, and mutual love. Faith is also shown to complete reason, to activate it with the rhetoric of persuasion even as it goes

Three Middle English Retellings of the Cecilia Legend," in *The Endless Knot. Essays on Old and Middle English in Honor of Marie Boroff*, ed. M. T. Tavormina and R. F. Yeager (Cambridge: Brewer, 1995), 177–200.

[45] For Wycliffite approaches to these matters, see Hudson, *Premature Reformation*, 302–303 and chap. 7.

[46] See Staley, "Chaucer's Tale of the Second Nun and Strategies of Dissent," *Studies in Philology* 89 (1992): 314–33 and Reames, "Artistry, Decorum, and Purpose."

[47] Staley, *Powers of the Holy*, 205.

beyond the boundaries of reason uninformed by faith. Cecilia embodies this from beginning to end, from the way she deals with marriage to her death sermons and final arrangements to have "of myn hous perpetually a cherche" (VIII.546).[48] As she has been "from hir cradel up fostred in the feith/ Of Crist (VIII.121–22), within the Church, she directs the virtues she practices in Rome to her and others' supernatural end, rather than to the ends given by absolute obedience "Unto a mortal man" and his very mortal projects (*Clerk's Tale*, IV.1149–50; see IV.361–64, 501–11, 646–47, 652–67). In this early Roman Church there are no conflicts between Church and the propagation of Christ's Gospel by the laity (including a woman), no conflicts between laity and priests. In Cecilia's version of Christian ethics the virtues' end informs their practice, as befits creatures who are "social and political animals" necessarily living in communities not only for survival but for their virtuous flourishing.[49]

But what are the consequences of such a version of Church, faith, and ethics? This was one of the questions Chaucer was examining in this legend. His own editing of the legend, as Sherry Reames has shown, highlights the focus on Cecilia, her agency, her preaching, and her trial.[50] Chaucer keeps material from the *Legenda Aurea* that has Cecilia "preaching authoritatively on Christian doctrines" but moves to other sources for her trial:

> for which he follows the Roman/ Franciscan abridgment, adding an occasional touch from *Legenda*. This scene, which tends to be greatly de-emphasized if not omitted altogether in English breviaries, is a prominent and dramatic part of both the continental sources he chose to use. But only the Roman/ Franciscan account turns it into the sole focus of the second half of the legend, by omitting or greatly condensing all the competing scenes. The emphasis on Cecilia's trial must have been part of what attracted Chaucer to this particular source.[51]

That is, "what attracted Chaucer to this particular source" was the way it brought out the necessarily political consequences of faith and ethics in the Church of Cecilia, Urban, Valerian, and Tiburce. This Church is a visible polity whose virtues conflict with those of the earthly city. The Roman authorities understand the challenge and seek to eliminate it: either Christians must conform or be exterminated. Almachius, the Roman prefect, has Cecilia brought to him. Noting her contempt of his power (VIII.428–41) he reminds her of its foundations:

---

[48] On her marriage and its spiritual offspring, Staley, *Powers of the Holy*, 205–207, with J. E. Grennen, "St. Cecilia's Chemical Wedding," *Journal of English and Germanic Philology* 65 (1966): 466–81. On spiritual marriage see Dyan Elliott, *Spiritual Marriage: Sexual Abstinence in Medieval Wedlock* (Princeton: Princeton University Press, 1993), esp. chaps. 4–5.

[49] St. Thomas Aquinas, *De Regimine Principum*, I.3–7 in *On the Government of Rulers*; see also Blythe's introduction, pp. 5–7.

[50] See Reames, "Artistry, Decorum, and Purpose," 178–99; also, Staley, *Powers of the Holy*, 207–208.

[51] Reames, "Artistry, Decorum, and Purpose," 193–94.

Wostow nat how oure myghty princes free
Han thus comanded and maad ordinauce
That every Cristen wight shal han penaunce
But if that he his Cristendom withseye,
And goon al quit, if he wole it reneye?   (VIII.444–48)

Almachius represents legitimate secular power, and the "myghty princes free" are the higher powers ordained by God, just those to whom Roman Christians owed subjection, according to St. Paul (Romans 13.1–5). St. Paul's text, taken out of context and adored by the magisterial reformers (until that adoration seemed to pose a threat to the very survival of Lutheran and Calvinist reformation[52]) did not trouble Cecilia or the *Second Nun's Tale*. The saint appeals to "conscience and good feith unfeyned," identifying all secular power as "mortal mannes power," a "bladdre ful of wynd" (VIII.434–41). She is totally confident that the Church within which she speaks has the authority to declare that "princes" and "nobleye" err and have passed insane laws (VIII.449–57, 463–67). In the light of this, she follows the lead of St. Peter and the apostles summoned before the high priest, the council, and the senate of Israel ("princeps sacerdotum et qui cum eo erant convocaverunt concilium et omnes seniores filiorum Israhel"): "We ought to obey God rather than men" (Acts 5.21–29). She also assumes that her Church's witness entails the rejection of conventional gender roles quite as much as the rejection of the princes' and nobles' authority.[53] The political consequences of such faith and ethics are that legitimate secular power and received social conventions are defined as "the world," a definition which instructs Christians to subject its authority to the traditions, practices, and ends of their own polity. There could be no reason for someone living in such a Church, participating in this City of God, to offer the kind of obedience to secular power that Griselda offers her sovereign. Chaucer thus seems to have answered his questions concerning the consequences of the version of faith and ethics cultivated in the early Church: evangelism, intransigent and joyful resistance to a secular power defending its own authority as it defended the empire's official religion ("oure goddes," VIII.491–92), and dismissal of conventional politics of gender. As for the secular powers' appeal to the "goddes" its citizens worship and to customary reverence for the "ymages" of their cult, this is dismissed by members of the Church as idolatry (VIII.493–511). We are certainly in the presence of a "stripping of the altars."[54] The Roman prefect consigns Cecilia to the fire, as Tiburce had anticipated

---

[52] An excellent introduction to this complex strand of Lutheran and Calvinist history is Quentin Skinner, *The Foundation of Modern Political Thought*, 2 vols. (Cambridge: Cambridge University Press, 1978), vol. 2, chaps. 3, 7, and 9.

[53] See Reames, "Artistry, Decorum, and Purpose," 178–81, 193; and Staley, *Powers of the Holy*, 207–208. On gender and the *Second Nun's Tale*, see Sherman, "Saints, Nuns, and Speech."

[54] For comparison of this aspect of the *Second Nun's Tale* with Chaucer's sources, see Reames, "Artistry, Decorum, and Purpose," 196–98. My quotation refers to Duffy's *The Stripping of the Altars*.

(VIII.313–18, 512–18). With the Church she represents, she is a rebel to secular authority and a rebel to the orthodox cult of the "goddes," a figure of sedition and heresy.

These are resonant images in late-medieval Europe. Both Reames and Staley have shown how Chaucer edited received versions of the story to emphasize these resonances.[55] In Staley's words, Chaucer's poem "mediates a set of problems ultimately relevant to the worldly status and hence to the spiritual authority of the church," and the saint's holiness "provides a screen for his exploration of otherwise charged subjects."[56] Within the *Canterbury Tales*, the Roman Church of Cecilia and Urban is juxtaposed with the Roman Curia of the *Clerk's Tale*, the contemporary Church of the Monk, Prioress, Pardoner, Friar, and Summoner in the *General Prologue*, the contemporary Church of the *Friar's Tale*, the *Summoner's Tale*, the *Shipman's Tale*, the *Pardoner's Prologue*, the *Canon Yeoman's Prologue and Tale*. Against these densely critical meditations on the contemporary Church, Chaucer sets the Parson of the *General Prologue* and the early Church of the *Second Nun's Tale*, a Church propagating what was taken as heresy and practicing what was understandably treated as sedition.

The resonances here have encouraged Sherry Reames to see the second half of the *Second Nun's Tale* as a satire on contemporary rulers "re-enacting the sins of such ancient Roman persecutors," and on "the English church authorities which condemned Wyclif and started persecuting his followers in the 1380s." Its force, she suggests, is on "behalf of the Wycliffites," despite the genre being one to which they objected.[57] Chaucer's explorations certainly move across terrain that includes his Church's campaign to have Wycliffite Christianity criminalized and then destroyed by the secular arm.[58] But I think their directions are not quite those indicated by Reames. Wyclif himself may help us see this. Despite advocating a radical change of criteria and a change of judges, Wyclif was prepared to defend the persecution of heretics. We can consider an example that seems relevant to Chaucer's own investigations in the *Second Nun's Tale*. In arguing for the disendowment of the Church and the direct subordination of ecclesiastics to the sovereign, God's vicar, Wyclif's *De Officio Regis* considers the tyrants who persecuted the early Church and killed Christians. Wyclif says that these rulers did so because they thought Christians were introducing a sacrilegious sect into the kingdom, disturbing the people, and enraging God against ruler and people for allowing such enemies to live with them. Wyclif's

---

[55] See Reames, "Artistry, Decorum, Purpose," 191, 193–99, and Staley, *Powers of the Holy*, 199–200, 207–12.

[56] Staley, *Powers of the Holy*, 200.

[57] Reames, "Artistry, Decorum, Purpose," 198.

[58] On this history see the works cited in n. 23. Also especially helpful here are the following: Gordon Leff, *Heresy in the Later Middle Ages*, 2 vols. (Manchester: Manchester University Press, 1967), vol. 2, chaps. 7–8; Margaret Aston, *Faith and Fire: Popular and Unpopular Religion, 1350–1600* (London: Hambledon, 1993), chap. 3; H. G. Richardson, "Heresy and the Lay Power under Richard II," *English Historical Review* 51 (1936): 1–28; Paul Strohm, *England's Empty Throne* (New Haven: Yale University Press, 1998), chapter 2.

judgment here is illuminating. If Christians had erred in their faith, killing them
would have been both licit and meritorious. The problem was that the rulers had
the wrong theological advisers and so themselves fell into heresy. This, so
Wyclif writes, shows how important it is for rulers to get the right theologians.
Who are these? They are theologians who understand that only people opposing
Scripture (not the decrees of the Church) are heretics. Once the king has chosen
such theologians as his advisers, he *must* remove heretics from his kingdom. In
seeking to do this the persecutors of early Christians were not wrong.
Correspondingly, the modern persecutors of Wycliffite Christians are not
wrong in principle: their error is in accepting inadequate theological advice
on who are heretics.[59] It should also be remembered that Wyclif's reformation
involved an exorbitant expansion of secular power with a massive diminishment
of the Church militant, in every way. *De Officio Regis*, *De Ecclesia*, and *De Officio
Pastorali* all make very clear the subordination of the visible Church and its
priests to the secular power.[60] Thomas Netter addresses this aspect of Wycliffite
Christianity when he writes that Wyclif and his followers clamored for secular
lords to become judges in matters of faith and ethics. Derisively, he goes on to
point out that when Henry V criminalized Wycliffism, Wycliffites proclaimed
this faithful ruler to be corrupt, naming him the prince of priests.[61] Netter here
puts his finger on one of the most ill-conceived strands of Wyclif's reformation
project albeit one with some deeper roots in his culture than his classification as
"heretic" has led many to assume. Langland entertained aspects of this idea of
reformation through the coercive force of the secular ruling classes, but his
explorations led him to abandon it, exposing its hollowness.[62] There is every
reason to think that Chaucer could also grasp such problems in Wyclif's
reformation program and that he had no wish to write "on behalf of" a
specifically Wycliffite version of secular power, Church, and reformation.

There is, however, an absence in the *Second Nun's Tale* that we should at least

[59] John Wyclif, *Tractatus De Officio Regis*, ed. A. W. Pollard and C. Sayle (London: Wyclif
Society, 1887), 71–72; see also pp. 125–26, 215, 228–29. For St. Thomas's insistence that
heretics should be killed by the secular power, treated under the theological virtue of faith,
see *ST* II–II.11, especially II–II.11.3 and 4. For the dating of Wyclif's works, Williel R.
Thomson, *The Latin Writings of John Wyclif: An Annotated Catalog* (Toronto: Pontifical
Institute of Medieval Studies, 1983). *De Officio Regis* is dated mid-1379 (60–61).
[60] On these issues, see chap. 6, below, where the relevant secondary literature will also be
cited.
[61] Thomas Netter, *Thomae Waldensis Doctrinale Antiquitatum Fidei Catholicae Ecclesiae*, ed. B.
Blanciotti, 3 vols. (Venice, 1757, facsimile Farnborough: Gregg, 1967), quoted by book
and chapter (and where more specific reference is needed the section will be added
followed by volume and column in parentheses): here II.46.6 (1, 485–86). See also II.63.3,
with its just observation on the irony of Wyclif's attack on "Caesarian" bishops from a
position which would create a completely "Caesarian" priesthood. On Netter, see
K. Ghosh, "'Authority' and 'Interpretation' in Wycliffite, Anti-Wycliffite, and Related
Texts c.1375–c.1430," Ph.D. diss., Cambridge University Press, 1996, chap. 6. This Ph.D.
is due to be published by Cambridge University Press.
[62] See *Piers Plowman*, X.279–333 and XV.551–62. Compare the sequence XVI–XX.

notice, even though our reflections on it will be inconclusive. The absence I have in mind is the eucharist. Understood, gazed upon, and received within the terms established by the doctrine of transubstantiation, this sacrament was central in the late-medieval Church and central in the experience of all orthodox people. Here the priest confected the very body of Christ that was tortured and crucified at the place called Golgotha; here the gazing faithful encountered Christ, on every altar and in a multitude of processions through their streets. The orthodox learnt that from their attendance at the eucharist abundant benefits flowed, both supernatural and thoroughly natural, thoroughly this-worldly. Richly documented historical studies by Miri Rubin and Eamon Duffy have made the relevant materials familiar, while the very different and out-standing works of cultural analysis focused on eucharistic devotion by Caroline Bynum and Sarah Beckwith have shown us its diverse, powerful roles in late-medieval culture and politics.[63] Their lead was followed in *Powers of the Holy*, which concentrated on the later fourteenth century when the doctrine of transubstantiation and the ritual forms and practices of the eucharist had attracted dissent of various kinds in England.[64] This dissent was fiercely resisted by the Church: the sacrament of unity in the one body of Christ became a major source of conflict between Christians. Refusal to accept the current hierarchy's formula for the way in which Christ is present in the eucharist was judged, from 1401, worthy of death by burning.[65] *In this particular context* the fact that we are not shown any sign of the eucharist in the versions of holiness elaborated in the *Second Nun's Tale*, let alone the kinds of eucharistic miracles proclaimed in John Mirk's *Festial* and Nicholas Love's treatise on the sacrament, becomes some-thing we should at least notice.[66] Again, in the particular web of discourses and conflicts out of which Chaucer wrote, we should also note that this absence is combined with an emphasis on the salvific role of preaching (by a woman) and baptism (priestly). This conjunction is one favored by Wyclif, who insisted, much against orthodox views and practice, that the task of preaching, not the consecration of the host, was the key task for priests concerned with their flock's final good.[67] When I write that we should notice the absence together

---

[63] I refer to the following: Miri Rubin, *Corpus Christi* (Cambridge: Cambridge University Press, 1991); Duffy, *The Stripping of the Altars*, chap. 3; Caroline W. Bynum, *Holy Feast and Holy Fast: The Religious Significance of Food to Medieval Women* (Berkeley: University of California Press, 1987) and her *Fragmentation and Redemption* (New York: Zone Books, 1991); Sarah Beckwith, *Christ's Body: Identity, Culture and Society in Late Medieval Writings* (London: Routledge, 1993). Also relevant are the essays by Beckwith and Rubin in *Culture and History 1350–1600*, ed. Aers (Hemel Hempstead: Harvester Wheatsheaf, 1992), chaps. 2 and 3.

[64] Aers and Staley, *Powers of the Holy*, chaps. 1 and 2.

[65] For the history here, see n. 23 and n. 58.

[66] On Mirk and Love in this context, see *Powers of the Holy*, 25–26.

[67] See Hudson, *Premature Reformation*, 353–58, 268–73, 281–90; see also *English Wycliffite Sermons*, 5 vols., ed. Pamela Gradon and Hudson (Oxford: Oxford University Press, 1983–96, 4:79–84, 50–56. For typical examples of Wyclif's downgrading of the priesthood in relation to secular rulers, see *De Officio Regis*, 143, 147–52.

with the conjunction just identified, I mean just that – notice. There is no sense in which the poem propounds, let alone proclaims, a neo-Wycliffite position on the eucharist and its relations to preaching, including women's preaching (itself a contested topic in the period, one to which Thomas Netter kept returning[68]). Indeed, I have made clear my own view that Chaucer's work maintains a clear detachment from the affirmative, constructive programs of Wyclif, while sharing many strands of the radical's account of the contemporary Church. We need to notice the absences and conjunctions at issue while acknowledging the work's resistance to any determinative interpretations.

Still, the further links in this sphere to Chaucer's idealized Parson in the *General Prologue* are plain. This Parson is the only ecclesiastic in the *Canterbury Tales* who seems to have been produced by the Church of Cecilia and Urban, the only ecclesiastic who would seem to belong in that fellowship (*General Prologue*, I.477–528). There has long been argument about the orthodoxy of this figure, argument initiated by Chaucer himself (II.1166–90). The *Riverside Chaucer* declares that "all the elements of the portrait can be found in contemporary discussions of the ideal requirements and failings of spiritual shepherds."[69] This is undoubtedly true but ignores questions it should at least address. There are huge areas of common ground in orthodox and Wycliffite accounts of the virtues, including the virtues needed by a good pastor. Wyclif and his followers were, after all, Christians trained in the scriptural narratives, traditions, and ethical practices of the Catholic Church. The question that needs addressing is about what could be expected to be present in an orthodox portrait of an ideal priest in the contexts traced above, contexts which included Wycliffism and the struggles against Wycliffism. What is absent? What has the writer chosen to exclude?[70] Chaucer foregrounds the following in his ideal priest: preaching, learning, and teaching; almsgiving to the local poor; an ascetic, dedicated and

[68] On the topic of women preachers: Hudson, *Premature Reformation*, 326–27; Claire Cross, "'Great Reasoners in Scripture': The Activities of Women Lollards, 1380–1530," in *Medieval Women*, ed. Derek Baker (Oxford: Blackwell, 1978), 359–80; Margaret Aston, "Lollard Women Priests?" in *Lollards and Reformers*, chap. 2. Walter Brut's statements and his adversaries' arguments are a fascinating part of the story. The proceedings of Brut's trial are in *Registrum Johannis Trefnant*, ed. W. W. Capes (London: Canterbury and York Society, 1916), 278ff. For translations of brief passages from this and from discussions of issues raised by Brut's case in BL MS Harley 31 see *Women Defamed and Women Defended*, ed. Alcuin Blamires (Oxford: Clarendon Press, 1992), 250–60. For argument against the emphasis of Cross and Aston, see Shannon McSheffrey, *Gender and Heresy: Women and Men in Lollard Communities 1420–1530* (Philadelphia: University of Pennsylvania Press, 1995).

[69] *Riverside Chaucer*, 819. For a summary of the literature on the Parson and Wycliffism, see *A Variorum Edition of the Works of Geoffrey Chaucer*, vol. 2, part 1 A and B, ed. Malcolm Andrew (Norman: University of Oklahoma Press, 1993). See here part 1, B, 431–32, 433–44. Only material up to 1985 was included (part 1, A, xi). Jill Mann's influential *Chaucer and Medieval Estates Satire* (Cambridge: Cambridge University Press, 1973) is content to note "The Parson is representative of what the estate of priesthood should be like" (66).

[70] Here I follow Hudson, *Premature Reformation*, 391: "What is omitted is, for the date, as significant as what is included: there is no mention of the Parson's administration of the mass, no allusion to his role as confessor."

exemplary form of life; freedom from any attachment to secular power and wealth; and indifference to the secular status of his subjects in his maintenance of discipline. Furthermore, we are told that his preaching consists of proclaiming "Cristes gospel trewely" and teaching "Cristes loore and his apostles twelve" (I.480–81, 527–28). In this he is distinctly unlike orthodox popular preaching of the period. The absence of "fables," emphasized later (X.31–36) and the concentration on "Cristes gospel" had become a mark of a peculiarly Wycliffite challenge to the Church.[71] The Host's suspicions that the Parson, who rebukes him for swearing by "Goddes bones" and "Goddes dignitee," is "a Lollere" who will give a "predicacioun," rather than a Canterbury fable, is at least understandable in the 1390s (II.1163–77). Yet, there remains an omission we have not yet discussed.

As in the *Second Nun's Tale*, Chaucer has decided to absent the eucharist. *In the particular contexts* of the late-medieval Catholic Church, its understanding of the priestly office, centered on the mass and the sacrament of the altar, and its current conflict with Wycliffite downgrading of the place of the eucharist in the economy of salvation, this is a remarkable choice. Chaucer's priest, in that context, has shed the crucial and contested distinctions that would show him to be a Catholic rather than a Wycliffite ideal of priesthood. In fact, the passage makes no mention of his role in any of the sacraments, not even baptism or penance. This silence should also be at least noticed. It is, once again, a silence that could be taken with a Wycliffite inflection in late-fourteenth-century England. Wyclif and his followers elaborated a wide-ranging critique of the Church's version of penance, while some also rejected the Catholic form of baptism. For example, Hawisia Mone of Loddon: "the sacrament of Baptem doon in watir in forme customed in the Churche is but a trufle and not to be pondred, for alle Cristis puple is sufficiently baptized in the blood of Crist, and so Cristis puple nedeth noon other baptem." As for the sacrament of penance: "confession shuld be maad oonly to God, and to noon other prest, for no prest hath poar to remitte synne ne to assoile a man of synne . . . . no man is bounde to do no penaunce whiche onyy prest enjoyneth hym to do."[72] Nevertheless, I wrote that these silences in the *General Prologue* "could be taken with a Wycliffite inflection," not that they necessarily should be. This reservation is not only sponsored by the *Parson's Tale*, to which I shall turn, but by the mode in which Chaucer chose to write. His mode allowed him to evoke questions, to conjure up hints of contemporary critiques, while avoiding determinations, avoiding the "*respondeo*." Still, an audience that included

---

[71] On the relevant contexts here see Spencer, *English Preaching*, and Katherine Little, "Reading for Christ: Interpretation and Instruction in Late-Medieval England" (Ph.D. diss., Duke University, 1998), chap. 1.

[72] *Heresy Trials in the Diocese of Norwich, 1428–31*, ed. Norman P. Tanner (London: Camden 4th series, vol. 20, Royal Historical Society, 1977), 140–141. For views on baptism similar to Hawisia Mone's, see 46, 52, 56, 60, 64, 66, 81, 86, 94–95, 107, 111, 121, 141. For penance, see index under "confession" (224).

people like Sir John Clanvowe, Sir John Montague, Sir Lewis Clifford, John Gower, and "philosophical Strode" would have been thoroughly alert to such hints and nuances.[73]

When it comes to ascribing a tale to the Parson the poet has him reject fables as a means of Christian instruction, as we noted above (X.22–54). In their place, he offers a manual on the sacrament of penance, remedying one of the absences noted in the *General Prologue*.[74] But only one, and not the most striking one we discussed in relation to the *Second Nun's Tale*. The time most medieval Christians confessed was at Easter in preparation for their annual communion: the sacrament of penance was closely bound up with the eucharist from which all sacraments flowed. Langland emphasized this in *Piers Plowman*, making the reception of the eucharist dependent on Christians having fulfilled the requirements of penance.[75] Chaucer makes as clear as Langland does that penance is done within the Church and involves at least the intention to confess to a priest, a clear contradiction of any unorthodox currents on this issue (X.85–88, 958–1027). But while much of the treatise is an exploration of sinful behavior (including attention to fashions in clothes, X.409–31), it never presents the eucharist as bound up with the sacrament of penance. The eucharist is not in fact mentioned until over a third of the way through the text, and then only as a subsidiary way of restraining venial sins. It is assimilated to the effects of holy water, alms-giving, the general confession at the opening of the mass and compline, the general blessing bestowed by bishops and priests, and miscellaneous good works (X.385–86). At its conclusion, the Parson's treatise moves to satisfaction which "stant moost generally in almesse and in bodily peyne" (X.1029), and the fruits of the sacrament of penance, "the endlees blisse of hevene" (X.1076). This men can purchase by "poverte espirituel," by humility, hunger, thirst, labor, "deeth and mortification of synne" (X.1080). The eucharist, the sacrament in which Christ in his real presence feeds the Church with the saving bread of life, the sacrament to which penance points, is not mentioned here. Nor is it mentioned in what seems to be designed as the final words of the *Canterbury Tales* (X.1081–92).

We have thus identified a displacement of the eucharist in areas of the *Canterbury Tales* where it might most be expected and where there can be no trace of irony being directed at putatively inadequate narrative voices. In the particular contexts we have described, this constitutes an especially striking displacement of a sacrament which is at the heart of Catholic faith, ethics, and

---

[73] The reference to Gower and Strode is from Chaucer's *Troilus and Criseyde*, V.1856–59. The other references point towards Wycliffite sympathizers at the court of Richard II. See n. 41.

[74] On the *Parson's Tale*, see Lee Patterson, "The *Parson's Tale* and the Quitting of the *Canterbury Tales*," *Traditio* 34 (1978): 331–80; see also Siegfried Wenzel's commentary in the *Riverside Chaucer*, 956–57.

[75] See *Piers Plowman*, XIX.360–408 and XX.228–33, 297–386. Here Langland may go beyond St. Thomas when St. Thomas denies that penitence is essential in preparation for the eucharist (*ST* III.65.2, *ad* 4). But he specifies this for those without mortal sin.

politics. But this also means that parodic and demonic versions of the eucharist in the *Canterbury Tales* are not set against their orthodox and divinely given fulfillment (see, for example, the *Pardoner's Tale*, VI.538–48, 795–97, 840–88[76]). Such displacements, such absences, would not be strange in a neo-Wycliffite work such as *The Two Ways*, by Chaucer's friend, Sir John Clanvowe.[77] But if Chaucer's Christianity is as obviously and consistently orthodox as most Chaucerians currently assume, the absences we have traced are very peculiar. But what kind of peculiarity? I will conclude this chapter with some tentative reflections on this question. There is no attempt to offer determinations where, as I have made clear, Chaucer's mode systematically resists these.

I have argued that Chaucer sets out from a traditional understanding of faith and ethics as described in chapter one. Faith, we observed, is given, received, and cultivated within the Church, the body of Christ, where the life-giving sacraments are found. In this tradition, faith is not some privatized, irrational leap in the dark. It entailed both inward and outward actions, heart and reason, will and intellect moved by God's grace within the Church, that sacrament of unity and God's chosen means of salvation. As St. Thomas maintained, whoever rejected the teaching of the Church, which was revealed by God and in Scripture, lacked the habit of faith and substituted his or her own will for faith.[78] This was seen as a catastrophic path, blazed by Lucifer. Christian ethics, we saw, were understood as the practice of distinctively Christian virtues, the exercise of right reason informed by grace in the Church, the individual agent pursuing the virtues (theological and cardinal) as a member of the mystical body of Christ. *Extra ecclesiam nulla salus.* In this tradition the creedal Church, the one holy, catholic, and apostolic Church that is believed (not believed "in") by Christians is visibly present and disclosed as the Roman Catholic Church. There is no sharp, let alone absolute, division between the invisible City of God and the visible Church militant. Insisting on an absolute division between the invisible, unknowable true Church of the eternally predestinate and the visible Church was among the founding principles of Wyclif's reformation program.[79]

[76] On these much discussed passages, see Peter Brown and Andrew Butcher, *The Age of Saturn: Literature and History in the Canterbury Tales* (Oxford: Blackwell, 1991), 138–41 together with the earlier literature they cite. Brown and Butcher, following Martin Stevens and Kathleen Fulvey (*Chaucer Review* 17 [1982]: 142–58), acknowledge that VI.538–548 is a "belittling" representation of the currently orthodox doctrine of transubstantiation, but they argue that the Pardoner's viciousness "undermines the force of his remarks on transubstantiation" (140–41). Possibly so. Nevertheless, orthodox doctrine *also* insisted, against Donatist heretics (past and present), that vicious officers may still mediate the graces and doctrines bestowed by God on the Church. As so often, Chaucer's fictions are extremely resistant to readings that would tease out determinations on theological and ecclesiological issues he insistently raised.

[77] See *The Works of Sir John Clanvowe*, ed. V. J. Scattergood (Cambridge: Brewer, 1975), 57–80.

[78] See, for example, *ST* II–II.5.3 *resp.* On will, grace, faith, and intellect, see II–II.2.9. An invaluable introduction to late-thirteenth-century discourse on the will is Bonnie Kent, *Virtues of the Will* (Washington, D.C.: Catholic University Press, 1995).

[79] An extended introduction to Wyclif's ecclesiology and its political implications is his *De*

The Church in which Chaucer was a member viewed the commitment to such a position as heretical.

But if Chaucer sets out within some version of the orthodox tradition outlined here, contemporary realities and conflicts put it under severe pressure, as I have indicated in chapters one and two. Chaucer inevitably contemplated such realities: the Great Schism, Bishop Despenser's crusade against fellow Christians who paid allegiance to the French pope (this was a crusade financed by the Church's indulgences exchanged for money), Wyclif's and Langland's broad critiques of the contemporary Church, and the persecutionary responses of that Church. It seems that his traditional understanding of the relations between the creedal Church and the visible Roman Church became a topic of critical reflection that went beyond the boundaries of conventional estates satire.[80] During the years Chaucer was writing, we can follow the consequences of such a loss of confidence in many different but overlapping texts: for example, work by Langland, Wyclif, Clanvowe, Walter Brut, William Swinderby, and the poem *Piers the Plowman's Crede*.[81] It certainly does not follow, nor is it implied, that Chaucer's loss of confidence in the identity of the contemporary Church led him to accept Wycliffite alternatives, whether theological, ecclesiological, or political. In this chapter I have suggested, on the contrary, that his own complex stories include critical reflection on possible consequences of a Wycliffite reformation. It seems to me, however, that Chaucer (compiling the *Canterbury Tales*) accepted the negative representations of the Roman Church elaborated in Langland's *Piers Plowman* (especially the Prologue, Passus XV, and Passus XIX–XX). These culminated, we recall, in a vision of this Church being overwhelmed by the forces of Antichrist, so that the Church becomes a force of delusion, enchanting Christians (XX.214–379). Chaucer, like Langland and Wyclif, also accepted the relevance of critical comparisons between the contemporary Church and the early Church in interrogating the former's identity. Pursuing such reflections, his work opened out some remarkable absences that we have followed in this chapter. These absences, especially of the eucharist, bespeak a diminished role of the sacraments in relation to their place in the tradition from within which Chaucer wrote, a remarkable shift in models of sanctification. Such shifts are always bound up with shifts in ecclesiology, but, as I have emphasized, Chaucer chose modes of writing that block any

Ecclesia, ed. J. Loserth (London: Wyclif Society, 1886). See chap. 6 below for a discussion of Wyclif's ecclesiology.

[80] Readily accessible examples of contemporary estates satire are John Gower's *Mirour de L'Omme (The Mirror of Mankind)*, trans. W. B. Wilson (East Lansing: Colleagues Press, 1992) and *Vox Clamantis* in *The Major Latin Works of John Gower*, trans. E. W. Stockton (Seattle: University of Washington Press, 1962). On Langland's relations to orthodox satire, see Wendy Scase, *Piers Plowman and the New Anticlericalism* (Cambridge: Cambridge University Press, 1989).

[81] For Brut and Swinderby, see *Registrum Johannis Trefnant*, 231ff., 278ff.; for *Piers the Plowman's Crede* see *Six Ecclesiastical Satires*, ed. James Dean (Kalamazoo: Medieval Institute Publications, TEAMS, 1991), 8–34.

determinate construals in this sphere of existence. Perhaps a plausible outcome for the idiosyncratic mixture of components analyzed in this chapter might be taken from the final passus of *Piers Plowman*. After the Church has been overwhelmed by the forces of Antichrist, Conscience continues to search for Piers, *Petrus id est Christus* (XV.212), but he does so by leaving the visible Church he has been defending (XX.380–86; XIX.256 – XX.379). As he does so, Will (figuring the poet and the faculty of volition, the rational appetite) remains, waiting. Waiting with Chaucer, perhaps. How would St. Cecilia or the Parson of the *General Prologue* fare in this Church? How would their evangelism, their utter disrespect for secular power and status, their strikingly minimal sacramentalism be received? Texts like the *Second Nun's Tale* or the portrait of the ideal priest in the *General Prologue*, written in later fourteenth-century England, insist on such questions being put. Did Chaucer or Clanvowe think of the potential fate of such evangelists as Wyclif did? Wyclif observed that if Jesus Christ visited England in his time as a "prelatus incognitus" and reiterated his gospel he would be excommunicated by the Roman Church's Curia: unless he abjured, he would be condemned to the flames as a heretic and blasphemer.[82] It is hard to imagine Chaucer or Langland demurring. But if Wyclif's scenario is all too plausible, a question follows: how can such a Church, currently maintaining two warring popes, be the bride and body of Christ, the Church Christians believe and outside of which is *nulla salus*? Whatever Chaucer's answers to these sharp and thoroughly contemporary questions, he did not follow Wyclif's programs.

He sought, rather, to sustain his inquiries from within the traditions outlined in the first chapter and summarized in this one. Yet we have seen how his writing also puts in question the understanding of the visible Church given in these traditions and produces certain absences which are, at the very least, alien to them. This is a source of serious tension in Chaucer's writing around the Church and Christian discipleship. He could not have resolved it in the 1390s without moving into positions he found unwarranted: either Wycliffite ones or the triumphalist, persecutionary orthodox ones led by the Archbishops of Canterbury, especially Arundel. The latter, very soon after Chaucer's death, achieved the agreement of the secular power to begin burning committed Wycliffites. The burning began with William Sawtry and John Badby, while the Church's devotional and pedagogic arm would be represented by Nicholas Love's *Mirror* and Arundel's Constitutions of 1409.[83] In extremely charged circumstances, Chaucer's multi-generic, polysemous modes in the *Canterbury Tales* enabled him to explore the substantial issues we have been following without resolving the tensions of his approaches into unwelcome positions. Had he unfolded and elaborated their ecclesiological implications, these would have

---

[82] Wyclif, *De Blasphemia*, ed. M. K. Dzewicki (London: Wyclif Society, 1893), 62: Thomson dates this to mid-1381 (*The Latin Writings of John Wyclyf*, 66). Oddly enough, Wyclif does not invoke Mark 12.1–12 here. Is this because his own theology and ecclesiology also prepare the way for an alliance of Rome and Jerusalem, which crucified Jesus? See chap. 6 below.

[83] On this history, see the works cited in n. 23 and n. 58.

been extremely disturbing for an orthodox Catholic, as orthodoxy was currently being shaped. But by conjuring up such issues while resisting determinate resolutions, Chaucer did not leave his tradition as he inherited it.

In her recent study, "Chaucer and the Postures of Sanctity," Lynn Staley drew attention to an aspect of the *Canterbury Tales* customarily ignored: "its political despair," its vision of a contemporary world in which "factions are held tenuously together by the need for power and prosperity and in which the sanctified is finally a commodity like any other."[84] It seems to me that the despair she has identified is inseparable from the vision of the Church and its sacraments we have traced above. One possible consequence of such a vision and "its political despair" could be a tendency to stoicize Christianity. The *Clerk's Tale* addresses this, so I have argued, as a critical problem, not as a resolution. But I wish to finish this chapter by reflecting on Chaucer's stoicizing lyrics, written outside his book of stories ascribed to Canterbury pilgrims.[85] Could stoical ethics and sensibilities be assimilated to Christian traditions without those traditions being seriously undermined?

Let us address the question by considering the "balade" now known as "Truth." The first stanza of this beautiful lyric advises readers to fly from the competitive world and "dwelle with sothfastnesse," settling for self-governance. Do this, and "trouthe thee shal delivere." This moral advice, "Bon Conseyle," might seem to be common ground between Stoic and Christian traditions, suggesting that assimilation will present the latter with no problems. However, there are some absences that should not be overlooked. The advice assumes that humans are agents who can flee from "the prees and dwelle with sothfastnesse" achieving self-rule autonomously, Once they have done this, "trouthe" will deliver them (1–7). The absences here can be summarized as the absence of sin, of Christ, and of the Church. The tradition Chaucer inherited taught that humans are fallen creatures with imprisoned, addictive wills, utterly dependent on the grace of their creator mediated through the life, death, and resurrection of Christ in the Church. Virtues that are distinctively Christian depend on grace and are bound up with the theological virtues in the way St. Thomas showed in his discussion of patience which we mentioned in our analysis of the *Clerk's Tale*. How does the "trouthe" that "shal delivere" in this

---

[84] Staley, *Powers of the Holy*, 182. See chap. 5 of this work, which justifies this view. Many aspects of Lee Patterson's reading of Chaucer in his *Chaucer and the Subject of History* (Madison: University of Wisconsin Press, 1991) are congruent with Staley's. However, Staley rejects Patterson's thesis on Chaucer's depoliticizing cultivation of inwardness and the aesthetic.

[85] The lyrics I have in mind are those conventionally entitled "Truth," "Gentilesse," "Lak of Stedfastnesse," "Former Age," and "Fortune." See *Riverside Chaucer*, 650–54 and the edition in *A Variorum Edition of the Works of Geoffrey Chaucer*, vol. 5, *The Minor Poems*, ed. George B. Pace and Alfred David (Norman: University of Oklahoma Press, 1982), 49–118. On the political contexts and meaning of "Lak of Stedfastnesse," see the illuminating essay by Paul Strohm in *Hochon's Arrow: The Imagination of Fourteenth-Century Texts* (Princeton: Princeton University Press, 1993), chap. 3; chap. 4 on Chaucer's "Purse" is also relevant here.

stanza relate to the truth that will "make you free" according to the Gospel (John 8.31–32), the figure of Jesus, "the way, and the truth, and the life" (John 14.6)? We need to see whether the remainder of the poem responds to these questions and absences.

The second stanza advises readers not to get involved in remedying what is wrong "al croked." This is the counsel of "political despair" identified by Staley as an aspect of Chaucer's *Canterbury Tales*. It is also a counsel of detachment from any contemporary movements of ecclesiastic reform: "Tempest thee noght al croked to redresse/ . . . Stryve not, as doth the crokke with the wal." The only rational way is to find "reste" in "litel besinesse" (8–12). Once more the poet assumes that the desired "reste" and self-rule are achieved by the autonomous individual and will then be rewarded by "trouthe" (13–14). The absences observed in the first stanza remain absences, the questions put in my comments remain unanswered. In addition, we now have the abandonment of both prophetic and eschatological visions intrinsic to Christianity. For example:

> And the book of Isaias the prophet was delivered unto him. And as he unfolded the book, he found the place where it was written: The spirit of the Lord is upon me. Wherefore he hath anointed me to preach the gospel to the poor: he hath sent me to heal the contrite of heart. To preach deliverance to the captives and sight to the blind, to set at liberty them that are bruised, to preach the acceptable year of the Lord and the day of reward. And when he had folded the book, he restored it to the minister and sat down . . . . And he began to say to them: This day is fulfilled this scripture in your ears (Luke 4.17–21).

The emphasis on the prophetic proclamation of the gospel pervades the New Testament and was as fundamental, in very different ways, to St. Francis as to John Wyclif. It was a faith quite incompatible with the individualistic, autonomous quest for "reste" by withdrawal which is the "Bon Conseyl" of "Truth." The poem's third stanza reinforces the sentiments of the first two before it exhorts its singular reader to become a pilgrim. He or she is a beast who should now leave its stall, know its divine homeland, become a pilgrim and hold to the high way led by its own spirit, knowing that truth will deliver him or her (15–21). These are eloquent generalizations. But they reproduce the absences already identified and raise questions already asked. What exactly is the "heye wey" envisaged here (18–20)? How, once again, does it relate to "the way" of John 14.6? How does a beast in a stall become a pilgrim who has discovered the way to her or his supernatural end? And how is this discovered before truth "shal delivere" the beast become pilgrim?

Recollecting a couple of passages from *Piers Plowman* can help us grasp the force and scope of the questions here. In Passus V, Langland brings "þe feld of folk," the community of the faithful, addicted sinners all, through the sacrament of penance. After the confessions, Repentance blesses the people with a profound and exquisite meditation on salvation history (V.477–509a). This long sequence sketches in most of the absences identified in Chaucer's "Bon Conseyl," but so does the ensuing passage:

> A þousand of men þo þrungen togideres,
> Cride vpward to Crist and to his clene moder,
> To haue grace to go to truþe, God leue þat þei moten.
> Ac þere was wye noon so wys þe way þider kouþe,
> But blustered forþe as beestes ouer baches and hilles (V.510–14).

Even after confession, a form of absolution, prayer, and attentive meditation on the redemption, "*Verbum caro factum est & habitavit in nobis* [the Word was made flesh and dwelt among us]" (V.500a, John 1.14), the community remains "as beestes." Chaucer's exhortations, "Forth pilgrim forth! Forth, beste, out of thy stal!" is placed in a distinctively Christian setting. There is nothing here to encourage any confidence in "Truth's" mixture of individualistic resignation, no faith in the ability of the allegedly autonomous will to step out of the "stal" into the "heye wey" and to dwell with "sothfastnesse." On the contrary, Langland's penitents confess the need of grace even to find "þe wey," let alone to travel on it. They are a community within the Church rightly seeking guidance from the Church. That is why Langland concentrates so remorselessly on the state of the contemporary Church, especially on its relations to its founding narratives and its administration of the sacrament of penance that precedes the eucharist.

The second passage I wish to recall from *Piers Plowman* confirms just how hard it is to get out of Chaucer's "stal." In Passus XVII we come across a man who has been so badly wounded by thieves that he cannot move or help himself in any way: he seems only half-alive. We are placed within Jesus's parable of the good samaritan as it was traditionally interpreted and reconfigured by Langland (XVII.50–126; Luke 10.25–37).[86] The "semyvif" man represents fallen humanity, ambushed by sins whose end is death. Only Christ, the good samaritan who is divine love incarnate, can help. He explains to Will, whose vision this is, how faith and hope can only help within and through his own saving actions. And these, he makes absolutely clear, are not appropriated by autonomous individuals but *within* the Church that he found in his own life, death, and resurrection. Healing calls for the sacraments of the Church:

> May no medicyne vnder mone þe man to hele brynge,
> Neiþer Feiþ ne fyn hope, so festred be hise woundes,
> Wiþouten þe blood of a barn born of a mayde.
> And he be baþed in þat blood, baptised as it were,
> And þanne plastred wiþ penaunce and passion of þat baby,
> He sholde stonde and steppe; ac stalworþe worþ he neuere
> Til he haue eten al þe barn and his blood ydronke (XVII.94–100).

[86] For traditional interpretations of this parable in relation to Langland's reconfiguration, see Ben Smith, *Traditional Imagery of Charity in Piers Plowman* (The Hague: Mouton, 1966), chap. 4.

Only within this dispensation can faith be the "forster [forester]" guiding wanderers in the wilderness and teaching them "þe wey;" only here can hope be the "Hostiler [inn-keeper]" healing with love "þoruȝ holy chirche bileue," only here, in the inn that is the Church (XVII.115–22: 66–82). The Church's sacraments, Christ the samaritan makes clear, are his crucial legacy: memorials, saving medicine and pledges of his return (XVII.122–26).

In this enactment of Chaucer's own tradition, it is forcefully revealed that Church and sacraments belong to a Christocentric, communitarian, and eschatological vision quite alien to the neo-stoicism of "Truth."[87] In the latter, any specifically Christian understanding of faith and ethics is dissolved. Stoicism shows itself to be a rival and pelagian tradition capable of assimilating the would-be assimilator. Nevertheless, slight as the neo-stoic lyrics are when set against the *Canterbury Tales*, they seem to suggest that at some moments Chaucer may have been drawn to this rival tradition. This would be an understandable response to the profoundly pessimistic representations of the contemporary Church in the *Canterbury Tales*. It might well have been strengthened by his rejection of Wyclif's model of ecclesiastic reform, inseparable from an exorbitant increase in secular power and its concentration in the hands of sovereigns like Walter.[88] That a Christian poet of Chaucer's powerful, searching intelligence was drawn at all to the rival tradition informing "Truth" is symptomatic of serious trouble in his own Christian tradition and its Church.

---

[87] One manuscript includes a fourth stanza addressed to Vache (*Riverside Chaucer*, 1189). This stanza acknowledges God as creator and counsels prayer for "hevenlich mede" (24–26). It does not address the questions and absences discussed above. Similar commentary could be developed for the other neo-stoic lyrics, but my aim is not "coverage"; for my purposes it is sufficient to raise the present issues, to identify absences, and to suggest their significance.

[88] Yet once more, see Staley, *Powers of the Holy*, 259; with this, Patterson, *Chaucer and the Subject of History*, 420.

3

Justice and Wage-labor after the Black Death: some Perplexities for William Langland

But þow lyue by loore of *Spiritus Iusticie*
The chief seed þat Piers sew, ysaued worstow neuere.
(William Langland, *Piers Plowman*)[1]

In the epigraph to this chapter Conscience is the speaker, and the seed invoked was sown under the divine guidance of Grace (XIX.274–318). It is a fitting comment on an author for whom individual salvation is inextricably bound up with the attempt to live a life that embodies the virtue of justice. Furthermore, the poet saw that such an attempt is inseparable from the forms of relationship encouraged by particular communities. His thinking here was shaped by Christian–Aristotelian tradition, and like St. Thomas Aquinas he sees repentance as allied to justice, a moral virtue without which sin cannot be forgiven.[2]

St. Thomas Aquinas argued that it is natural for human beings to live in association with each other.[3] Only in relationships with others can we learn what Will so desperately searches for, "Dowel," the virtues that constitute good human beings. To lead a good life, St. Thomas maintained, we need both to act and to have a sufficiency of the temporal goods that are necessary for virtuous action.[4] Since we are all necessarily part of some political community, it is impossible to be good unless we act in accord with the common good (*ST* I–II.92.1, especially *ad* 3). So if a community is organized in a manner opposed to the pursuit of the virtues, it would foster "good" citizens (that is, ones obedient to its laws) whose goodness would actually foster, even demand, wickedness – take the example of a "good" Nazi citizen in Germany during the

---

[1] The edition of *Piers Plowman* cited in the text of this essay, unless otherwise stated, is *Piers Plowman: The B-version*, ed. George Kane and Talbot Donaldson (London: Athlone, 1988). For the C-version I use *Piers Plowman: An Edition of the C-text*, ed. Derek Pearsall (London: Arnold, 1978).

[2] See St. Thomas Aquinas, *Summa Theologiae* III.85–86. The Latin text used here is *Summa Theologica* [*sic*],·4 vols. in 6 (Rome: Forzanus 1894). For an English translation, see the Blackfriars' parallel text edition in 61 vols. (London: Blackfriars, 1964–81). Hereafter the *Summa* is cited as *ST* in the text.

[3] See St. Thomas in *On the Government of Rulers: "De Regimine Principum": Ptolemy of Lucca with Portions Attributed to Thomas Aquinas*, trans. James M. Blythe (Philadelphia: University of Pennsylvania Press, 1997).

[4] *De Regimine* I.16.4.

1930s and 1940s. As Aristotle says in the *Nicomachean Ethics*, "it is not always the same thing to be a good man and a good citizen." St. Thomas himself offers the example of a community of robbers. The community is evil and pursues evil ends, but one could speak of a "good" robber adapted to the ends of that evil community.[5]

Justice, the *Summa Theologiae* tells us, regulates human action according to a standard of right reason rendering it good and directing us to our final good (God). It is a disposition to render to each what is due, a virtue that leads the will towards perfection.[6] Religion itself is understood as part of the cardinal virtue of justice, directing us to render what we owe to God.[7] From within this tradition Langland decided to make *redde quod debes* one of the most prominent refrains throughout his poem.[8] The risen Christ himself stresses that the powers of forgiveness and mercy he bestows on Piers are conditional upon *redde quod debes* (XIX.182–87), a condition confirmed, not surprisingly, by Grace (XIX.258–61). The point is that justice is actually constitutive of the good life under the new dispensation. Not that St. Thomas suggests that justice can lead to beatitude uninformed by the supernatural virtue of charity, a gift he treats before addressing justice and the other cardinal virtues.[9] Nevertheless, it would make no sense, in this tradition, to make a move that has become familiar in Langland scholarship. This move involves identifying the demands of justice with a punitive legalism, allegedly the mark of an "Old Testament" totally superseded in the Christian dispensation, a supersession allegedly figured forth from the sixteenth passus of *Piers Plowman*.[10] But Langland does not align the virtue of justice and its demands with an un-Christian or unacceptably

---

[5] See Aristotle, *Ethics*, trans. J. A. K. Thomson, rev. H. Tredennick (Harmondsworth: Penguin, 1976), vol. 2, 1130 G 25–29, p. 176. See St. Thomas's comment on this in his *Commentary on Aristotle's Nicomachean Ethics*, trans. C. I. Litzinger (Notre Dame: Dumb Ox Books, 1993), V.926, pp. 291–92. For St. Thomas on the robbers, see *ST* I–II.92.1; also relevant are the reflections on unjust laws and taxation, *ST* I–II.96.4.

[6] See especially *ST* II–II.57; 80; 123.1; 44.6; and also *ST* I–II.90–91. This is congruent with Langland's own approach to the journey of Will in *Piers Plowman*. On Langland and justice, see the following: M. W. Bloomfield, *Piers Plowman as a Fourteenth-Century Apocalypse* (New Brunswick: Rutgers University Press, 1961), 127–43; P. M. Kean, "Love Law, and *Lewte* in *Piers Plowman*," *Review of English Studies* 15 (1964): 241–61 and "Justice, Kingship and the Good Life in the Second Part of *Piers Plowman*," chap. 3 in *Piers Plowman: Critical Approaches*, ed. S. S. Hussey (London: Methuen, 1969); Myra Stokes, *Justice and Mercy in Piers Plowman* (London: Croom Helm, 1984).

[7] *ST* II–II.81; II.79.1.

[8] Much has been written about this: especially see Bloomfield in n. 6 and R. W. Frank, *Piers Plowman and the Scheme of Salvation* (New Haven: Yale University Press, 1957), 100–109; Britton J. Harwood, *Piers Plowman and the Problem of Belief* (Toronto: University of Toronto Press, 1992), 43–44, 114–16, 130–32, 151. Also relevant is Anna Baldwin, "The Debt Narrative in *Piers Plowman*," in *Art and Context in Late Medieval English Narrative*, ed. Robert Edwards (Cambridge: Brewer 1994), 37–50; and Kean, "Justice, Kingship and the Good Life."

[9] *ST* II–II.23–44; II–II.47–168.

[10] This kind of argument tends to make Piers in B V–VI a figure representing the "Old Law,"

"pelagian" ethos superseded in the Christian dispensation. On the contrary, his own commitment to this virtue and its place in human salvation is affirmed at all stages of the poem and through a wide range of speakers including, as we have just noted, Christ and the Holy Spirit. I see no reason to think that Langland dissented from St. Thomas's view that the order of justice is not superseded in the Christian dispensation but is in fact strengthened.[11] This accords with St. Augustine's argument in the *De Trinitate* that to live justly is to render to all what we owe them and to love one another. Indeed, we ought to love one another because those we love are just or may become just; and our love for ourselves should be on the same grounds.[12] The power of the eucharist, we are shown in *Piers Plowman*, is conditional upon the recipient having "ypaied/ To Piers pardon þe Plowman *redde quod debes*" (XIX.389–90). Even the Holy Spirit's own commands include the establishment of an agency for enforcing the demands of justice on those who reject justice: "*Spiritus Iusticie* spareþ noȝt to spille þe gilty" (XIX.302). This may well involve the use of force, even of "Foluyles lawes" (XIX.245–47).[13] If individuals are to lead the life of the virtues, they need communities committed to enabling and safe-guarding such a life.

If a tradition is to survive, it will not be as a closed, static system serenely transcending economic, political, demographic, and military changes, serenely ignoring new challenges. The maker of *Piers Plowman* grasped this clearly, and part of his poem's greatness is its tenacious engagement with contemporary circumstances which were posing some new and perplexing challenges to the tradition I have so crudely outlined above. As James Simpson notes, *Piers Plowman* is committed to a spirituality that "can be realized only through 'true' social relationships of interdependent labor," a poem "concerned to examine the institutions that nourish the individual."[14]

the "Old Testament"; for a typical example, see Barbara Raw, "Piers and the Image of God in Man," chap. 6 in *Piers Plowman: Critical Approaches*, ed. Hussey, 145–46, 163–65, 168.

11 *ST* II–II.104.6.

12 See St. Augustine's *De Trinitate*, VIII.6.9; also closely related VIII.7.10, VIII.9.13, and IX.9.14. On the continuity of justice in the next life, see XIV.9.12. For the most recent English translation, see vol. 5 of *The Works of St. Augustine*, ed. and trans. Edmund Hill (Brooklyn: New York City Press, 1991). In the *Confessions* he observes that we are not only bound to restrain our desires for certain things, but also to maintain justice, directing our love, and love demands that we help those oppressed by injustice: see X.37.61 and XIII.17.21. The English translation of the *Confessions* used here is by Henry Chadwick (Oxford: Oxford University Press, 1992). Here I draw on Alasdair MacIntyre, *Whose Justice? Which Rationality?* (London: Duckworth, 1988), 153–54.

13 On "Foluyles lawes" see Pearsall's notes to C XXI.247 (p. 351 of his edition of *Piers Plowman*, cited n. 1) and Anna Baldwin, *The Theme of Government in Piers Plowman* (Cambridge: Brewer, 1981), 39–40.

14 James Simpson, *Piers Plowman: An Introduction to the B-text* (London: Longman, 1991), 71, 220; see similarly 88, 161–65. Important approaches along congruent lines are by Anne Middleton, "William Langland's 'Kynde Name,'" chap. 1 in *Literary Practice and Social Change in Britain 1380–1530*, ed. Lee Patterson (Berkley: University of California Press, 1990); and, most recently, Middleton, "Acts of Vagrancy: The C-Version 'Autobiography' and the

The problems addressed in the present chapter are those posed around the practices of wage-labor after the Black Death. Here Langland's moral tradition was confronting a major challenge. The poet shows us how the option he had initially favored would not be compatible with that tradition, even if it could have solved the current economic and political conflicts he was considering. This option is the one chosen by the ruling elites. They passed the first *national* legislation on wages and their own control of laborers; they sought to enforce it through the existing coercive apparatus; and they evolved a rhetoric of abuse in which those who resisted this self-interested legislation were identified as able-bodied mendicants, dangerous vagrants, idle parasites with endless sums of money to spend in the ale-houses of England, and, in the language of the poet's contribution to this assault, wasters, embodiments of injustice and lawlessness. Elsewhere I have analyzed the ideological moves made by the poet here and their relations to contemporary conflicts between employers and the "laborers" who struggled "ayeins þe statut" (VI.313–20).[15] I have no wish to rehearse that account of the complex and shifting ideological strategies in Langland's construction of "wasters" and the work ethic in passus VI, nor of the basic texts such as the Statute of Labourers (1351) and the commons' petition against vagrants (1376). Although these are points of reference in the present chapter, the main question here is how and why the sale of labor-power after the Black Death could bring the poet's powerful tradition of moral inquiry under severe pressure. A related question is the consequence of such pressure for that tradition.

That slavery is in no sense "natural" to human beings, but the product of human contrivance, was a commonplace of Christian doctrine.[16] And there were certainly masses of women and men in Langland's England who were convinced that serfdom was not compatible with natural reason or a just society. For them the time had come to sweep it away, however clerics might gloss the story of Ham or preach that God "made man soget & þral to man for þe synne of Adam, as seyth Sent Austyn."[17] The events and explicit demands of June 1381

Statute of 1388," in *Written Work: Langland, Labor and Authorship*, ed. Steven Justice and Kathryn Kerby-Fulton (Philadelphia: University of Pennsylvania Press, 1997), 208–317.

[15] Aers, *Community, Gender, and Individual Identity* (London: Routledge, 1988), 20–40. Since this was published, Anne Middleton has studied the relations between the 1388 version of the Statute and the "autobiographical" addition to the C-text in passus 5; see "Acts of Vagrancy" (n. 14). I am completely unpersuaded by Lawrence Clopper's approach to the poem's political and social reading of the Statutes and the conflicts to which they belong, as I am completely unpersuaded by his attempt to present *Piers Plowman* as a "coterie" poem written by a radical Franciscan for Franciscans (*"Songs of Rechlessnesse": Langland and the Franciscans* [Ann Arbor: University of Michigan Press, 1997], 166–76 for the former, 320, 325, 333 and *passim* for the latter).

[16] See *ST* II–II.57 and I–II.94; Augustine, *City of God*, XIX.15 trans. Marcus Dods (New York: Modern Library, 1950), 693–94; also, *City of God*, trans. Henry Betterson (London: Penguin, 1984), 874–75.

[17] On Ham see *Dives and Pauper*, ed. P. H Barnum (EETS 275, 1976), IV.1, vol. 1: 305–306; quoting here from vol. 2: 125–26.

were only the most concentrated, forceful, and dramatic manifestations of these convictions.[18] Yet it is neither the long-term decline of serfdom nor the conflict over villein tenure and status that draws the poet's attention. He seems to take its continuation for granted – and to approve of this continuation. For him bondage represents a world where workers' mobility is completely dependent on the will of the lord, where they have no right to make a charter and where they not only have no right to sell land but no right even to dispose of what they saw as their own personal goods – without permission of the lord (XI.127–30: C XII.60–63).[19] The poet took for granted this mode of production, its forms of dominion, and its extremely heavy exploitation of villeins' resources.[20] These extractions are allegedly sanctioned by "lawe," "reson," and "conscience" (XI.127, 131, 132). Similarly, he assumes that if the social order is as it should be, then the lord will be free to fine his tenants at will – a mark of villein tenure and the state of serfdom. That is why the lord can only be exhorted to exercise this franchise with whatever he counts as "mercy," even as he is exhorted not to oppress or torment these people unless "truþe" assents (VI.37–40). The poet occludes the fact that villeins themselves lived in communities which were self-regulating, self-policing, and the repositories of their own versions of tradition and custom. Their own understanding of "truþe," as 1381 showed with especial clarity, might not coincide with their lords'. In reality, the terms of "mercy" and "truþe" in these relationships were negotiated within a complex web of forces and decisions, including the major demographic changes caused by the Black Death and succeeding plagues. Despite this, the customary appearance of servile forms of tenure and status, the family formations they determined and their embeddedness in the culture's learned languages, enabled the poet to perceive them as somehow static, securely trans-historical. This was, as already observed, not a universally

[18] On the 1381 rising the literature is now immense. Especially helpful are the following: R. B. Dobson's superb anthology, *The Peasants' Revolt of 1381* (London: Macmillan, 1970, rev. 1986); R. H. Hilton, *Bond Men Made Free* (London: Methuen, 1973); E. B. Fryde, chap. 8 in *The Agrarian History of England and Wales*, ed. Edward Miller (Cambridge: Cambridge University Press, 1991); Nicholas Brooks, "The Organization and Achievements of the Peasants of Kent and Essex in 1381," in *Studies in Medieval History Presented to R. H. C. Davis*, ed. H. Mayr-Harting and R. I. Moore (London: Hambledon, 1985); Caroline Barron, *Revolt in London: 11th to 15th June 1381* (London: Museum of London, 1981); T. Prescott, "London in the Peasants' Revolt," *London Journal* 7 (1981): 125–43; L. R. Poos, *A Rural Society after the Black Death* (Cambridge: Cambridge University Press, 1991), chap. 11. In studying the political and ideological contexts of the rising, Richard W. Kaeuper's work is invaluable, *War, Justice, and Public Order: England and France in the Later Middle Ages* (Oxford: Clarendon Press, 1988).
[19] On the traditions here and the fourteenth-century situation, Hilton, *Bond Men* and *The Decline of Serfdom in Medieval England* (London: Macmillan, 1969); L. R. Poos and L. Bonfield, "Law and Individualism in Medieval England," *Social History* 11 (1986): 287–301.
[20] For a good account of this domain, see J. R. Maddicott, *Law and Lordship: Royal Justices as Retainers in Thirteenth and Fourteenth-century England* (Oxford: Past and Present Society, 1978); also Kaeuper, *War, Justice, and Public Order*, chap. 4 and pp. 104–17.

"medieval" perception but a class-determined one demonstrably not shared by many contemporaries, those who fought covertly and openly against villeinage and persuaded King Richard, on that memorable day in June 1381, to abolish serfdom.[21] Nevertheless, Langland himself seems unperturbed by what some observers see as the core of the conflicts leading into the great rising and the demands made at Mile End.[22] Nor do the poet's revisions to a poem that had been used by some of those involved in the rising show any significant changes to his assumptions in *this* area. The fact is contemporary villeins, bondmen and bondwomen, are marginal, shadowy but striking absences in *Piers Plowman*. What takes their place in the poet's representation of productive labor, and why?

The answer to this question is that in *Piers Plowman* the villeins of England are displaced by wage-laborers, craftspeople, and small scale traders. What kind of presence did such people have in the late medieval system of production and exchange? All attempts to quantify forms of work in this period, even the attempt to make the classifications on which calculations must be based, are fraught with methodological and empirical difficulties. Granting this, recent studies of different regions have used a wide range of evidence and controls to come up with some rough figures that can, at least, serve as indicators of the scale of wage-labor one might find in various areas of England. Here are a few very rough examples: in Suffolk and Essex between 50% and 63%, while not *more* than a quarter of families in central and northern Essex "derived their livelihood from agriculture or their own properties" and half or more "were substantially dependent upon wages;" in Cuxham (Oxfordshire), a small village, the proportion of wage-earners was in excess of 30%, in Gloucestershire in excess of 40%. In a town such as Coventry, even when the city was in decline, wage-laborers would make up over half the working population.[23] We also need to recall that precise definitions of forms of most working people's livelihood are hazardous because of the fluidity of forms of work, the changing forms appropriate to different phases of peoples' life-cycles, and the decisive role of gender. Nevertheless, the research of recent years has demonstrated that despite sharp regional differences, despite crucial gender differences, and despite the fact that one person's life-cycle was very likely to include a multiplicity of forms of work, "wage earning was widely diffused in English society," both rural and urban, in Langland's lifetime.[24]

---

[21] On the abolition of serfdom in 1381, see Hilton, *Decline*, 42; Dobson, *Peasants' Revolt*, 161.

[22] The key attack, however, was on the administrators of current law. See on this topic Alan Harding, "The Revolt against the Justices," chap. 7 in *The English Rising of 1381*, ed. R. H. Hilton and T. H. Aston (Cambridge: Cambridge University Press, 1984).

[23] Figures here are drawn from the following work: Christopher Dyer in *Agrarian History*, ed. Miller, 645–46, and Dyer, *Standards of Living in the Later Middle Ages* (Cambridge: Cambridge University Press, 1989), 211–12, 214 (Coventry); Hilton, *Bond Men*, 171–72; Poos, *A Rural Society*, 18–31, quoting from 23–24. On women in this context, Dyer, *Standards*, 212, and especially Judith Bennett, *Women in the Medieval English Countryside* (New York: Oxford University Press, 1987), 32–33, 52–57, 82–84.

[24] Dyer, *Standards*, 214.

Were this not the case, there would not have been the national legislation on wages and the mobility of laborers after the Black Death, nor would there have been the sustained attempt to enforce this legislation with all the means of central and local power. True enough, in the long run this coercion failed. However, people do not live "in the long run," nor are their struggles conducted "in the long run." We need to remember that the elites' coercive activity seems to have succeeded up to the second great plague of 1361, which killed about a further 10% of the population. It was this, together with the sharp fall in grain prices from 1376, which seems to have provided the determining factor in this particular struggle between wage-laborers and employers.[25] Since those who were prosecuted and fined in the 1350s, 1360s, and 1370s could see no end to any "long run," we should not use the "long run" to obscure either the intensity of the employers' coercive efforts in the forty years after the Black Death or its significant role in the network of factors leading to the rising of 1381.

The few examples of indictments I shall now offer were commonplace during the period in which Langland wrote and re-wrote *Piers Plowman*. They were so commonplace that in 1352 there are surviving records of 7,556 people being fined in Essex alone under the terms of the Statute of Labourers.[26] In his study of north and central Essex, L. R. Poos calculated that "roughly one in seven Essex people older than their mid-teens, or nearly one in four Essex males in the same age-range, were fined for violating the labour legislation in a single year."[27] Elizabeth Furber earlier had found that in 1377–79 "two hundred of the two hundred and eighty extant indictments before the justices of the peace [in Essex] involved labour offences," while Poos found, in one series of Essex indictments in 1389, 791 fines against the Statute of Labourers.[28] His comment is especially relevant to the concerns of the present chapter:

> The sheer numerical weight of Statute enforcement in the county . . . makes much more vividly comprehensible the ferocity directed towards the county-level agents of law enforcement (like Bampton, Gildesburgh and Sewale) by a rural society so heavily infused with wage labour and rural industry.[29]

The standard charge, experienced by many thousands of English workers acting "ayeins þe statut" (VI.320), went along lines such as these:

---

[25] On the Statutes of Labour and the ensuing struggles see the classic work by Bertha Putnam, *The Enforcement of the Statutes of Labourers* (New York: Columbia University Press, 1908); Poos, *A Rural Society*, chap. 10 is an important recent study.

[26] Poos, *A Rural Society*, 220–21; 20% were women.

[27] Poos, *A Rural Society*, 241; see too Elizabeth Furber, *Essex Sessions of the Peace 1351, 1377–79* (Colchester: Essex Archaeological Society, 1953), 68–69.

[28] Furber, *Essex Sessions of the Peace*, 69; Poos, *A Rural Society*, 241.

[29] Poos, *A Rural Society*, 241; see too Nora Kenyon, "Labour Conditions in Essex in the Reign of Richard II," *Economic History Review* 4 (1934): 429–51.

they present that Alicia Gylot (from the same place) takes excessive wage in autumn, that is 4d., and also moves from place to place . . . they present that Emma Shepherd (from the same place) does the same . . . they present that John Mory of Castle Hedingham moves from place to place in autumn for excess wages . . . they present that Henry atte Watere (ploughman) takes 20s. a year from William Andrew, 4 days use of a plough, one new tunic and grain, namely a quarter of corn every twelve weeks, against the statute . . . they present that Richard Waterford is a good ploughman and refused that work [we can see how Langland's Piers would have seemed to his local justice in passus VII] . . . they present that John Loue of High Easter is a common reaper and moves from place to place for excessive wages, and gets others to act in the same way against the statute . . . they present that Robert Craddok (of Thaxted), labourer, takes 2 d. a day and food.[30]

In her still indispensable study of the enforcement of the Statute of Labourers, Bertha Putnam observed that, "The constables report long lists of labourers who are rebellious and refuse to take oaths of obedience to the statutes."[31]

On top of this an important factor relevant to *Piers Plowman* was the clergy's involvement in the nexus of wage-labor and legislation. In her study of the proceedings before the Justices of the Peace, Bertha Putnam produced evidence of the King's Bench removing a case from Hertfordshire against a vicar and a hermit for "preaching that the statutes of labour are wicked and that there is nothing to prevent labourers from taking what wages they please."[32] Such a vicar and such a hermit, it needs recalling, are as much part of late medieval mentalities, as "representative," as are prescriptive texts composed by orthodox preachers or by John Gower. Furthermore, the clerisy included not only employers of wage-labor but also those whose situation was precisely analogous to wage-laborers'. We find an Essex jury presenting a vicar for charging excessive prices for his labor-power in administering the sacraments.[33] Similarly in Wiltshire we find John Bryan, clerk, being presented for taking excessive wages for his labor.[34] In 1362 the commons' petition include complaints about the costs of priests: "les Chapelleins sont devenuz si chers q'ils ne voillent demurrer ove nuly meins que dys marcz ou dusze, a grant grevance & oppression du poeple."[35] The king's response agrees to fix wages of such priests and to restrain their mobility, to stop them "passant d'une Diocise a

---

[30] These examples are taken from Furber, *Essex Sessions of the Peace*, 159–60, 164, 168, 170; see too 171, 176–77; she prints the Latin and gives an English version which I have occasionally adapted as I think appropriate. For some Suffolk examples, Aers, *Community, Gender, and Individual Identity*, 28–29.

[31] Putnam, *Enforcement*, 76.

[32] Bertha Putnam, *Proceedings before the Justices of the Peace in the Fourteenth and Fifteenth Centuries* (London: Spottiswoode, 1938), cxxv.

[33] Harding, "The Revolt against the Justices," 186.

[34] "Offenders against the Statute of Labourers in Wiltshire," trans. E. M. Thompson, *Wiltshire and Natural History Magazine* 33 (1903–04), 384–409, here p. 387.

[35] *Rotuli Parliamentorum*, 6 vols. (London, 1783), 36 Edward II, vol 2: 271.

autre."[36] Langland himself joined in with this complaint too, one levied against himself in the C version by Reason and Conscience.[37] Such complaints and resolutions are a good reminder of how integrated were the lower clergy in standard practices and relations of wage-labor. On this topic Bertha Putnam made yet another indispensable study. There she traces the "growing demand for stipendiary priests at just the time when the supply was being diminished both by the plague and by promotion of many of them to fill the gaps in the ranks of rectors and vicars." She described the social and economic "gulf" between a mass of unbeneficed clergy and "the beneficed clergy, whose employees they normally were," a gulf she found close to that "between the labourers and the governing classes." The changes in supply and demand led to substantial increases in the wages these unbeneficed men could claim. The response of the *ecclesiastical* establishment was to pass "clerical statutes of labourers," ones whose working Putnam investigated.[38] This legislation fixed rates, giving penalties for charges classified as excessive, forbad priests to leave the diocese without a bishop's letter, and chose the same rhetorical strategies as the parliamentary legislators used against secular wage-laborers. In 1354 Bishop Grandisson complained about the "exorbitant salaries" demanded by his priests – they too, like Langland's "wasters," seem to inhabit taverns more than churches.[39] But the unbeneficed clerical wage-laborers did not necessarily accept their masters' legislation. For example, in 1364 a royal commission of oyer and terminer was directed against chaplains in the archdeaconry of Leicester. The commission was

> to investigate the assault made by chaplains on the parsons [i.e. rectors] who had been deputed to act as the bishop's commissaries in enforcing the second *effranata*. The chaplains, bound together by oaths, had broken up the parsons' sessions by horrible words, almost killing them and even lying in wait for the bishop himself.[40]

Stirring times indeed, ones in which we can never assume that a classification such as "clerical" entails a predictably conservative, consistently orthodox, and obedient set of attitudes in a homogeneous social and ideological group. We can hardly assume that what constituted "traditional religion" in these circumstances was obvious and uncontested.

What we are now in a position to see is how wage-labor after the Black Death carried an extremely rich and troubling range of meanings for Langland, ones

---

[36] *Rotuli Parliamentorum*, vol. 2: 271.

[37] On mobile priests seeking better pay, *Piers Plowman* Pr.83–86; see too the friars there, Pr.58–63. His own self-representations are discussed below. On this passus (C V) see *Written Work*, essays by Hanna, Pearsall, and Middleton.

[38] Bertha Putnam, "Maximum Wage-Laws for Priests after the Black Death, 1348–1381," *American History Review* 21 (1915–16): 12–32; quotations here come from pp. 14 and 15.

[39] Ibid., 20–21 and 24.

[40] Ibid., 25 (*Calendar of Patent Rolls 1364–67*, 4 September 1364).

that were ethical and political in the broadest sense. Wage-labor suggested to the poet a culture of independence, assertiveness, and anti-authoritarianism. Nor were his impressions unwarranted. It seems no coincidence that Essex, the region with probably the highest level of wage-labor in England, was found by L. R. Poos to be "the centre of a deeply rooted strain of anti-authoritarianism during the later fourteenth and fifteenth centuries, which manifested itself both in rural revolts and uprisings and in a persistent subculture of religious non-conformity."[41] Langland was certainly interested in wage-labor and found it more disturbing than the traditional forms of conflict between rural villeins and the seigneurial classes. His vision shares something with Bertha Putnam's closing comment to her study on the enforcement of the Statute of Labourers: "the statutes of labourers must not be regarded as having created a new system or a new set of economic relations, but as affording proof that radical changes had occurred, ushering in a new era."[42] The grounds for such a strong claim were not only that the Statutes were the first attempt of "the central authorities to apply to the country as a whole, uniform legislation on wages and prices." More important still, in the contexts of the present essay, was the fact that in the past, "wages of agricultural labourers were apparently regulated by custom."[43] That is, relations around wage-labor now presented an exceptionally sharp challenge to a nexus of traditional practices, understandings, and negotiations. Langland was acutely conscious of the implications this carried for his tradition's version of the cardinal virtue of justice.[44]

An important part of Mede's prominent role in the first vision of *Piers Plowman* is to dramatize some of these implications. From passus II to passus IV Mede symbolizes a culture in which not only production but all human relations become exchanges in a market for commodities. The figure's gender is given in accord with conventional stereotypes of received misogynistic discourses. These identified the letter, carnality, instability, insatiability, and supplementary with "femininity," the "other" against which "masculine" identity could be defined

---

[41] Poos, *A Rural Society*, 229; see chaps. 11 and 12. On the incidence of wage-labor in this part of Essex, chaps. 1 and 10; on mobility, chap. 8; see too Hilton, *Bond Men*, 171–75, 190–92. This context should highlight the grave inadequacies of modern literary histories that assume that any challenge to "social distinctions" in this period *must* have struck all medieval people as "an impious affront to the ordained order of the universe." This simply ignores the number of people actually making such challenges at many different levels of society, rural and urban. The quotation here is from Stokes, *Justice and Mercy*, 211. See too the vehement attack on laborers resisting employers, p. 212, an attack that, presumably, coincided with the Thatcherite government's attack on sustained strikes by British miners in defense of their work.

[42] Putnam, *Enforcement*, 223.

[43] Ibid., 3, 156. For Wyclif's version of this "new era" and its "central authorities" see chap. 6 below.

[44] His vision would have been sharpened by life in one of the greatest North European markets, London. On Langland as "a London poet" see Caroline Barron, chap. 5 in *Chaucer's England: Literature in Historical Context*, ed. Barbara Hanawalt (Minneapolis: University of Minnesota Press, 1992).

but which, simultaneously and always, threatened to subvert this identity from without and from within.[45] Mede is both powerful courtly lady and ubiquitous common prostitute, a "baude," a "hore," as "commune as þe Cartwey to knaue and to alle," totally uninterested in social status.[46] The "female" figure thus becomes the symbol for Langland's vision of communities in which, as the Wife of Bath observed, "al is for to selle."[47] She figures forth a culture determined by the kind of exchange St. Thomas had viewed with such grave misgivings, one shaped not by what he considered the quest for the "necessities of life" but for "profit." Such motivation deserves blame, he maintained, because it fosters "the greed for gain," and this "knows no limit and tends to infinity" (*ST* II–II.71.4). This is the economy and culture symbolized by Mede. Not surprisingly then, Mede is presented as the dissolvent of just relations in all domains.[48] "Mede oucrmaistreþ lawe," observes the reforming king (IV.176), and neither Reason nor Conscience dissents from this view.

In representing Mede as ubiquitous, the poet evokes a community with no boundaries, with no cogent moral principles, with no criteria other. than pragmatic response to profit and loss in the market. Here there can be no common project to foster institutions, relations, and laws that could help people cultivate the virtues in pursuit of their final good, as understood by the tradition to which the poet belonged. In a community driven by what Mede symbolizes, it is not at all clear that we would even understand what *redde quod debes* could mean, let alone act on it as a decisive imperative. And it is to just this version of society that the poet returns in the courageous final vision of *Piers Plowman*. There, quite explicitly, "þe comune" rejects the cardinal virtues and the demands of Conscience to pursue them: whatever does not contribute to financial profit, to "wynnyng" is unreal.[49] In such a community, however

---

[45] On this now familiar material, see, for example, Carolyn Dinshaw, *Chaucer's Sexual Poetics* (Madison: University of Wisconsin Press, 1989), intro. and chap. 1; Elaine Tuttle Hansen, *Chaucer and the Fictions of Gender* (Berkeley: University of California Press, 1992); R. H. Bloch, "Medieval Misogyny," *Representations* 20 (1987): 1–24; and its elaboration and enrichment in *Medieval Misogyny and the Invention of Western Romantic Love* (Chicago: University of Chicago Press, 1991).

[46] Here see III.129, IV.166, III.131–35. On Mede see especially J. A. Yunck, *The Lineage of Lady Meed* (Notre Dame: University of Notre Dame Press, 1963). On Mede and the politics of gender, see Aers, "Class, Gender, Medieval Criticism, and *Piers Plowman*," and Clare Lees, "Gender and Exchange in *Piers Plowman*," both in *Class and Gender in Early English Literature*, ed. Britton J. Harwood and Gillian R. Overing (Bloomington: Indiana University Press, 1994), 59–75 and 112–30.

[47] *Wife of Bath's Prologue*, 414 (*Riverside Chaucer*, ed. L. B. Benson [Boston: Houghton Mifflin, 1987]).

[48] See III.136–69; IV.47–107; IV.149–56; IV.171–76; also Kaeuper, *War, Justice, and Public Order*, 334–35. On the problems of this use of gender in *Piers Plowman*, see Aers and Lees cited in n. 46. See too Stephanie Trigg, "The Traffic in Medieval Women: Alice Perrers, Feminist Criticism and *Piers Plowman*," *YLS* 12 (1998), 5–29.

[49] See XIX.45–53: there is no reason to question the accuracy of the vicar's perceptions here since they accord with what the poet shows us in passus XIX–XX, XV, VI, II–IV, and Prologue. They confirm Holy Church's gloomy observation at I.5–9.

gradually, however celebrated as a desirable liberation from fetters (as at III.137–39), all ethical discriminations will become incoherent, even impossible. No-one will be able to know, "Wheiþer he wynne wiþ right, wiþ wrong or wiþ vsure" (XIX.350). Once again, we are forced to ask how anyone could know what *redde quod debes* might entail in such a society.

How will we be able to determine, in good conscience, what constitutes a just wage and just conditions of employment? There will never be problems in offering rationalizations of self-interest, no problem in developing rhetoric to demonize those whose interests conflict with one's own. Nor will there be much problem for those in command of the legal and coercive apparatus to pass "laws" in their own interests and to set about enforcing them as best as they can, classifying all opponents as people hostile to God, Reason, and Justice (see VI.312–18). This, however, has nothing to do with the understanding of justice in the Christian-Aristotelian tradition from which the poet came. As St. Thomas argued, and as not all commentators on the *Clerk's Tale* have remembered, legislators who make tyrannical laws have no legitimate claim to obedience. Tyrannical law, he insists, is not truly law because it only serves private interests and harms the people, setting up forms of life at odds with their true end – the life of the virtues in accord with reason. Most pertinently for the present context, he argues that to rebel against a tyrannical government is *not* illicit, since such a government denies the ends of government and impedes the citizens' pursuit of the good.[50] If the employers' legislation was narrowly self-interested, as it was, what did it have to do with justice and what moral force could it have? What good moral reasons could be offered against the vicar and the hermit of Hertfordshire who were charged with telling laborers that the legislation in question had no moral force? The relevant questions had indeed become extremely difficult to answer. As *Dives* says to his instructor in *Dives and Pauper*, "It is hard to knowyn what is þe ry3te value of a þing."[51] It was especially hard when that "þing" was a peculiar commodity capable of turning over the tables on which it was displayed for sale. In *Dives and Pauper* the instructor gives the answer taught by St. Thomas and others, one that was standard enough:

þe ry3te value & þe iust prys of a þing is aftir þat þe comoun merket goth þat tyme, & so a þing is as mychil worþ as it may ben sold so be [*sic*] comoun merket – tanti valet quanti vendi potest . . .[52]

The issue here is central to the present chapter. As St. Thomas argued, " it is an act of justice to give a just price for anything received . . . an act of justice to make a return for work or toil" (*ST* I–II.114.1, *resp*). In relation to wages and labor-power, however, the definition of the just price given in *Dives and Pauper*

---

[50] *ST* I–II. 92.1; II–II.42.2; see too *De Regimine* I.4. These issues have been addressed above in chapters 1 and 2.

[51] *Dives and Pauper*, II.154 (written c. 1405–10).

[52] Ibid., II.154.

held unwelcome consequences for employers and legislators after the Black Death. This is so because its definition assumes a *free market*. The "just prys" is the price a commodity fetches on an open market, "þe comoun market," a market free from manipulation by monopolizers, forestallers, or any other self-interested person or groups. Along these lines, fixing prices by a small minority in their own interests could not be defended, and those who resisted their attempts to rig the market in this way could reasonably claim to be acting rationally and justly. Perhaps it was an attempt to think coherently along the lines of this tradition that led the vicar and hermit in Hertfordshire to tell local people the Statutes of Labourers "are wicked."[53] Perhaps John Ball, first recorded as being in trouble with the authorities in 1366, had been a Christian-Aristotelian who had no need to hear Wyclif before challenging the justice of current ruling class policies of legislation and taxation.

Langland's line is, of course, hardly that of the vicar from Hertfordshire. In a much-discussed passage, greatly elaborated in the C version, he had Conscience address the problems of labor and the just wage.[54] In relation to earthly relations, Conscience seeks to distinguish the culture of Mede from what is here called "measurable hire." This, he emphasizes, is "no manere Mede." Because our world knows the disasters consequent upon the long-term pursuit of Mede in a society where Mede rules, because we can now see its catastrophic teleology, I have great sympathy with Langland's ethical intentions in trying to address the complex problems of limits and justice in this domain. But sympathy should not obscure the unresolved difficulties concealed in the "solution" he attributes to Conscience. It sounds fine to attack priests who "taken Mede and moneie for masses þat þei syngeþ" (III.253). After all, this certainly looks like simony, what Chaucer's Parson describes as "Espiritueel marchandise."[55] But the situation was actually not so simple, and attacking priests who sang masses for money was not necessarily fine. As we have already noticed, this was a period of increasing demand for unbeneficed clergy, for chantry priests, for the service of priests without the security of a regular living or independent funds – priests, in fact, with nothing to live on but the "mede" they obtained for the religious services they performed. As we also noted, these priests were subject to ecclesiastical legislation and prosecution similar to that imposed on their brothers and sisters who were secular laborers. But how does the poet expect unbeneficed priests to go on singing masses and offering other

---

[53] Discussed above: Putnam, *Proceedings*, cxxv.

[54] See B III.230–58 which is discussed here; the C expansion is substantial and reflects the poet's continuing attempt to deal with the vexed issue, C III.285–405. On the C version here much has now been written, but see Janet Coleman, *Medieval Readers and Writers, 1350–1400* (London: Hutchinson, 1981), 252–61.

[55] *Parson's Tale*, X.781–83. Here we enter one of the fiercely contested areas to which both Chaucer and Langland contributed, in their very different ways. For the central dispute see John Wyclif, *De Simonia*, ed. S. Herzberg-Fränkel and M. H. Dziewicki (London: Wyclif Society, 1898); *On Simony*, trans. T. A. McVeigh (New York: Fordham University Press, 1992).

spiritual services if not by taking "moneie for masses?" If he concedes that such wages are not, after all, simony, how then should the just price be fixed? Through an open market for priests and their performances? That sounds bad, for it suggests profoundly unspiritual market negotiations over the means of grace. But if not that, then, once more, by what principle should the just wage here be reached? The problems were stark and fresh, bound up with the massive demographic collapse of the Black Death and the plague of 1361, and bound up too with corresponding shifts in expectations and aspirations that could not necessarily be answered by appeals to customary rates in a web of contexts that were now far from customary. There *is* one answer here that the poet, given his commitment to orthodox traditions, could not consider, although it was clearly articulated by some Lollards in the later fourteenth century and thereafter – namely, declare the priesthood of all believers and cure both the shortage of priests and the "sale" of spiritual gifts at a stroke![56]

A similar set of problems emerges in the poet's treatment of secular wage-labor at this point. Conscience teaches that what "labourers" take "is no more manere Mede but a mesurable hire."[57] This sounds both traditional and reasonable. Yet in passus VI the poet supports the employers' labor legislation with such vehemence that he even suggests, deploying his own prophetic idiom, that "werkmen" who resist the Statute of Labourers are leading England to some divinely sent chastisement in which the plague of famine will be "Iustice" (VI.312–31).[58] Now the many people prosecuted under the new legislation hardly saw their wages as "Mede mesureless," especially when they looked at the worldly consumption of those judging and taxing them. This is plain enough both from their sustained resistance and from their demands for a fully free market in labor and wages made at Mile End in June 1381.[59] So the question returns: by what principles are we to resolve the competing versions of a just wage, of "mesurable hire" in the circumstances after the Black Death? Why should we now abandon the guidelines for establishing the just price so lucidly articulated by St. Thomas and reproduced in texts such as *Dives and Pauper*, quoted above? The only answer can be that those who abandon the received framework at this juncture do so to defend the employers' material interests in a context where the market in labor,

[56] Examples of Lollard claims concerning the priesthood of all believers can be found among the East Anglian people rounded up in the persecutions of 1428–31, *Heresy Trials in the Diocese of Norwich, 1428–31*, ed. Norman P. Tanner (Camden fourth series, vol. 20, London: Royal Historical Society, 1977), 52, 57, 73, 142. On this teaching in Lollardy, see too Anne Hudson, *The Premature Reformation: Wycliffite Texts and Lollard History* (Oxford: Clarendon Press, 1988), 325–27. The problems and ambivalences in Wyclif's own theology and ecclesiology here are addressed in this book's final chapter.

[57] See III.255–56. Compare Mede at III.217–18, and Theology at II.119–23.

[58] See Aers, *Community, Gender, and Individual Identity*, 47–49. Compare the works by Middleton and Clopper cited in n. 15.

[59] See *The Anonimalle Chronicle*, ed. V. H. Galbraith (Manchester: Manchester University Press, 1927), 144–45; at Mile End, he notes, the demands include the following: "et que nulle ne deveroit servire ascune homme mes a sa volunte de mesmes et par covenant taille"; trans. in Dobson, *Peasants' Revolt*, 161.

and after 1376 in grain prices, is unfavorable to them. But this takes us, or should take us, back to the Thomistic account of a tyrannical legislation, already outlined, an account that teaches us that our own material self-interests may not actually be identical with the common good and the virtue of justice. This is not a comfortable lesson for anyone. One could pursue the difficulties here further, but we have reached one of those moments where the poet turns out to have explored a major moral and political issue to a point where the force of the questions he has raised and dramatized is in excess of any solution anyone could find. The employers' legislation was a pragmatic self-interested response which failed. It also failed to meet the demands of justice and the terms of the just price in the tradition to which Langland belonged. But the laborers' demands for a free market in labor-power and wages, understandable as they are, did not offer a satisfactory solution either. Although they were in fact grounded in a pragmatic opportunism similar to their opponents', they may in theory seem closer to the traditional idea of how the just price should be established. However, when the commodity is human labor-power and human lives there are massive moral problems at stake. One has only to look forward to the appalling situation of wage-laborers in the very different demographic and market situation of the sixteenth century to begin unpacking the grave inadequacies of their ancestors' solutions in the later fourteenth century. *Piers Plowman* here dramatizes a genuine aporia for the poet's tradition in the new circumstances with which the poem engages so admirably. The problems Langland was exploring have turned out to be quite as recalcitrant to the paradigms dominant in our own liberal, unprecedentedly secular, and capitalist societies.[60]

Langland himself emphasized how intractable he found the cluster of problems I have been addressing. He did so not only returning to the issues they raise but in the haunting self-representations he weaves in his own poem. Having launched attacks on mobile clerics and on mobile wage-laborers who resist the employers' work ethos and legislation, he shows himself as lacking land, lacking traditional occupation, always on the move, a vagrant whom we encounter as he goes "by þe wey" (XX.1), a wanderer who confesses "forþ I gan walke/ In manere of a mendynaunt many yer" (XIII.2–3), one who "romed aboute" (VIII.1), "In habite as an heremite, vnholy of werkes,/ Wente wide in þis world wondres to here" (Pr.3–4).[61] The dazzling new self-referential passage in the C version (V.1–108) elaborates these passing depictions to bring out the ways in which his form of life cannot be understood in terms of any traditional version of the just life in which one renders to others their due in a web of reciprocal and known obligations. Reason sees him as an "ydel man . . . a spille

[60] Profound studies of the changes in moral paradigms at issue here are in two books by Alasdair MacIntyre, *After Virtue: A Study in Moral Theory* (Notre Dame: University of Notre Dame Press, 1984) and *Whose Justice? Which Rationality?*

[61] See Middleton, "William Langland's 'Kynde Name,'" and Lawrence M. Clopper, "Need Men and Women Labor? Langland's Wanderer and the Labor Ordinances," chap. 6 in *Chaucer's England*, ed. Hanawalt. The major study of these issues in C V is Middleton, "Acts of Vagrancy."

tyme," and to stress the implications of a life led in defiance of traditional versions of justice, the poet invokes Christ's words of warning: "*Reddet unicuique iuxta opera sua*" (He will render to each one according to his works, Matthew 16.27). Although we and our communities may reject the terms of *redde quod debes*, making them virtually incomprehensible, the warning is that we will nevertheless be held responsible and answerable within its framework. The projected self of the poet represents precisely what he cannot assimilate to his own tradition. It is no wonder that he was more gripped by the problems of wage-labor and market exchanges in relation to traditional accounts of justice than he was by current struggles between villeins and lords over services and status. His own identity, elusive and mobile, is convicted, in his own eyes, by God's umpires, Reason and Conscience (C V.92–93, 102–4). That is, he himself, a kind of clerical laborer, represents his own understanding of the dissolution of the good and the just community, both effect and cause. In this he is another Haukyn.[62] Like that figure, Will is painfully struggling towards a conversion but, again like that figure, it remains quite unclear what form of life he would, or could, pursue. Converted in a community under the domination of Mede, what will his options be? At one point in the B version he claims that if he knew what the virtues were he would "neuere do werk" – precisely what Reason and Conscience attack him for in C V – "but wende to holi chirche/ And þere bidde my bedes" (XII.25–28). In the end, he remains an isolated man, immobilized by age (XX.183–98), on the verge of death (XX.199–202), with a disintegrating Church under Antichrist's forces and still asking *how* to combine the evangelical commands to love with a licit way of obtaining the necessities of embodied life in this community (XX.204–11: cf. XX.322–86). It is worth stressing that the collapse of the Christian communities founded by the Holy Spirit and Piers in the poem's final passus is directly related to the pressures we have been studying. In conclusion I will discuss some aspects of this founding activity and its catastrophic reversal.

The Holy Spirit gives a diversity of graces to the first Christian communities (XIX.225–61: 1 Corinthians 12.4–31).[63] James Simpson sees this passage as an attempt to incorporate "Labour, or works . . . in the scheme of salvation," to see how "labour can find a place in the scheme of salvation."[64] For the final time the

---

[62] On Haukyn, XIII.220–XIV.335. On C V and the 1388 Parliament, see Middleton, "Acts of Vagrancy."

[63] Langland's emphasis that this is the early Church does not fit James Simpson's view that the poet is here representing "a renewed apostolic Church" in "a renewed society" (*Piers Plowman*, 223, similarly, 220, 224). Langland is clear that the passage in question follows immediately on the first pentecost, with Piers now figuring St. Peter, the first and true Pope.

[64] Simpson, *Piers Plowman*, 224. On the profound processes involved here, not part of Simpson's interests, see Jacques Le Goff, *Time, Work, and Culture in the Middle Ages*, trans. Arthur Goldhammer (Chicago: University of Chicago Press, 1980), esp. 43–52, 58–70, 107–21; Sylvia Thrupp, *The Merchant Class of Medieval London*, 2nd edn. (Ann Arbor: University of Michigan Press, 1989).

poet returns to one of the issues that most perplexed him, only now he tries to imagine an originary moment that could serve as a corrective model for his own intractable present. In an interesting reading of this passage, James Simpson has argued that Langland keeps his attention on "the fundamental questions of social hierarchy and labour that he had confronted in passus VI," while he finally displaces the "hierarchical or coercive . . . feudal structure" assumed earlier in the poem.[65] In response to this claim, the first question to ask is the following: if by "feudal" Simpson means a social formation in which the dominant and basic form of production is carried out by "agriculturists"[66] holding land (much of it in villein tenure) from lords in a political regime legitimizing a massive extraction of services and money from these tenants, while excluding the vast majority of people from any political voice, then what form of labor is envisaged as replacing the traditional agriculturist in her/his web of obligations, fines, taxes, and suit at the lord's court? Simpson's answer is that we now see "Langland's renewed vision of society as modeled on urban horizontal structures, despite the manorial and hierarchical images which are also employed."[67] By "urban horizontal structures" Simpson means "trade guilds, craft guilds." Indeed, he claims that "the bourgeois model of the 'crafte' (XIX.236, 242) or guild is invoked as a model of brotherly love."[68] This seems a little surprising, for at least two reasons. Firstly, Grace is offering a prophetic admonition to the future craft guilds of Langland's own world:

> And alle he lered to be lele, and ech a craft loue oþer,
> Ne boost ne debat among hem alle. (XIX.250–51)

As is the way with utopian forms, the negation ("Ne . . . ne") is directed against present norms and practices. It is mistaken to think that *present* institutions are being used "as a model of brotherly love." Indeed, Simpson himself acknowledges that "the guilds of Langland's London were in fierce rivalry" – and not only, he might well have added, of London.[69] Langland was as well placed as

[65] Simpson, *Piers Plowman*, 225 and 224.

[66] On this term and its uses in current controversies over the "peasantry" in England, see Poos, *A Rural Society*, 21 and 43–51. For a useful introduction to the debates on feudalism and transitions from it, see John E. Martin, *Feudalism to Capitalism*, rev. edn. (Basingstoke: Macmillan, 1986); R. H. Hilton, *Class Conflict and the Crisis of Feudalism* (London: Hambledon Press, 1985), esp. chaps. 18–19, 22–23; R. Brenner, "Agrarian Class Structure and Economic Development in Pre-Industrial Europe," *Past and Present* 70 (1976): 30–75 and "The Agrarian Roots of European Capitalism," *Past and Present* 97 (1982): 16–113. For a collection of essays in *Past and Present* related to Brenner's work, see *The Brenner Debate: Agrarian Class Structure and Economic Development in Pre-Industrial Europe* (Cambridge: Past and Present Publications, 1985).

[67] Simpson, *Piers Plowman*, 225.

[68] Ibid., 225–26.

[69] Ibid., 226–27. For examples of the conflicts, see M. James, "Ritual, Drama, and the Social Body in the Late Medieval English Town," *Past and Present* 98 (1983): 3–29; Ruth Bird, *The Turbulent London of Richard II* (London: Longmans Green, 1949); R. B. Dobson, "The Risings in York, Beverly, and Scarborough," in *The English Rising*, ed. Hilton and Aston; on

Thomas Usk to see how easily the rhetoric of fraternity turned into the practice of fratricide, and perhaps he would not have been entirely surprised: "For soþest word þat euer god seide was þo he seide *Nemo bonus*" (X.447 [Luke 18.18]). Furthermore, the craft guilds were committedly exclusivist, hierarchical, and authoritarian organizations designed to serve the political and economic interests of a minority of males.[70] *Piers Plowman* gives us no reason to think that "urban" forms of production, competition, and exchange were admired by a poet for whom the practices and institutions of the markets, including the crucial markets in labor-power, were profoundly disturbing.

It seems to me that in the passage attributed to the Holy Spirit the poet does not, in fact, really address what Simpson calls "the fundamental questions" about forms of labor. What Pentecost and Grace give us is a divine vision that sets aside "the fundamental questions" thrown up by economic and social relations in England after the Black Death. In Grace's oration we meet, for example, the following: those who earn their licit livelihood "by labour of tongue" (some hope here for the poet given such a bad time by Ymaginatif in the B version and by Reason and Conscience in C?); licit market exchange; wage labor – but wage-labor that is "lele" and classifiable as "trewe" (whatever that would mean in the 1370s); tilling, making haycocks, and thatching (whether these are villein services, sale of labor-power, or work on a family's free-holding is not specified); astrology; asceticism; and a multitude of cooperating, loving crafts (XIX.229–51). The poet has thus *bracketed* the most vexing problems about justice, wages, conditions, and work, while, understandably enough, choosing not to go back to the most challenging vision of early Christian community found in the Acts of the Apostles and given such striking application by early fifteenth-century Taborites and by seventeenth-century Diggers. If one sought, in Simpson's manner, to apply the passage to "fundamental questions" about work after the Black Death, its vagueness might seem to sanction almost all current practices – as long as they are part of "a lele life and a trewe" (XIX.237). The problem, as we have seen, was that the constitution of "lele," "trewe" forms of labor and wages was in serious dispute. The vision of harmony Holy Spirit offers here is admirable, but it does nothing to address the profound difficulty of ascertaining what constitutes a just

the political force and composition of craft guilds, especially useful is Heather Swanson, *Medieval Artisans: An Urban Class in Late Medieval England* (Oxford: Blackwell, 1989). See also Steven A. Epstein, *Wage Labor and Guilds in Medieval Europe* (Chapel Hill: University of North Carolina Press, 1991) and A. C. Black, *Guilds and Civil Society* (Ithaca: Cornell University Press, 1984).

[70] On this dimension, see Swanson, *Medieval Artisans*, and Martha Howell, *Women, Production, and Patriarchy in Late-Medieval Cities* (Chicago: University of Chicago Press, 1986); an excellent introduction here is Judith Bennett, "Medieval Women, Modern Women: Across the Great Divide," chap. 5 in *Culture and History 1350–1600*, ed. Aers (Hemel Hempstead: Harvester, 1992). Although it lacks sustained attention to issues of guilds and gender, see too P. J. P. Goldberg, *Women, Work, and Life Cycle in a Medieval Economy* (Oxford: Clarendon Press, 1992), chap. 3.

price and what constitutes a coherent application of the tradition's understanding of justice in the poet's society. It thus does not address some issues that are major topics of exploration in *Piers Plowman*. Indeed, and contrary to Simpson's optimistic account, we find that Holy Spirit sanctions, even in this utopian vision, the existence of a mounted (hence elite) law-enforcement agency (XIX.245–47).

Nor does the poet leave us with this Pentecostal vision. In the same passus he invents a scene in which "al þe comune," showing unusual solidarity, rejects the fundamental imperative of justice, *redde quod debes* (XIX.309–92). Here, alas, is the "horizontal" fraternalism James Simpson was looking for, a solidarity in the rejection of the Christian–Aristotelian tradition the poet wished to bring into contact with new and extremely testing circumstances. It is a solidarity Holy Church herself had already articulated with memorable clarity (I.5–9).[71] But coming towards the end of the poem, *after* the great shewings of Christ, his teachings of *kindness* (XVII.215–64), his living exemplification of love and saving solidarity with humankind (B XVIII), coming after the Pentecostal graces (B XIX), this has a far more disturbing resonance than it could in the poem's opening passus. The poet actually reinforces this with the aggressive and shocking intervention of one of the commodity producers so recently, and so blandly, sanctioned in the poet's utopian vision:

> "Ye? baw!" quod a Brewer, "I wol noȝt be ruled,
> By Iesu! For al youre Ianglynge, wiþ *Spiritus Iusticie*,
> Ne after Conscience, by crist! While I kan selle
> Boþe dregges and draf and drawe at oon hole
> Thikke ale and þynne ale; þat is my kynde,
> And noȝt hakke after holynesse; hold þi tongue, Conscience!
> Of *Spiritus Iusticie* þow spekest much on ydel."   (XIX.396–402)

This brilliantly inventive rhetoric shows us how a fixed and deludedly autonomous individual can be produced by a certain kind of community, one in which the market is god: such individuals are persuaded that the pursuit of profit and self-interest constitutes rationality and felicity, even as they are persuaded to deny the roots of creatureliness and the fluid contingency of the self. The Incarnation, the crucifixion, and resurrection so memorably explored in passus XVI–XIX count for nothing here. Unlike the poem's Will, so remorselessly castigated, such a self feels no need to search, to search for the virtues and their end. The passage dramatizes how certain forms of work and community can transform someone's *kynde*, persuading them that the teaching of the Samaritan/Christ, of Grace, and of Piers is vapid. In Langland's terms, the collective rejection of justice in passus XIX and XX displays a terrifying rejection of the final good disclosed by the good Samaritan, by the life of Christ and the salvific promises he makes in the Harrowing of Hell.

[71] On this Guy Bourquin, *Piers Plowman*, 2 vols. (Lille: University of Lille, 1978), 183.

Probably worst of all for the poet, the Church, the ark of salvation, is now assimilated to the brewer's community, fulfilling the darkest prognostications of passus XV. Once more, the refusal to meet the demands of justice, of *redde quod debes*, seems to be decisive (XX.306–72). Throughout the poem, as in the teaching it follows, the sacrament of penance is allied to justice (*ST* III.85–86); so with the contemptuous rejections of the tradition in which justice is articulated goes the rejection of penitence, of *redde quod debes*, a practice, for this poet, essential to any serious commitment to Christian discipleship. Not surprisingly then, when Conscience appreciates, belatedly enough (such is indeed the way of our consciences), what he has colluded in, he *leaves the Church* to search for Piers and Grace outside the ark.[72] This means that Conscience must become an isolated, wandering, mobile, independent searcher, someone who might well fall on the wrong side of the labor legislation and the commons' petition against the vagrants of 1376. Langland gives no indication of the search's outcome, but we should note that the aged Will, the figure for the poet, apparently remains in the Church. Even if it seems overwhelmed by the forces of Antichrist, this is where he has been directed to wait, in love (XX.204–208). Perhaps the poet and Will could remember William of Ockham's *Letter to the Friars Minor* [*Epistola ad Fratres Minores*]: "the whole Christian faith, and all Christ's promises about the Catholic faith lasting to the end of the age, and the whole Church of God, could be preserved in a few, indeed in one."[73] That, however, is an extremely bleak vision.

---

[72] On the ending of the poem, see Simpson, *Piers Plowman*, 242, 243.

[73] William of Ockham, *A Letter to the Friars Minor and Other Writings*, ed. Arthur S. McGrade and John Kilcullen, trans. Kilcullen (Cambridge: Cambridge University Press, 1995), 13; see similarly *A Dialogue*, part 3, tract 1, III.11, p. 218 in the same volume.

4

Christianity for Courtly Subjects: or Pelagius Redivivus. Reflections on the *Gawain*-poet

> For here we are with the nineteenth book in hand on the subject of the City of God; and how could that City have made its first start; how could it have advanced along its course; how could it attain its appointed goal, if the life of the saints were not social? (Augustine, *City of God*).[1]

This chapter on the ecclesiology, ethics, and forms of faith in the *Gawain*-poet sets out from *Piers Plowman*. Langland's poem interweaves an individual quest for salvation ("tel me þis ilke, How I may saue my soule," I.83–84)[2] with a sustained critical exploration of English institutions and communities after the Black Death.[3] Langland's treatment of penance, a major preoccupation, exemplifies the ways in which interiority and spirituality are formed within determinate institutions and social networks. These, in the poet's view, are shaped by market values. Law itself is commodified and the poet's satire comes from and contributes to an increasingly widespread conviction that there was a general crisis of both order and legitimacy.[4] But the Church itself, at all levels, so *Piers Plowman* maintains, had become assimilated to current market relations and the secular powers these sustained (for example Pr. 81–86, XV.80–145, 539–67).[5] The sacrament of penance, without which the eucharist should not be received (as Conscience notes, XIX.385–90), is explored as a crucial example of this process. Its critical, reforming force abandoned, it can work to naturalize and internalize current social relations and goals that Langland saw as major obstructions on the journey to God (for example, III.32–63, XIX.383–409).

---

[1] St. Augustine, *City of God*, trans. Henry Betterson (London: Penguine, 1984), XIX.5, 858; see also XXI.25, 1008.

[2] References to *Piers Plowman* are to *Piers Plowman: The B-Version*, ed. George Kane and E. Talbot Donaldson (revised ed., London: Athlone, 1988).

[3] See Aers, *Chaucer, Langland, and the Creative Imagination* (London: Routledge, 1980), chaps. 1–3; James Simpson, *Piers Plowman: An Introduction* (London: Longman, 1991).

[4] See Richard W. Kaeuper, *War, Justice, and Public Order: England and France in the Later Middle Ages* (Oxford: Clarendon Press, 1988), chaps. 2–4; A. Harding, "The Revolt against the Justices," in *The English Rising of 1381*, ed. R. H. Hilton and T. Aston (Cambridge: Cambridge University Press, 1984), 165–93; Steven Justice, *Writing and Rebellion* (Berkeley: University of California Press, 1994), chap. 4.

[5] Aers, *Chaucer, Langland*, chap. 2; Wendy Scase, *Piers Plowman and the New Anticlericalism* (Cambridge: Cambridge University Press, 1989).

CHRISTIANITY FOR COURTLY SUBJECTS

Against this, the poet draws on a tradition that saw penance as "a public act" demanding a transformation of both inner and outer forms of life.[6] This is why restitution becomes a divisive demand in the poem.[7] It is inextricably bound up with a traditional conception of justice that itself unites inner and outer, individual and collective, private and public, contingent particular and divine teleology. No transformation of self can be achieved in isolation from changes in social practices (V.270–71). Restoration of justice in the soul entails a transformation of relations in the community, and the demands of this transformation may certainly be radical (for example, XV.80–145, 538–67). Similarly, resistance to reforming justice in social relations proves to be an overwhelming impediment to interior transformations (as in XIX–XX). This Christian-Aristotelian vision is then driven by Langland to confront (and not only once) the possibility that contemporary communities, including the Church, are such that practical reason becomes lost and no-one knows what constitutes just action, what one owes to one's neighbors. The penitent Haukyn is left weeping but still without a clear sense of how to live justly in his world (XIV.323–35) while by the end of the work we encounter a culture actually rejecting *Spiritus Iusticie*, the "chief seed þat Piers sew," the virtue without which none will find salvation (XIX.405–6). The register within which Langland represents this is not without interest to readers of the *Gawain*-poet and his courtly language of piety. Peace resists the kind of penitential practice that the poem has repeatedly depicted as indicative of the Church's assimilation by the existing structures of profit and power. But Peace is overruled and, significantly enough, by *hende speche* (XX.348–54). The culture of Christian discourse here is courtly as the confessor speaks "curteisly" and impresses Conscience who empowers him to take over the sacrament of penance. The forms of courtesy are integrated with "pryvee paiment," echoing the earlier exchange between Mede and her confessor (III.32–63). This combination certainly consoles Christians. But it also induces the final catastrophe of the poem, showing itself to be the fantasy and illusion of a demented optimism (XX.355–79). Conscience now confronts the effects of his actions and abandons the Church to seek for the sources of salvation outside the ark. Although the ark designated itself as that outside of which there could be no salvation, it is shown here to have become an impediment to the activity of grace, an institution now shaped by Antichrist's forces (XX.51–386). Langland's struggles to see how Christian-Aristotelian traditions of justice and penance could withstand certain corrosive forces in his culture, including, finally, its "hende speche," can help us focus on strategies through which the *Gawain*-poet addressed this culture. *Piers Plowman*

---

[6] John Bossy, *Christianity in the West, 1400–1700* (Oxford: Oxford University Press, 1985), 47–48, and chap. 3 *passim*. For a more realistic account of the practice of confession see W. David Myers, *"Poor Sinning Folk": Confession and Conscience in Counter-Reformation Germany* (Ithaca: Cornell University Press, 1996), part one.

[7] R. W. Frank, *Piers Plowman and the Scheme of Salvation* (New Haven: Yale University Press, 1957), 100–109; Anna Baldwin, "The Debt Narrative in *Piers Plowman*," in *Art and Context in Late Medieval English Narrative*, ed. Robert R. Edwards (Cambridge: Brewer, 1994), 37–50.

can also encourage appreciation of some of the consequences of the *Gawain*-poet's strategies, so different to Langland's.

I. *Sir Gawain and the Green Knight*

Some influential studies have read *Sir Gawain and the Green Knight* as a poem sharply focused on aspects of the culture approached in this chapter through Langland's troubled meditations. Al Shoaf, for example, maintains that the poet sought to reconcile "the old values of chivalry and feudalism" with "the abstract market forces" of "commercialism in the fourteenth century."[8] The poem shows that all humans live "in a web of relations largely commercial" (47) and that all "value" is the product of "human subjectivity" (32). Sir Gawain must learn that he, like all humans, is "subject to a pricing," "enmeshed in the market," and "a commodity" (37–39). At Hautedesert he engages in "business transaction" with Sir Bertilak and becomes "enmeshed in commerce" (61). Jill Mann too argues that the poem explores "the fundamental realities of mercantile life" from within "the tradition of Aristotelian commentary" and fuses "knightly and mercantile values," while Stephanie Trigg relates its examination of exchange and value to "political instability" in late fourteenth-century England.[9]

Is the poet concerned to examine and revise received Christian-Aristotelian teaching in the face of contemporary "commerce" and "mercantile life"? We should recall that in this tradition exchanges for profit, as St. Thomas Aquinas argued, are justly censured since they are devoted to the acquisition of gain that knows no boundaries and tends to infinity ("deservit cupiditati lucri, quae terminum nescit, sed infinitum tendit").[10] St. Thomas allies this judgment with a qualification that was certainly to have an important life in the Middle Ages: the lack of a virtuous end in gain ("lucrum") does not mean that in itself gain is necessarily vicious. This being so, "lucrum" can be ordered to a good end. What does he have in mind? In transactions that are aimed at moderate "lucrum" to support a household, to support the poor ("indigentibus") or to serve the common welfare ("propter publicam utilitatem"), "lucrum" becomes a just wage for labor rather than an end, a goal (II–II.77.4 *resp*). This is certainly the framework within which Langland strives to analyze the problems he encounters in his culture, and we can see a deployment of St. Thomas's qualification to

[8] R. A. Shoaf, *The Poem as Green Girdle: Commercium in Sir Gawain and the Green Knight* (Gainesville: University of Florida Press, 1984), 3. Hereafter references appear in the text.

[9] Jill Mann, "Price and Value in *Sir Gawain and the Green Knight*," *Essays in Criticism* 36 (1986): 294–318, here 313, 294, 314; and Stephanie Trigg, "The Romance of Exchange: *Sir Gawain and the Green Knight*," *Viator* 22 (1991): 251–66, here 265–66. See also P. B. Taylor, "Commerce and Comedy in *Sir Gawain and the Green Knight*," *Philological Quarterly* 50 (1971): 1–15.

[10] The edition of St. Thomas's *Summa Theologiae* used here is *Summa Theologica* [*sic*], 4 vols. in 6 (Rome: Forzanus, 1894), II–II.77.4 *resp*. Hereafter references appear in the text.

the condemnation of commercial pursuits in *Piers Plowman* (VII.22–39). Yet Langland's work should help us grasp just how this is definitely not the ethical and political terrain on which the *Gawain*-poet's attention is fixed, either in *Sir Gawain and the Green Knight* or anywhere else, even in the parable of the discontented laborers in *Pearl*, a text that certainly could have encouraged engagement with the Statute of Labourers and conflicts over the just price of labor and commodities.[11] Markets, market values, and the English ruling elites' profound involvement both in the profits generated through market trans-actions and the profits of war, including the investment in mercenaries, none of this was at all novel in the period after the Black Death.[12] What was novel was the consequences of the demographic collapse, combined from the 1370s with lower prices of food, consequences that involved a shift in the balance of forces between classes to which the Statute of Labourers and the great Rising of 1381 were responses.[13] Yet *Sir Gawain and the Green Knight* carefully brackets all these areas of ruling class experience, both traditional and novel. No fourteenth-century aristocrat, no prince, could be as removed from the conflicts catalyzed by effects of the Black Death. While Sir Gawain's military skills turn out to be of little interest to the poet, it should be noted that the other weapons of his class, political, legal, and economic, weapons as essential to its identity, are rendered invisible. The poem carefully occludes all contemporary conflicts over the extraction and distribution of "lucrum."

How then should we read the vocabulary of exchanges, of "chaffer," "chevisaunce," "prys," and "pay," one to which scholars such as Taylor, Shoaf, and Mann have drawn attention? Any reading should at least take note of what we have already observed: namely, that this vocabulary belongs, in this poem, to a discourse from which the realities of fourteenth-century commodity production and exchange have been purged, a discourse *without* production and *without* the producers who were proving forceful opponents to gentry and courtly elites in the years around 1381. In this context, something that could certainly have been purchased as a commodity in contemporary markets, something like a jeweled girdle, venison, fish, or a kiss, ceases, in fact, to belong to what Mann calls the "fundamental realities of mercantile life." They are, instead, located in courtly worlds where exchanges (of clothing, food, kisses, or blows) are exchanges of gifts, not, carefully and precisely not exchanges of

---

[11] See Aers, "*Piers Plowman*: Poverty, Work, and Community," in *Community, Gender, and Individual Identity* (London: Routledge, 1988), chap. 1; see also Andrew W. Cole, "Trifunctionality and the Tree of Charity: Literary and Social Practice in *Piers Plowman*," *English Literary History* 62 (1995): 1–27.

[12] See E. Miller and John Hatcher, *Medieval England: Rural Society and Economic Change 1086–1348* (London: Longman, 1978), 173–97; Hatcher, "England in the Aftermath of the Black Death," *Past and Present* 144 (1994): 3–35; *The Black Death*, ed. Rosemary Horrox (Manchester: Manchester University Press, 1994), esp. part 7; on the war, C. T. Allmand, *The Hundred Years War* (Cambridge: Cambridge University Press, 1988), 73–76, 102–11, 120–35.

[13] See especially Hatcher, "England in the Aftermath."

commodities in fourteenth-century commerce. As Britton Harwood has observed, drawing on the work of Marcel Mauss and Pierre Bourdieu, the poet's model is an "economy of the gift."[14] This economy had rules that mediated fierce competition for power and status, an economy that remained, in part, though only part, of the culture and self-identity of those Mervyn James describes as "honourmen."[15] So when the poet's extensive descriptions of the immense luxury of Arthur's court include a reference to the fact that the royal tapestries were embroidered with the best jewels that money could buy (74– 90),[16] there is no concern to focus on this reference as a topic for reflection. Indeed, making this a topic for reflection, in the poet's culture, would mean an engagement with problems around the just price, the sale of labor power, and contemporary law, problems faced in *Piers Plowman* (III, VI–VII and C III.290– 405). Unlike Langland, the *Gawain*-poet simply sets aside what Mann calls "the world of the market."[17]

If the poet's relations to his culture are such as I have outlined, what becomes of the Church and its administration of the sacraments? Especially what becomes of the one so central to *Piers Plowman*, the one which, in the words of Jean Gerson, "gives life back to the dead," the sacrament of penance?[18] The Church, like the communities of Camelot and Hautdesert, is extracted from its place in the networks of contemporary markets, networks that so fascinated Chaucer and appalled Langland. It becomes a Church totally assimilated to the poem's version of courtly existence. There are no signs of any gaps between the secular elites and the Church's ministers, no tensions between the elite forms of life (including the readiness to kill in sport, as at lines 96–99) and the Church's teachings or liturgy. Nor are there any signs of criticism being directed against the poem's priests, whether the bishop feasting at Arthur's high table in a place of honor (109–15) or at chaplains so fully integrated to the life of courtly abundance and display, one that is a feature of the chapel itself (917, 928–74).[19] At both Camelot and Hautdesert Christianity is thoroughly assimilated to the celebration of forms of life aspired to by contemporary gentry and nobles. The pentangle itself, far from being an emblem of unworldly transcendentalism, enshrines exclusively upper class

---

[14] Britton J. Harwood, "Gawain and the Gift," *PMLA* 106 (1991): 483–99.

[15] Mervyn James, *English Politics and the Concept of Honour, 1485–1642* (Oxford: Past and Present Supplement 3, 1978).

[16] For the *Gawain*-poet's works I use *The Poems of the Pearl Manuscript*, ed. Malcolm Andrew and Ron Waldron (London: Arnold, 1978; rev. edn., Exeter: Exeter University Press, 1987).

[17] Mann, "Price and Value," 297; cf. Harwood, "Gawain and the Gift," 486.

[18] D. Catherine Brown, *Pastor and Laity in the Theology of Jean Gerson* (Cambridge: Cambridge University Press, 1987), 56. Chapters 3–5 are an illuminating commentary on the issues here.

[19] See. J. W. Nicholls, *The Matter of Courtesy: Medieval Courtesy Books and the* Gawain-*poet* (Cambridge: Brewer, 1985); see also Derek Brewer, "Feasts" in *A Companion to the Gawain-Poet*, ed. Derek Brewer and J. Gibson (Cambridge: Brewer, 1997), 131–42.

virtues ("fraunchyse," "cortaysye") and draws the term "clannes" into the same domain, as John Burrow has shown.[20] In this form of Christianity the five wounds of Christ and the figure of the Virgin Mary sacralize the values of the secular nobility in the poet's own culture. The wounds of Christ and the image of Mary are placed on the very symbol of class power, privilege, and violence – the warrior's shield. Indeed, Gawain is said to draw his knightly fierceness and courage in battle from the image of the Virgin Mary (644–50). Sir Robert Knolles, Sir Hugh Calveley, John of Gaunt, or Henry V, like most late medieval knights, would have identified with this version of the Church and Christianity.[21] True enough, by the end of the poem, the girdle supersedes the pentangle as Gawain's emblem. But this, as we shall see, involves no transformation of the Church or of the Christianity to which the poem's elites subscribe, elites that continue to include Gawain.

Before discussing the poem's ending, however, I wish to consider the sacrament of penance in this text. The first scene of confession is an emphatically orthodox one between Gawain and a priest that culminates in the knights's absolution (1876–84). The account of this episode seems one of the most unequivocal pieces of writing in the poem. We are told that Gawain sought out a priest in the chapel to hear his confession, confessed himself completely, shewing all his misdeeds, begged for mercy, and begged for absolution. The priest absolves him, an absolution carefully and strikingly recounted by the poet:

> And he asoyled hym surely and sette hym so clene
> As dome3day schulde haf been di3t on þe morn   (1883–84).

These words emphasize that the priest accepts the confession as a good one, an adequately complete one carried out with due contrition. They also show the poet stressing the *efficacy* of the Church's sacrament. Gawain seems far more secure in the face of death and the last judgment than Langland's penitents in Passus V, Haukyn in Passus XIV, or Will in Passus XX. Yet this scene has generated a substantial literature, a veritable encyclopedia of scholastic teaching on confession and penance.[22]

There are good reasons for this. First, there is the fact that Gawain did not

---

[20] John Burrow, *A Reading of Sir Gawain and the Green Knight* (London: Routledge, 1965): 47–48; see *GGK*, 607–14, 651–55.

[21] On the relevant forms of life here, see Maurice Keen, *Chivalry* (New Haven: Yale University Press, 1984); P. R. Coss, *The Knight in Medieval England, 1000–1400* (Stroud: Sutton, 1993), chaps. 3–6; M. J. Bennett, *Community, Class, and Careerism: Cheshire and Lancashire Society in the Age of Sir Gawain and the Green Knight* (Cambridge: Cambridge University Press, 1983); Bennett, "The Historical Background," in *A Companion to the Gawain-Poet*, ed. Brewer and Gibson, chap. 3.

[22] Burrow, *Sir Gawain*, 104–10; W. R. J. Barron, *Trawthe and Treason: The Sin of Sir Gawain Reconsidered* (Manchester: Manchester University Press, 1980), 87 ff. and 121–29; G. Morgan, *Sir Gawain and the Green Knight and the Idea of Righteousness* (Dublin: Irish Academic Press, 1991), 133–42.

give the gift of the girdle to Bertilak, thus breaking the agreement made in a game he was playing with his host. This has made many critics doubt that the poet could have meant what he wrote: namely, that Gawain's confession is complete, a sound one, and that he received valid absolution. Second, there is Gawain's later mortified reaction when the Green Knight draws attention to his retention of the girdle (2331–438). The last thing Gawain seems to have here is the feeling of being "clene," although this was what the priest had pronounced him the day before, when he had clearly determined to keep the girdle.[23] It is certainly tempting to join in this inquiry, to begin one's own *summa de casibus conscientiae*: for example, to observe that as major an authority as Jean Gerson insisted that penitents need not confess venial sins and warned confessors against fostering a destructive scrupulousness,[24] or to speculate about whether an undetected offence in a game must be taken to a confessor. However, it seems to me that these temptations should be resisted. As Wendy Clein argues, the poet himself refuses "to indicate that there is anything sinful in Gawain's intention to conceal the girdle from the host."[25] The confession is presented as valid and the priest's absolution as being in accord with the Church's teachings on the saving powers of this sacrament.

If there is a question here, it runs as follows: could a canonically sound confession and absolution be both licit and spiritually quite worthless or irrelevant? And if so, is Gawain's an example of this, one symptomatic of a massive gap between orthodox claims about the sacrament of penance and spiritual realities? Could it be that the fusion of "chivalric" and "Christian" values has consequences less than helpful on the journey to the creature's end?[26] Could such a fusion have transformed the sacrament of penance into a therapeutic social form devoid of sacramental power, devoid too of the ability to encourage the kind of inward journey described by Piers (V.592–629)? It is certainly striking that Gawain's confession opens out no inner spaces of the kind we have seen emerging in his time at Hautdesert.[27] As for the sacraments, they incorporated Christians into the body of Christ, extending Christ's merits to his members so that Christians could live in Christ and Christ live in Christians.[28] They were necessary to human salvation, the expression and constitution of "a life of love between Christians and God."[29] Yet what happens *immediately* after Gawain's confession is not designed to suggest that his attention, his heart, has been directed in ways such as this:

---

[23] Burrow, *Sir Gawain*, 110.

[24] Brown, *Pastor and Laity*, 63–64, 68–72.

[25] W. Clein, *Concepts of Chivalry in Sir Gawain and the Green Knight* (Norman: University of Oklahoma Press, 1987), 114.

[26] Burrow, *Sir Gawain*, 105.

[27] Aers, *Community, Gender, and Individual Identity*, 162–66.

[28] St. Thomas, *ST*, III.19.7, III.60–64.

[29] *ST* III.61.1 *resp*; and see Brian Davies, *The Thought of Thomas Aquinas* (Oxford: Clarendon Press, 1993), 357.

And syþen he mace hym as mery among þi fre ladyes,
With comlych caroles and alle kynnes joye (1885–86).

Such behavior is certainly appropriate to a great nobleman and is not, of course, incompatible with a love directed by sacramental grace towards Christ. Nevertheless, the poet has given us a striking sequence whose juxtapositions offer a powerful image of the way this Church and its sacrament of penance is immersed in, even subordinate to, courtly forms of life and the court's erotic games.

The questions posed above, concerning not whether Gawain's confession was sound or unsound but addressing the spiritual efficacy of the Church's sacrament, cannot simply be dismissed as historically impossible, as anachronistic. Far from it; a radical attack on the Church's claims for its sacrament of penance was part of both Waldensianism and Wycliffism, forms of Christianity that radically undermined traditional legitimations of the Church's power, authority, and wealth.[30] Could the *Gawain*-poet's relations to his culture include some elusive convergences with such critical views on the late medieval Church and its sacramental powers? Before my own answer to this question emerges the second confessional scene needs to be recalled.

There Gawain confronts a knight who seems to have powers of surveillance that a penitent would ascribe to God. What Gawain had experienced as private, secret space turns out to have been subject to another's gaze.[31] This, as John Burrow observed, leads into a passage, "especially rich in penitential matter," one that "follows closely the actual order of the confessional."[32] Burrow demonstrated how the dialogue between the Green Knight and Gawain elicits "confessional self-analysis," a request for penance, "an act of restitution," and a concluding "absolution."[33] Other scholars have elaborated and qualified Burrow's reading, even identifying the Green Knight with Christ, the judge who is merciful and strong.[34] But what is especially intriguing about Burrow's analysis, in the present context, is its conclusion. He decides that although the exchange between the Green Knight and Gawain follows conventional penitential forms and has a penitential effect far greater than the one enacted with the priest, it is "not a 'real' confession." How does Burrow know this? He

---

[30] See Gordon Leff, *Heresy in the Later Middle Ages*, 2 vols. (Manchester: Manchester University Press, 1967), 2:452–85, especially 457, 463, 479; and Anne Hudson, *The Premature Reformation: Wycliffite Texts and Lollard History* (Oxford: Clarendon Press, 1988), 294–301 and chap. 6.

[31] A different set of preoccupations around the "gaze" are explored by Sarah Stanbury, *Seeing the Gawain Poet: Description and the Act of Perception* (Philadelphia: University of Pennsylvania Press, 1991), chap. 5.

[32] Burrow, *Sir Gawain*, 127; see *GGK*, 2341–93.

[33] Burrow, *Sir Gawain*, 128–32.

[34] See Harwood, "Gawain and the Gift," 152–61; Clein, *Concepts of Chivalry*, 122–24; A. C. Spearing, *The Gawain-Poet: A Critical Study* (Cambridge: Cambridge University Press, 1970), 219–29; Spearing, *Readings in Medieval Poetry* (Cambridge: Cambridge University Press, 1987), 201–6.

knows it because "Bercilak, being a layman, has no power of absolution." All we have, finally, is a "pretend secular confession" which, "theologically speaking," cannot remedy the "inadequacies of a sacramental one."[35] Two points need to be made here. The first is that it was certainly orthodox teaching that in an emergency "if no priest is available, one can gain God's forgiveness if one desires it and confesses one's crime to one's lay companion [secundum tamen Augustinum tanta est virtus confessionis quod si deest copia sacerdotis meretur tamen ex voluntate veniam a Deo qui crimen confitetur socio]," as in the *Fasciculus Morum*.[36] Perhaps Gawain's situation is one that would legitimize and sacralize confession to his companion. The second point takes a very different direction. Even if one concedes that it was traditional to allow confession to a layman in the absence of a priest, the challenge of Wycliffite ideas and practices in later fourteenth-century England gave such strands of orthodoxy a very different resonance. For example, the Lollard preacher William Thorpe, defending his radical views on confession against Archbishop Arundel, invokes just the tradition noted by the author of *Fasciculus Morum* above.[37] For a Wycliffite this was a logical step on the path to the doctrine that absolution can only be licit if it is declarative of God's prior and quite independent forgiveness (82), a doctrine incorporated in a cluster of beliefs profoundly subversive of the Roman church.

Furthermore, one might recall that in the four decades before Arundel's *Constitutions* (1409) it was possible for those belonging to the elite to have, and show, sympathy with positions that challenged the Church's power and authority, as the "Lollard" knights testify.[38] In these contexts, it becomes plausible for someone to suggest that the *Gawain*-poet might have entertained some perspectives that could be unfolded in directions incompatible with Catholic orthodoxy. Perhaps a ruling class layman could fulfill a priestly role far more effectively than the official minister of the Church. It is the layman, not the priest, after all, who is shown to stimulate self-scrutiny and acknowledgment of moral vulnerability (2433–36). The distance between such perspectives and those of Sir John Clanvowe's treatise *The Two Ways*,[39] or even more determinedly Wycliffite ones, need not be great, Yet although the distance might not be great, the poet chose not to travel it. Whatever the critical potential some of his poem's perspectives could have held for some late fourteenth-century readers brooding about the Church, its alignments with the wealthy, its pastoral activities, and its administration of penance, the poet himself chose not to

---

[35] Quotations from Burrow, *Sir Gawain*, 132–33; see also Davenport, *Art of the Gawain-Poet*, 174.

[36] *Fasciculus Morum: A Fourteenth-Century Preacher's Handbook*, ed. and trans. Siegfried Wenzel (University Park: Pennsylvania State University Press), 466–67.

[37] *Two Wycliffite Texts*, ed. Anne Hudson (EETS, 301, Oxford: Oxford University Press, 1993), 83 (lines 1919–22). Hereafter references appear in the text.

[38] See K. B. McFarlane, *Lancastrian Kings and Lollard Knights* (Oxford: Oxford University Press, 1972).

[39] *The Works of Sir John Clanvowe*, ed. V. J. Scattergood (Cambridge: Brewer, 1975).

actualize them. His modes of writing leave us in considerable doubt even as to what would constitute satisfaction, the third part of penance, that which pertains especially to justice, "the virtue that gives to each his own [satisfactio stat cum illa virtute cardinali que dicitur justicia]," in the *Fasciculus Morum*.[40] What does Gawain actually owe, and in what form, to his aunt ("Morgne þe godes")[41] . . . to the lady . . . to his court . . . to his Church . . . to Christ? How does the return to Camelot deal with this? For the court there are no problems. The "broþerhede" has survived the tests instigated by Morgan la Fay, tests that challenged the virtues appropriate to a community of Christian "honourmen." Joyfully it assimilates its courageous and chaste representative together with his story and new emblem. The court's traditions and forms of life are adequately vindicated, a vindication to which neither Bishop Bawdewyn nor Gawain offer objections (2913–21). Nor, contrary to the views of some modern scholars, does the poet. And how could he, with any cogency? For he himself offers not the slightest hint of alternative forms of life for the chivalric classes to pursue, not the slightest hint of forms of Christianity outside the court Church. There are, it seems, no alternatives. Not even for Gawain. However pronounced his public display of "schame" as he tells his story (2501–5), its moral, psychological, and theological dimensions are undecidable.[42] Whatever it may seem, it too is readily assimilated by the knight's community, an assimilation perfectly congruent with Gawain's prior decision to continue with the chivalric life and the pursuit of "prowes of armes" (2433–38). Whoever added the motto of Edward III's order of the garter after the poem's ending ("Hony soyt qui mal y pence") responded appropriately to these aspects, assimilating Gawain's "schame" to the values and language of a contemporary royal court.

This ending tells us much about the poem's relations to contemporary culture, its ethical and political orientations. The poet is suggesting that whether knights display the psychological, moral, and introspective tendencies represented by Gawain or the apparently different ones represented by Arthur and the rest of the "broþerhede," whether the sacrament of penance is spiritually powerful or not, whether a priest or a nobleman may stimulate a more contrite disposition, whether the Church is more or less thoroughly incorporated in the elites' worlds, even whether there are large domains of indeterminacy and undecidability or not, none of this is of much consequence since nothing much will change anyway. Nor is this a matter for lamentation or complaint. That too

[40] *Fasciculus Morum*, 496–97.
[41] On Morgan and her powerful, repressed role, see Aers, *Community, Gender, and Individual Identity*, 170–73; Geraldine Heng, "Feminine Knots and the Other: *Sir Gawain and the Green Knight*," *PMLA* 106 (1991): 500–14; E. D. Scala, "The Wanting Words of *Sir Gawain and the Green Knight*: Narrative Past, Present, and Absent," *Exemplaria* 6 (1994): 304–38.
[42] See Spearing, *The Gawain-Poet*, 236, and *Readings in Medieval Poetry*, 203–7; Clein, *Concepts of Chivalry*, 125–38; Stanbury, *Seeing the Gawain-Poet*, 109–13; for tellingly *antithetical* determinations compare Harwood, "Gawain and the Gift" and C. David Benson, "The Lost Honor of Sir Gawain," in *De Gustibus: Essays for Alain Renoir*, ed. J. M. Foley (New York: Garland, 1992), 30–39.

would have little consequence, as Gawain's own lamentations illustrate so nicely. True enough, the lamentations in his case involve taking a new emblem, but, as we have just seen, that turns out to have no consequences for knightly forms of life, including Gawain's. The poet suggests that while there are potentially tricky conflicts within the elites' codes, and while there are some potentially threatening family relationships from a darker past, one need not worry about these very much, because even if one does, the worrying will change nothing, nor could it. There are no alternatives, and none are necessary. The existing codes of honormen, with their virtually Christless Christianity, are good enough for this world. And they are unequivocally sanctioned by the one Church, by Bishop Bawdewyn and his clergy. How then, asking Langland's question again, may I "saue my soule" (I.83)? Certainly you don't need to worry about the world in which most people lived, about the forms of justice in existing communities, or about current debates on the role of the Church. You should respect the general values of "honormen" but don't feel bad about being a lot more pragmatic and a lot less perfectionist than Gawain (550–65, 2505–30). Do, however, follow Gawain in maintaining a certain sexual discipline. Indeed, the poet links the possibility of adultery with an ensuing exchange between the two knights that would now go beyond their nightly kissing to an act exposing them to the homophobic and annihilating rage of God against the people of Sodom, people whose acts so fascinated this poet.[43]

II. *Pearl*

Pearl is an immensely complex religious work, an exquisitely composed dream vision.[44] It deals with loss and mourning, with the fragile but tenacious attempts to shore up familiar identities in the face of death and the supernatural, with the specifically courtly makings of masculine identity and desire. I have addressed the poem's treatment of the mourning, courtly self elsewhere, and here I will focus on the place of the Church in its account of faith.[45]

As we have observed, from the book's opening chapter, orthodox Christianity of the Middle Ages saw individual salvation as inseparably bound up with belonging to the Church, a community envisaged as the body of Christ, the saving ark and also as a city, the new Jerusalem. It was through participating in the sacramental life of the church that people lived in Christ and Christ in them, through sacraments, especially the eucharist, which actually constituted

---

[43] See Elizabeth B. Keiser, *Courtly Desire and Medieval Homophobia: The Legitimation of Sexual Pleasure in "Cleanness" and its Contexts* (New Haven: Yale University Press, 1997); Carolyn Dinshaw, "A Kiss is just a Kiss: Heterosexuality and its Consolation in *Sir Gawain and the Green Knight*," *Diacritics* 24 (1994): 204–26; Allen Frantzen, "The Disclosure of Sodomy in *Cleanness*," *PMLA* 111 (1996): 451–64.

[44] For *Pearl* as for *Cleanness* and *Patience*, I continue to use the Andrew and Waldron edition cited in n. 16.

[45] Aers, "The Self Mourning: Reflections on *Pearl*," *Speculum* 68 (1993): 54–73.

the spiritual life they symbolized. *Extra ecclesiam nulla salus.*[46] Langland's agonized and wrathful relationship with the Church is founded on just these assumptions. But one of the most striking features of *Pearl*, a dramatic meditation on death, mourning, and a Christian vision of salvation is the absence of the Church.

The poem opens with the narrator mourning in isolation from the Church and from any community, even though he observes that the day is a festival during harvest time (1–40).[47] Such isolation is certainly a consequence of the melancholic despair threatening to overwhelm the narrator. But although he is then granted a divine vision in which the lost child appears as his redeemed teacher, the ensuing dialogue does not bring the Church into its traditional place in the economy of salvation. The dreamer's concerns remain doggedly fixed on his lost child, the object of a love constituted in thoroughly courtly forms, while his teacher struggles to free him from this earthly attachment, actually an attachment to himself, and from modes of perception which are profoundly incongruent with any serious acknowledgment of spiritual realities, in particular the new creation in Christ (2 Corinthians 5.14–19).[48] Throughout the vision the dreamer's perspectives remain incorrigibly individualistic. The competitive individualism intrinsic to courtly life is remorselessly projected onto the spiritual realm (for example, 409–92, 913–18, 925–36).[49] Nothing in his experience enables him to make any sense of the Pauline idea of Christian community invoked by his celestial teacher (459–66), and certainly there is no sense of the Church as the mystical body of Christ in which Christians discover a salvation that is simultaneously individual and corporate. At the beginning of this chapter I noted that the parable of the vineyard and the lord's discontented workers (494–648) readily suggested contemporary conflicts that the poet carefully blocks out, ones memorably addressed in *Piers Plowman*.[50] More interesting in the present context, however, is the way in which this passage reveals the narrator's simple and thoroughly unselfconscious disregard for the Church and its authority even when the issue is the interpretation of Scripture (589–600). Under pressure from Wyclif and his followers this had become an increasingly conflictual domain.[51] Yet he shows no awareness that interpretation is an activity conducted within a particular community and within particular traditions, in the present case, the Church within which the canon was formed. Instead he assumes that he, the autonomous interpreter, is the measure of licit interpretation. His own version of reason has sufficient authority to dismiss both Christ's

---

[46] See chap. 2, n. 19.

[47] On the "heyȝ seysoun" in August, see the note by Andrew and Waldron to lines 39ff.

[48] On this, see Spearing, *The Gawain-Poet*, chap. 4.

[49] Ibid., 137–65.

[50] *Piers Plowman*, VI; see Aers, *Community, Gender, and Individual Identity*, 20–49.

[51] On these developments, Hudson, *Premature Reformation*, chap. 5, and K. Ghosh, "'Authority' and 'Interpretation' in Wycliffite, Anti-Wycliffite, and Related Texts c.1375–1430" (Ph.D. diss., Cambridge University, 1996; due to be published by Cambridge University Press).

parable and the exegesis of his sanctified teacher as so "vnresounable" that they would turn "holy wryt" into a mere "fable" (589–592). In maintaining this response he invokes another scriptural text and handles it with complete disregard both of its contexts and of the Church's teaching that one's own "desserte" can in no way merit salvation (593–96). His teacher strenuously resists his assumptions about God, merit, reward, and grace (601–744), but it is striking that she has nothing to say about the Church, about tradition, and about ecclesiastical authority. She does not even mention that the vineyard of Matthew 20.1–16 was habitually taken as a figure of the Church.[52] In the contexts of later fourteenth-century England this is a remarkable silence. In a crucial area it allows the narrator's horizons to shape the discourse. This is something she habitually resists. Time and again she challenges his horizons so that they become visible, making him uncomfortably aware of their presence and effects, de-naturalizing them. Only through such a process of dislocation can she hope to open his perception to worlds beyond these horizons. But not here, not where the Church is concerned.

Does the poem's conclusion remedy this lack? It certainly includes both a vision of the celestial city, taken from the Apocalypse with its medieval illuminations, and a closing reference to the priest showing Christ to Christians in the sacrament of the altar (973–1152, 1205–12).[53] But the dreamer finally rejects the former in favor of his own quest for his lost child (1145–64).[54] This is represented as a false, rebellious move that ends the vision and cannot gain him the object of his desire. God's will cannot be circumvented: "mad hit arn þat agayn þe stryuen" (1165–1200). This acknowledgment leads into the closing reference to the eucharist. The narrator commits the pearl to God with his blessing and Christ's, invoking Christ's presence:

> þat in þe forme of bred and wyn
> þe prest vus schewez vch a daye   (1206–9).

Christ, replacing the lost pearl of the narrator's desires, is mediated in the form of bread and wine consecrated and elevated by the priest. At last we are shown that the narrator does belong to the Church where the priest displays Christ to "vus" each day. This can be read as a final reincorporation of the isolated mourner in the Christian community, an incorporation that affirms

---

[52] On traditional figurative readings of the parable, see D. W. Robertson, "The Heresy of *The Pearl*," *Modern Language Notes* 65 (1950): 152–55; T. Bogdanos, *Pearl: Image of the Ineffable* (University Park: Pennsylvania State University Press, 1983), 91–98; Lynn Staley Johnson, *The Voice of the Gawain-Poet* (Madison: University of Wisconsin Press, 1984), 185–90. On the exegesis of the Virgin Mary as a type of the Church in the Song of Songs, see E. Ann Matter, *The Voice of my Beloved: The Song of Songs in Western Medieval Christianity* (Philadelphia: University of Pennsylvania Press, 1990), 86.

[53] On the apocalypse here, see R. Field, "The Heavenly Jerusalem in *Pearl*," *Modern Language Review* 81 (1986): 7–17.

[54] See Aers, "The Self Mourning," 67–70.

the ultimate centrality of the Church so marginalized in *Pearl*.[55] Such a reading is perfectly reasonable. But we need to make two qualifications. First: the marginalized Church has made a strangely belated appearance. Second: what is entailed in practice by the narrator's reincorporation is left thoroughly, perhaps studiedly, vague. Does Christian discipleship, being Christ's "homly hyne" (1211) call for anything more in practice, than recognizing that Christ is shown by the priest in the consecrated elements? Does reflection on the conflict of Scriptural interpretation staged by his own poem remind readers that there are conflicting models of Christian discipleship in the late fourteenth-century English Church? Such issues were currently being addressed by others, as we have observed,[56] but the poet sets them aside, here and elsewhere. This is a significant decision.

In their place his conclusion makes an extraordinary claim, stunning in its breezy optimism. It maintains that to please God, or to find peace with God, is very easy for the good Christian:

> To pay the Prince oþer sete saȝte
> Hit is fule eþe to þe god Krystyin   (1201–2).

This is a surprising assertion in the light of the poem's dramatization of the powerful resistances to the way of reconciliation offered by the heavenly teacher. It is even more surprising in the face of traditions of Christianity out of which the poet writes. These traditions were sensitive to the excruciating difficulties obstructing the transformation of wills addicted to loveless, unkind, egotistical habits, emphatic on the needs of fallen creatures for prevenient grace, repentance, and forgiveness in the Church. How can we account for the two lines just quoted from *Pearl* (1201–2)? In my view they respond to a lack of specificity in the poem's representations of the virtues and contemporary impediments to their flourishing, a lack of specificity that is bound up with the marginalization of the Church and the consequent occlusion of substantial problems currently troubling it. What practical difference does Christian discipleship and membership in the Church make in someone's life; what distinctive virtues are called for? The ending of *Pearl* suggests that besides acknowledging Christ's presence in the eucharist, the only demand made on a "good" Christian is for a patient resignation (1195–1200) which seems as stoic and abstractly individualist as it is Christian. There is much here that is congruent with the ending of *Sir Gawain and the Green Knight* discussed in section one. In the end, "Hit is ful eþe to þe god Krystyin": so keep an eye on the eucharist; do not become irrationally attached to what you know is impermanent; do not worry

---

[55] See especially A. C. Spearing, *Medieval Dream-Poetry* (Cambridge: Cambridge University Press, 1976), 129 and 122; and Spearing, *Readings in Medieval Poetry*, 213–15; on the eucharist here, Bogdanos, *Pearl*, 145–47.

[56] See chapters 1–2 above and 6 below; also Aers and Lynn Staley, *Powers of the Holy: Religion, Politics, and Gender in Late Medieval English Culture* (University Park: Pennsylvania State University Press, 1996).

about justice and the need for beneficent communities if the life of the virtues is to flourish; and just go on doing what comes "naturally," accepting the unwelcome with resignation, with patience.

III. *Cleanness* and *Patience*

Does the homiletic poetry from the *Pearl* manuscript call for a substantially different account of faith, ethics, and the Church?[57] I will try to answer this question, beginning with reflections on *Cleanness*. On the face of it, we seem to enter a different universe of Christian discourse with this poem. It represents, often exultingly, massive and punitive destruction that is alien to *Pearl* and *Sir Gawain and the Green Knight*. First, most animals and all but eight humans are killed by God in "malys mercyles" (25); next Sodom and other cities are subjected to mass destruction; then the citizens of Jerusalem are massacred by God's chosen army: the massacre is described with collusive zest and includes images of babies having their brains beaten out and women having their wombs cut open so that the contents flow in the ditches; and, finally, we read of Belshazzar's slaughter. So prominent is this violence that David Wallace has described the poet's strategies as a "masterful terrorizing of the reader."[58] To what purpose is this "terrorizing?" Wallace answers that the poet wishes his readers to acknowledge God's absolute power in a way that any moral objection to his "arbitrary, barbaric" behavior "can only rebound upon the accuser."[59] We seem to have met an early version of the "persecutory imagination" ascribed to English Calvinism by John Stachniewski but one, as recent criticism has emphasized, shaped by virulent homophobia.[60]

As A. C. Spearing observed, the God of *Cleanness* "is shown above all as angry and destructive" in a poem "concerned mainly with impurity."[61] What exactly is

[57] Although I call *Cleanness* a homiletic poet, its "kind" is plainly plural; see Keiser, *Courtly Desire*, chap. 1.

[58] David Wallace, "*Cleanness* and the Terms of Terror," in *Text and Matter: New Critical Perspectives on the Pearl-Poet*, ed. Robert J. Blanch, Miriam Youngerman Miller, and Julian N. Wasserman (Troy: Whitston, 1991), 93–104. The violence against Jews and Jerusalem should be studied alongside the *Siege of Jerusalem*, ed. E. Kölbing and M. Day, EETS o.s. 188 (London, 1932). On this see Ralph Hanna, "Contextualizing *The Siege of Jerusalem*," *Yearbook of Langland Studies* 6 (1992): 109–21 and Christine Chism, "*The Siege of Jerusalem*: Liquidating Assets," *Journal of Medieval and Early Modern Studies* 28 (1998): 309–40.

[59] Wallace, "*Cleanness*," 95.

[60] See John Stachniewski, *The Persecutory Imagination: English Puritanism and the Literature of Religious Despair* (Oxford: Clarendon Press, 1991); for illuminating studies focusing on the text's "homophobia" see Keiser, *Courtly Desire*; Frantzen, "The Disclosure" (both cited in n. 43); and Michael Calabrese and Eric Eliason, "The Rhetorics of Sexual Pleasure and Intolerance in the Middle English *Cleanness*," *Modern Language Quarterly* 56 (1995): 247–75.

[61] Spearing, *The Gawain-Poet*, 65 and 71. See also Spearing's influential Douglasian reading of "filth" in *Readings in Medieval Poetry*, chap. 7.

this "impurity that elicits such rage from God that even the poet describes him as mad ("wod," 204)? And, a related question, what is the form of life humans should pursue if they are to avoid this destructive wrath? What, specifically, is the "clannesse" they should follow if they are to "loke on oure Lord with a leue chere" (23–28: Matthew 5.8)? In *Cleanness* the "fylþe" (6) that continually engages the poet and his God is a figure for all that he classifies as "perversion or pollution."[62] Such "perversion" elicits immense disgust in God and triggers his fits of destruction, a destruction that, of course, legitimizes the poet's own construction of what is to count as the perverse.[63] We need to see now if we can answer the questions put in this paragraph concerning the specific forms of vice and virtue.

The poet's category of "perversion" is constructed around sexual acts that he judges to be "against nature [agayn kynde]" (265–72, 671–1048) and around devotional acts that reject the divine terrorist, "oure Fader" (1174; see 1157–1260, 1333–1804). The construction of the "perverse" around sexual acts is focused on an unusually extensive, particularizing fascination with Sodom, one that includes a voyeuristic, and equally unusual, attention to the beauty of the angels whom the men of Sodom wish to rape (see especially, 691–96, 709–12, 781–96, 833–90). The unusual features of the poem's representation of virulent homophobia were admirably explicated by Allen Frantzen and have now been thoroughly investigated by Elizabeth Keiser.[64] It is worth recalling a more conventional treatment, exemplified from the fourteenth-century preacher's manual, *Fasciculus Morum*.[65] Here the writer addresses sodomy as one of the branches of lechery (*luxuria*). He introduces it as "the diabolical sin against nature called sodomy [illa diabolica contra naturam, que sodoma dicitur]" and immediately comments, "I pass it over in horror and leave it to others to describe it" (*FM*, 686–87). Nevertheless, he offers two episodes to exemplify the sin. First he selects the rape of Cassandra, Minerva's prophetess, by Ajax. He allegorizes this to make Cassandra figure any woman who fornicates against the will of God and the Church. He understands Minerva, who takes revenge on Ajax by organizing his death with all his company, as Christ. The story teaches that Christ will take revenge on both "simple fornication" and on "that vile and abominable sin against nature that is not to be named [vile peccatum contra naturam abhominabile et innominandum]" (*FM*, 686–87). Sodomy is here figured by a heterosexual act, and there is no sign of the movements of fantasy comparable to those we find in *Cleanness*. Here Sodomy is *luxuria* without bounds. The second episode chosen is Genesis 19, the destruction of Sodom

---

[62] Spearing, *Readings in Medieval Poetry*, 181.

[63] Ibid., 181–82, 183–84, 189–90. See also the studies by Keiser, Dinshaw, and Frantzen cited in n. 43. There is also another relevant essay by Frantzen, "Between the Lines: Queer Theory, the History of Homosexuality, and Anglo-Saxon Penitentials," *Journal of Medieval and Early Modern Studies* 26 (1996): 255–96.

[64] Cited in n. 43. See especially Frantzen, "The Disclosure," 457–59.

[65] *Fasciculus Morum* (n. 36). Hereafter references occur in the text parenthetically.

and other cities. Whatever this sin "against nature that is not to be named" enacts, "God hated this vice so much that, seeing it being committed by men before his incarnation, he almost refrained from becoming a man" (*FM*, 689). Once again the reticence of the *Fasciculus Morum* contrasts with the detailed attention of *Cleanness*. The aim there is not only to present the sin "against nature" as the other of conventional heterosexual union, but to celebrate the latter in a manner that "is a startlingly unusual attitude to find in a medieval homiletic poem – particularly as the poet gives these words to God."[66] God recalls that he invented "a kynde crafte" and taught it secretly to humans (697–98). This natural ("kynde") activity is heterosexual union in blissful joy, love-making that is the "play of paramorez" in a paradise where the flames of love are blazing hot and able to overwhelm all earth's troubles (699–708). These are sentiments one might expect from the hero or heroine of a courtly romance, but not in a homily. The passage, famously enough, includes none of the traditional Christian teaching on the true ends of sexual union which alone legitimize sexual activity. As we recalled in chapter two, following Chaucer's *Parson's Tale*, marriage ordered sexual activity towards people's final end. A "ful greet sacrement" of the Church, it "clenseth fornicacioun and replenysseth hooly chirche of good lynage, for that is the ende of mariage" (*Canterbury Tales*, X.918, 920).Thus the teleology is made clear. Sexuality is envisaged as a Christian virtue in the Church. It is a sacrament established by God "in paradys," confirmed by Christ in his birth, sanctified at Cana and "figured bitwixe Crist and holy chirche" (X.917–22).[67] A marital union in which sexual pleasure became an end in itself was sinful and judged as a form of adultery. This traditional teaching is reiterated by the Parson: "The thridde spece of avowtrie is somtyme bitwixe a man and his wyf, and that is whan they take no reward in hire assemblynge but oonly to hire fleshly delit . . . . in swich folk hath the devel power . . . for in hire assemblynge they putten Jhesu Crist out of hire herte" (X.904–906). The Parson emphasizes that the sacrament and the virtues it elicits are Christocentric. They are to inform and order sexual practice. What makes the passage from *Cleanness* so "startlingly unusual" is not only that homiletic writing does not celebrate "þe play of paramorez," the "merþe" of sexual intercourse. It is also, more significantly in the contexts of this book, remarkable for abandoning the teleological and Christian account of the virtues. *Cleanness* has God subvert tradition in favor of a vision of sexuality that isolates its agents from the webs of community, so emphasized in confessional instruction, as the *Parson's Tale*, and

---

[66] Andrew and Waldron, *Pearl Manuscript*, note to 697–708.

[67] Still invaluable sources for exploring the relevant traditions concerning this sacrament are John T. Noonan, *Contraception: A History of its Treatment by the Catholic Theologians and Canonists* (New York: New American Library, 1967); H. A. Kelly, *Love and Marriage in the Age of Chaucer* (Ithaca: Cornell University Press, 1975); D. L. D'Avray and M. Tausche, "Marriage Sermons in *Ad Status* Collections of the Central Middle Ages," *Archives d'histoire doctrinale et littéraire du Moyen Age* 46 (1980): 71–119. Keiser addresses this material in *Courtly Desire*, chap. 2, especially 59–70.

completely ignores the Church, with the sacrament of marriage. The only condition God seems to demand for heterosexual "merþe" is that the couple "moȝt honestly ayþer oþer welde,/ At a stylle stollen steuen, vnstered with syȝt" (705–706). This seems to call for "proper" sexual action and the kind of secrecy pervading courtly romance.[68] Were the homilist a priest he would be an exceptionally liberal confessor of heterosexual couples, one who side-lined traditional understanding of individuals as belonging to a social, political, and mystical body in and through which they were to find their supernatural end, an end immanent in the practices of the present. He would also be one totally careless of the contexts in which children were to be born. This marginalization of Church and its traditional confessional texts is congruent with the aspects of *Pearl* and *Sir Gawain* explored in this chapter. Of course, as recent commentators have observed, the liberal invitation to do what comes "naturally" as God's gift is bound up with the massive violence that surrounds the passage, violence against that which is "against nature."

There is a similar structure in the poet's treatment of licit and illicit devotion. Noah, Abraham, Lot, the converted Nebuchadnezzar, and Daniel exemplify the former. What does one have to do to belong to this group of survivors? As we have seen, one must not stray from the liberally construed pleasures of a thoroughly individualistic heterosexuality. What else? One must fear God. That is not a very difficult task given his propensity to avowedly mad wrath backed up by the massive destructive powers he has demonstrated his willingness to use. Noah is a model of saving fear (295). One must also follow the customary rules of hospitality, unlike Lot's fellow-citizens. One must believe God's words although dismissive incredulity such as that expressed by Sarah is not necessarily met by rage, especially if such rage would destroy a divine promise (653–70). If one is not a Jew, there seems no need for conversion: all one must do is desist from actually deriding God's power, from setting oneself up as an autonomous superpower. If one follows these undemanding guidelines, one will be an acceptable ruler and one's empire is likely to expand. However, if one begins to direct "blasfemy" against God he will respond – not as ferociously as against bi-sexual people of Sodom or as against those acting "against nature" before the flood, but forcefully enough to persuade a Babylonian ruler to acknowledge and love this Lord as the one, unquestionable superpower. This is the story of Nebuchadnezzar as interpreted in *Cleanness* (1149–1332, 1643–1708). In all these stories of "ryȝtwys" action (294) the content of the virtues is extremely thin and the form of life they cultivate strikingly non-specific. Do whatever comes naturally (if you wish to mate with a "male" in "femmalez wyse" [695–96], remember that is defined as "against nature"); be hospitable; don't mock God; and don't actually desecrate vessels devoted to him. As for political order, any

---

[68] Andrew and Waldron translate the condition as follows: "provided that they would possess each other in a proper manner, at a quiet secret meeting, undisturbed by sight" (*Pearl Manuscript*, note to 705–708). On this passage, including a slightly different translation, see Keiser, *Courtly Desire*, 66–70.

regime will do: there is no conviction that virtuous lives are fostered by certain kinds of community. *Cleanness* is perfectly happy with the Babylonian empire, and happy with its massacre of Jews. There are no criteria for thinking its author would be unhappy with any imaginable regime. He has abandoned the exploration of justice and the life of the virtues in communities ordered to their flourishing that was intrinsic to the Christian-Aristotelian tradition we have seen some of his contemporaries striving to explore and maintain under severe difficulties.

The passages in which *Cleanness* addressed Christianity directly do not change this picture. The poet decides to follow God's second act of mass destruction with a celebration of the Incarnation (1049–1148). Following the kinds of questions pursued in the first two sections of this chapter, what is the version of Christ now produced in *Cleanness* and what version of Christian discipleship does it entail? What ethical consequences do the life, death, and resurrection of Christ have for Christians? Do they develop a form of virtues that is distinctly Christian or can Nebuchadnezzar or Lot remain adequate models? One would expect the poem to answer this last question with a clear affirmation, for it opened with a recollection of the beatitudes from Matthew's Gospel (23–28). But keeping this and the previous questions in mind I shall now consider the poem's representation of Christ (1065–1110).

The passage on the Incarnation opens as a reflection on the destruction of Sodom and the other cities.[69] The readers are reminded of the wreck God inflicts on "fylþe" and that if they wish to achieve the vision of God, to be known in his court, then the best advice they can be given is that they should be "clene" (1049–56). The incarnate Christ is the model of how we should be "clene" (1065–1110). Christ was "ful cortays." He hated most horribly ("ful lodly") everything connected with evil, and because of the "nobleye of His norture" he refused to touch anything that was vile ("vngoderly") or contained filth ("ordure"). This is a striking set of choices with which to introduce the life and teaching of the one who insisted that he came to call sinners and to heal the sick, who proclaimed and practiced the kingdom of God in a manner that led to his execution. We can recall a characteristic episode:

> But the Pharisees and scribes murmured, saying to his disciples: Why do you eat and drink with publicans and sinners? And Jesus answering, said to them: They that are whole need not the physician: but they that are sick. I came not to call the just, but sinners to penance   (Luke 5.30–31).

In the words of Matthew's Gospel, "Jesus went about all Galilee, teaching in the synagogues and preaching the gospel of the kingdom and healing all manner of

---

[69] *Cleanness*, 1001–48; 1049–56. We should recollect *Fasciculus Morum*, 689: "God hated this vice so much that, seeing it being committed by men before the incarnation, he almost refrained from becoming man." The poet of *Cleanness* would have enjoyed this statement and its congruence to his own sequence here. On the sequence here see especially Keiser, *Courtly Desire*, chap. 7, 184–90; also Calabrese and Eliason, "The Rhetorics," 266–68.

sickness and every infirmity among the people" (4.23). This mobile prophet seems rather removed from the courtly figure composed in *Cleanness*. True enough, the poem does move to Jesus healing "lazares monye" and those suffering from various illnesses (1093–1100). But it does so in a manner that occludes the theological, political, and ecclesiological significance of these actions in the Gospels. Having noted the "lodly" (loathsome, horrible) people coming to Christ, the poet writes that Jesus healed them "wyth kynde [courteous] speche" and with "hende" touch. Indeed, Jesus's fingers were so refined that he needed no knife to break bread cleanly in his "fayre honde" (1092–1108). Even here, then, Jesus is predominantly a courtly figure who models "clannesse" in distinctly courtly directions, despite its initial alignment (23–27) with the sixth beatitude, "Blessed are the clean of heart [Beati mundo corde]" (Matthew 5.8). As the poem emphasizes, "þus is He kyryous and clene þat þou His court askes," a line the editors translate as, "To that extent is He whose court you seek fastidious and pure" (1109).[70] The open table and community of Jesus, a new creation, has been transformed into one resonant of the exclusiveness of late medieval courts. This is a remarkable revision. It is impossible to imagine this Jesus founding the new community that is to be the Church figured forth in Luke's Acts of the Apostles and in Chaucer's *Second Nun's Tale*, discussed in chapter two. It is also impossible to imagine him or his disciples, past or present, coming into the kinds of conflicts with secular power that would result in torture and execution. To *make* this impossible is a work of political and ecclesiological imagination, the work of composing a Christianity for courtly subjects in the poet's culture.

Before *Cleanness* leaves its fashioning of Jesus and turns to Nebuchadnezzar and Belshazzar the poet addresses a question he himself has put: if Jesus Christ is so "kyryous and clene," how can sinful and unclean ("sovly") humans come to his court (1109–12)? Despite the evidence of his own poem he answers that God is "mercyable" to sinful, unclean humans (1113–14). The unclean sinner can become a shining pearl through confession and penance (1115–16). Just as a pearl can be cleansed from "fylþe" so can people who are "sulped [polluted] in saule" be polished by the priest in penance (1117–32). This is conventional teaching. And yet, in the contexts provided by *Cleanness*, there is something ghostly and strange about it. This ghostliness comes from the lack of any sense of specifiable community with the occupations, relations, and social webs so prominent in confessional manuals such as Thomas of Chobham's *Summa Confessorum* or their refractions in *Piers Plowman*.[71] As we saw in chapter three,

---

[70] The translation of 1109 is in Andrew and Waldron, *Pearl Manuscript*, 157. On courtliness in the *Gawain*-poet see Nicholls, *Matter of Courtesy*; Keiser, *Courtly Desire*; John M. Bowers, "*Pearl* in its Royal Setting: Ricardian Poetry Revisited," *SAC* 17 (1995): 111–55.

[71] See Thomas of Chobham, *Summa Confessorum*, ed. F. Broomfield (Louvain: Edition Nauwelaerts, 1968); *Piers Plowman* V and XIII.313–459. For an illuminating treatment of Haukyn's filthy clothes in these contexts, see Calabrese and Eliason, "The Rhetorics," 261–65. A still starker contrast could be developed by closely comparing the treatment of clothing in Julian of Norwich's great parable of the lord and the servant in her *Revelation*,

penance was bound up with restitution, the restoration of justice, and its mending of bonds broken by sin. It is fulfilled in the eucharist. In *Cleanness*, however, the eucharist is conspicuously lacking. As the subject in this passage is the means of grace by which fallen human life is transformed, one might expect the poet to introduce the eucharistic body of Christ present in the Church. He does nothing of the sort. Furthermore, he moves directly from the cleansing force of penance to a sharp warning. If you sin after penance, you so displease God that the "mercyable" master will hate you more fiercely than if you had sinned without penance (1133–38). God apparently feels about post-penance sinners what he feels about consecrated vessels and their abuse, one of the themes followed in the ensuing treatment of Baltazar's feast (1333–1650, 1709–1804). Post-penance sin is viewed as a theft that arouses God's wrath at the newly "vnclene" creature (1139–48). Given that the poem is replete with accounts of the mass destruction that follows when God's "wraþ is achaufed" (1143), we are in no doubt about the meaning of this statement. Yet behind this violent threat are assumptions that seem thoroughly pelagian. The poet imagines that the habits of sin and the difficulties of cultivating Christian virtues, in the community that is the Church, can be swept aside, once and for all, by a single act of penance. Yet his own tradition actually taught that in this life people would always be in need of forgiveness, always in need of the sacraments of penance and the altar. The rigorous, ruthless judgementalism here is also an extraordinarily optimistic and bland pelagianism. But this is perfectly congruent with the claim that to please God and be reconciled to God is "ful eþe to þe god Krystyin" (*Pearl*, 1201–202, discussed in section two of this chapter).

Although the eucharist is absent from the passage on Christ, sin and penance, it had been invoked near the poem's opening. We should consider the mode in which this is done. *Cleanness* begins with the wish to praise cleanness and reflection on the wondrous wrath of God against "fylþe" in his creatures (1–6). Priests are then chosen to exemplify such "fylþe." This is because they belong to God, serve at the altar, and handle his body ("hondel þer His aune body and vsen hit boþe," 7–11). If priests are "in clannes" they receive great reward ("mede"). But if they lack "cortaysye" and are inwardly "alle fylþez," then they are defiling God and his consecrated vessels. This drives God to wrath. After all, he himself, in his own court, is so "clene" and so "scoymous and skyg [scrupulous and fastidious]" (12–22). These priests prefigure the post-penance sinners we have discussed and the sacred vessels polluted by Baltazar. With this,

chap. 51, *A Book of Showings*, ed. E. Colledge and J. Walsh, 2 vols. (Toronto: Pontifical Institute, 1978), 2: 513–45. For a different but congruent criticism of "Deficient Images of Sin and Penance in *Cleanness*," see Keiser, *Courtly Desire*, 195–200. Probably the major source of difference in our readings here is that Keiser remains within the perspectives established by the poem's occlusion of the Church so that this cannot become a topic of reflection. It also seems that her work's anti-Augustinian and liberal perspective, from which Augustine is labeled as "pessimistic" (31) and as advocating "dualism" (140), has not prepared one for the Augustinian assumptions in the treatment of *Cleanness*'s "deficient" treatment of sin and "the persistent human inclination to prefer evil" (197).

the eucharist is left and the poet pursues his version of cleanness, filth, and God's wrathful judgments against a few, very few, forms of "fylþe."

This brief mention of the eucharist splits it off from its crucial role in the economy of salvation. It is introduced and treated as a measure of cleanness/ filth in priests, itself a topic brought in to illustrate the general theses concerning God's pleasure in cleanness and his violent dislike of "fylþe." The eucharist is not represented as the sacrament of union between creatures, of union between creatures and Christ in the life of grace within that new creation, the Church.[72] Indeed, one has no sense that in the eucharistic meal, flowing from Jesus's open table, the local congregation, in all the particularities with which we saw Langland struggling, becomes the Church. Despite the divine terrorism directed against those constituted by the poet as perverse, the actual content of the virtuous life has become as thin and depoliticized as any that flows from a Kantian categorical imperative, while the sacraments have become spectral simulacra. This is certainly a drastic transformation of Christian tradition. But it may be one that the courtly and pelagianizing subjects it fashions would find congenial.

Patience is a comedic homily centered on a telling of Jonah's story in an inventive mixture of literary modes.[73] It could be read as a distinctively Christian version of the virtue from which it begins, patience, a contrast to the Griseldan version analyzed with help from Aquinas in chapter two. This is a particularly plausible reading if we concentrate on the narrative of Jonah, the bulk of the poem. As scholarship on *Patience* has shown, Jonah's rebellions against God are displays of impatience that are implicitly contrasted with the redemptive patience of Jesus. The Book of Jonah has accumulated a densely allegorical tradition of exegesis setting out from the Gospels' treatment of Jonah as a figure of Christ (Matthew 12.39–41; Luke 11.29–32). In such exegesis every detail of the text could be assimilated to the grand allegory: for example, Jonah's journey to Joppa is allegorized as Christ's Incarnation.[74] While *Patience* is not a mechanical reproduction of such exegetical practices, it does select a story

---

72 On these dimensions of traditional eucharistic teaching, see St. Thomas, *ST*, III.73 and 79. On the eucharist in *Cleanness* Keiser comments, justly, that the poem "jettisons any identification with the Creator's most intimate sharing of human flesh and so any understanding of what is salvific about the Eucharist or penance" (*Courtly Desire* 198; see also 24–29).

73 On *Patience* I have found the following especially helpful: Spearing, "*Patience* and the *Gawain*-poet," *Anglia* 84 (1966): 305–29, assimilated in his *The Gawain-Poet*, chap. 3; Stanbury, *Seeing the Gawain-Poet*, chap. 4; Staley Johnson, *The Voice of the Gawain-Poet*, chap. 1; Elizabeth Kirk, "Who Suffreth More than God? Narrative Redefinition of Patience in *Patience* and *Piers Plowman*," in *The Triumph of Patience*, ed. Gerald J. Schiffhorst (Orlando: University Presses of Florida, 1978), 85–104.

74 See Malcolm Andrew, "Jonah and Christ in *Patience*," *Modern Philology* 70 (1973): 230–33 and Staley Johnson, *The Voice of the Gawain-Poet*, 3–6, 10–11, 14–15, 23–24, 34. On medieval scriptural commentary and allegory, see Henri de Lubac, *Exégèse Médiévale*, 4 vols. (Paris: Aubier, 1959–63).

that had long been appropriated as an allegorical prefiguration of salvation in Christian tradition. From this perspective it is a Christocentric allegory: Jonah's vices are figurations of their recapitulative remedy in Christ, the model for Christian virtues. So when Jonah angrily, impatiently, rejects the possibility of martyrdom on the cross ("naked dispoyled, / On rode rwly torent with rybaudes mony"), while God sits in comfortable glory (93–96), the passage "clearly suggests the crucifixion" and "sets Jonah's conduct in comparison to Christ's."[75]

Patience may also seem to have an interest in the social and political dimensions of the virtue it seeks to exemplify. We are shown two communities moving to a trust in God that demands immediate decisions. The first is on the boat (97–241), itself a traditional image of a polity; the second is Nineveh (351–408). In the first episode, the poem shows that Jonah's lack of patient obedience to God has potentially disastrous consequences for others. It contrasts his own isolating egotism with the generous human solidarity out of which the gentiles do all they can to avoid ejecting Jonah. The second episode includes an aspect with potentially sharp contemporary political resonance. We are shown a prophetic challenge to a city's faith and practices followed by collective penance and divine forgiveness. The political resonances are generated by the fact that in later fourteenth-century England, a Wycliffite sympathizer or an anti-Wycliffite could find special significance in the role of the secular lord in this collective penance (378–406). It is the king who issues "a decre" of repentance through his "serjauntes" (385–404), while the clergy, "uche prest, and prelates alle," simply obey the royal decree: they neither initiate nor lead the saving activity. This, in its contexts, could open out a political and ecclesiological chain of reflections linked with those developed by John Wyclif in *De Ecclesia* or by William Langland in *Piers Plowman*.[76] However, the poem does nothing to encourage the pursuit of such issues, let alone their pursuit in neo-Wycliffite directions: on the contrary.

This reservation leads me to suggest some continuities between the treatment of virtues in *Patience* and their hollowing out in other poems we have considered in this chapter. Even when the ethical choices are allegedly matters of life and death, in this world and the next, the virtues are depicted in so parsimonious a manner that their content is left extremely vague. This is a parsimony we have described in all the other poems in the manuscript. God's initial attack in Patience is against what he describes as wickedness and malice so great that he cannot but take revenge against the "vilanye and venym" of Nineveh's citizens (66–71). Having just read *Cleanness*, which precedes *Patience* in the manuscript containing these poems, we may think we know what these people must have done to draw God's furious attention onto themselves – "her malys is so much,

---

[75] Andrew and Waldron, *Pearl Manuscript*, note to 95 ff., p. 189. See Staley Johnson, *The Voice of the Gawain-Poet*, 7–8.

[76] For Wyclif and *De Ecclesia* see chapter 6 below; for *Piers Plowman*, X.317–33, XV.531–69.

I may not abide" (70). But we actually know nothing of the sort. The poet who is ready to elaborate narratives from the Old Testament when he wishes to do so, adds no indications here to his source. The Ninevites believe Jonah's warning of imminent mass destruction and repent in terror. They put on hair shirts, dust, ashes, and sackcloth while they weep and fast (359–406). Seeing this, God withdraws his "vengaunce," thus overturning his promise (408). Yet we do not know what is entailed by the Ninevites' penance: the virtues of the new life remain a blank. Such a lack of specificity concerning virtues and vices is remarkable in a work allegedly teaching its readers about virtue. But read alongside the other poems in the manuscript it seems less than surprising.

Despite this treatment of the narrative, one might expect the homily's introduction to include some consideration of what is entailed by Christian patience in a Christian community. *Patience* begins by claiming that "Suffraunce" can overcome all evil and malice (1–8). The narrator (presenting himself in isolation from any determinate community) sees such patience as especially appropriate to his own involuntary poverty. Patience teaches him to endure this "destyné" without complaint, since complaint will merely lead to more trouble, as it would if he questioned the apparently arbitrary orders of his secular "lege lord" (35–56). As Elizabeth Kirk has noted, this is a thoroughly stoicizing version of patience,[77] and even the beatitudes are revised to fit. In Matthew's Gospel, which the poet invokes as his source (9–10), Jesus says, "Blessed are the peacemakers [Beati pacifici]: for they shall be called the children of God" (Matthew 5.9). The poet renders this as:

> They are happen also þat halden her pese,
> For þay þe gracious God sunes schal godly be called   (24–25).

Where Jesus blesses those who *make* peace, the poet blesses those who hold their own peace, who "remain quiet."[78] This is a small but telling transformation of the Gospel. An active, communitarian virtue is turned into an internalized, withdrawing virtue, a virtue of inner stillness. The poet does something similar with another beatitude. Matthew's Jesus says, "Blessed are they that suffer persecution for justice's sake [beati qui persecutionem patiuntur propter iustitiam]: for theirs is the kingdom of heaven (Matthew 5.10). The poet translates this as:

---

[77] See Kirk, "Who Suffreth," 90, 90–91, 95. Throughout her essay she *assumes* that there is no collusion whatsoever between the poet's views and the narrator's "highly stoic attitude" (90). I can find no warrants for such a clear and sharp division, and her essay provides none.

[78] Andrew and Waldron's translation, *Pearl Manuscript*, n. 25, p. 186. On the "liturgical context" evoked in *Patience* 9, see Staley Johnson, *The Voice of the Gawain-Poet*, 25 and 241–43 (n. 19). For traditional explication of the relevant beatitude see ibid., 25–30, 241–42 (notes 20–21). Also relevant here is Ralph Hanna, "Some Medieval Commonplaces of Late Medieval Patience Discussions," in *The Triumph of Patience*, 65–87; and Kirk, "Who Suffreth," 91, 95–97.

þay ar happen also þat con her hert stere,
For hores is þe heven-ryche, as I er sayde   (27–28).

Here the transformations of Jesus's words are even more marked, although they are in precisely the same direction as the one just discussed. Jesus blesses those who are persecuted for a political practice, the pursuit of justice within a determinate community. The poet turns the beatitude away from the social activity to self-control, away from a cardinal virtue that is concerned with relationships in a community to an inner, personal self-governance. The editors translate the phrase, "þat can her hert stere" as "who can control their hearts" and comment that the poet's "alteration places emphasis on self-control and moderation."[79] True enough, but one needs to add that while the practice of justice calls for "self-control and moderation" it calls for much *more* than this, and it is the "more" that the poet has occluded. He has privatized a virtue in which inner and outer agency are fused. He has also deleted the implication that being a disciple of Christ may call for resistance to social powers that have the force to persecute, powers that in late fourteenth-century England could be secular or ecclesiastic. Such deletion, in that context, was a thoroughly topical move, especially given the great emphasis Wyclif placed on persecution as a major constituent of Christian discipleship.[80]

The poet's alterations to the beatitudes fit the introduction's neo-stoic version of patience, one that does not take up the allegorical and Christocentric potentials of the story he tells. Attention is turned away from the life of the virtues in contemporary communities and their institutions, including the Church. This anticipates the poem's refusal to specify the relevant virtues, to particularize practices, even when they are allegedly a matter of life and death. The combination here generates a pelagian and courtly vision perfectly compatible with the treatment of faith, ethics, and Church in *Sir Gawain and the Green Knight*, *Pearl*, and *Cleanness*.[81]

It is appropriate to conclude this chapter with a memory of St. Augustine.

---

[79] Andrew and Waldron, *Pearl Manuscript*, n. 27, p. 186; on the poet's translation Kirk comments: "Positive action for a great cause is transformed into control of the feelings" ("Who Suffreth," 90).

[80] On this see Michael Wilks, "Wyclif and the Great Persecution," in *Prophecy and Eschatology*, ed. Wilks (Oxford: Blackwell, 1994), 39–64.

[81] The final lines of *Patience* reflect on the story of Jonah and God's closing words (520–31). As in the opening lines that they carefully echo, the poet advocated a still acceptance and endurance of what cannot be avoided (529). I say the poet for the reason given at the end of n. 77 above. Elizabeth Kirk rightly notes that St. Thomas argues that there can be no patience without grace (*ST* II–II.136.3), and that he "places patience in a very different light from the stoical one" ("Who Suffreth," 95). But whereas she assumes that the Thomistic account of the virtues is equivalent to the poet's version of patience, one opposed to the narrator of *Patience*, my own reading is that St. Thomas provides an illuminating contrast to *Patience*. It is this *contrast* that can help us focus on the ways in which the poet produces a version of the virtues that side-lines the Church and distinctive aspects of Christian tradition in this domain.

Writing about patience, he emphasized that Christian ("true") patience does not come from the strength of the human will, from our own "free will." Augustine maintains that it is a gift of the Holy Spirit poured into our hearts (Romans 5.5). Without the gift of charity there cannot be true patience. He notes that "bad men" are perfectly capable of enduring pain and adversity but this endurance is generated by the human will outside grace. It is charity that is patient (1 Corinthians 13.4) and there is no true, Christian patience without charity which is the love of God. Furthermore, this is bound up with "the unity of the spirit and the bond of peace whereby the Catholic Church is gathered and knit together."[82] This approach to patience offers a resonant contrast to the one we have followed in *Patience*. I will conclude with some related observations from St. Augustine's *De Gratia Christi*. Against Pelagius, he maintains that the law forces us to recognize our need for Christ's grace. The divinely given moral law cannot bring us to life, cannot justify us, and its fulfillment is in charity. Charity, the love of God, however is not poured into our hearts by the law, but by the Holy Spirit who is given to us (Romans 5.5). The tree that brings forth good fruits does so because it has received the grace of God in Christ.[83]

[82] From *De Patientia* in *Seventeen Short Treatises of St. Augustine* trans. by members of the English Church (Oxford: Parker, 1847), 543–62, *seriatim*, 15.12, 23.20 (with 6.5 and 17.14), 17.14, 32.20, 25.23. This text is used by St. Thomas in *ST* II–II.136.3, proof that it is impossible to have patience without grace; see n. 81 above.

[83] I paraphrase from *De Gratia Christi*, 8.9, 9.10, and 19.20 in *Select Anti-Pelagian Treatises of St. Augustine and the Acts of the Second Council of Orange*, ed. W. Bright (Oxford: Clarendon Press, 1880), 208–209, 216. In the final sentence Augustine is using Matt. 17.18. For a useful selection of anti-Pelagian works by Augustine, although not including *De Gratia Christi*, see *St. Augustine: Four Anti-Pelagian Writings*, trans. J. A. Mourant and W. J. Collinge (Washington, D.C.: Catholic University of America Press, 1992).

5

Reflections on Gower as "*Sapiens* in Ethics and Politics"

Recent scholarship on Gower has been marked not only by its erudition but also by the extremely strong claims made for the subtlety and coherence of Gower's moral and political thought, especially in the *Confessio Amantis*.[1] Because this chapter explores aspects of Gower's ethics it seems appropriate to begin with a few examples of the kinds of claims I have in mind. These examples are from recent works which have done a great deal to encourage serious engagement with Gower's writing.

Characteristic of such work is Alastair Minnis's influential essay "'Moral Gower' and Medieval Literary Theory," which sought to demonstrate how

---

[1] Examples of the work I have in mind are well represented by the following: Jane Chance Nietzsche, *The Genius Figure in Antiquity and the Middle Ages* (New York: Columbia University Press, 1975), 125–30; A. J. Minnis, "John Gower, *Sapiens* in Ethics and Politics," *Medium Aevum* 49 (1980): 207–29, repr. in Peter Nicholson, ed., *Gower's "Confessio Amantis"* (Cambridge: Brewer, 1991), 158–80; Minnis, "'Moral Gower' and Medieval Literary Theory," in ed. Minnis, *Gower's "Confessio Amantis": Responses and Reassessments* (Cambridge: Brewer, 1983), 50–78; E. Porter, "Gower's Ethical Microcosm and Political Macrocosm," in ed. Minnis, *Gower's "Confessio Amantis"* (cited above), 135–62; K. Olsson, *John Gower and the Structures of Conversion* (Cambridge: Brewer, 1992); R. F. Yeager, *John Gower's Poetics* (Cambridge: Brewer, 1990); James Simpson, *Science and the Self in Medieval Poetry* (Cambridge: Cambridge University Press, 1995), chaps. 1, 5–9; Larry Scanlon, *Narrative, Authority and Power* (Cambridge: Cambridge University Press), chap. 9; Kathryn Lynch, *The High Medieval Dream Vision* (Stanford: Stanford University Press, 1988), chap. 6; John H. Fisher, *John Gower: Moral Philosopher and Friend of Chaucer* (New York: New York University Press). For an attempt to show the coherence and specificity of Gower's political fictions and comments, together with claims that in both *Vox Clamantis* and *Confessio Amantis* "Gower *was* [author's italics] speaking for – on behalf of and in defence of – the people," see Judith Ferster, *Fictions of Advice: The Literature and Politics of Counsel in Late Medieval England* (Philadelphia: University of Pennsylvania Press, 1996), chap. 7: here, 132. Relevant to the concerns of the present essay, and in some ways in dialogue with them, is Frank Grady's "The Lancastrian Gower and the Limits of Exemplarity," *Speculum* 70 (1995): 552–75; and N. Zeeman, "The Verse of Courtly Love in the Framing Narrative of the *Confessio Amantis*," *Medium Aevum* 60 (1991): 222–40. The Gower texts that I refer to in this essay are the following: *The English Works of John Gower*, ed. G. C. Macaulay, 2 vols. EETS e.s. 81 and 82 (1900 and 1901); *The Latin Works*, vol. 4 of *The Complete Works*, ed. G. C. Macaulay (Oxford: Clarendon Press, 1902); The English translation of *Vox Clamantis* in *The Major Latin Works of John Gower*, trans. E. W. Stockton (Seattle: University of Washington Press, 1962).

coherently Gower's *Confessio Amantis* fulfilled the criteria for "ethical poetry" inherited from Christian-Aristotelian traditions. Minnis noted that "Gower's *principalis materia* falls within the subject area of ethics" and that "Gower has taken upon himself the function of *ethicus*, the role of *sapiens* with a special expertise in ethics and politics."[2] This is the Gower Minnis had described in an earlier article, "John Gower, *Sapiens* in Ethics and Politics," where it was argued that Gower's *Confessio Amantis* was an ethical treatise that included substantial political argument.[3] Similarly, R. F. Yeager's book on Gower's poetics presented a poet who completely meets the "medieval moralist's imperative" to apply traditional teaching to "edifying use" in present circumstances. Yeager showed how "public ethics and poetry were never unrelated in Gower's estimation." The *Confessio Amantis* was the product of a "poet of moral and political reform," one with a cogent "political program," a profound "program for societal unity and growth" incorporating a strong tendency to a "pacifist" ethic.[4] Kurt Olsson's book, *John Gower and the Structures of Conversion*, also saw Gower as successfully "reshaping the values of Ricardian England" as he freed his readers from "facile morality."[5]

The dominant version of Gower in current Gower studies, a brilliant dialogic and utterly coherent moral and political poet, is tenaciously maintained in James Simpson's explication of Gower's *Confessio Amantis* in *Sciences and the Self in Medieval Poetry*. Simpson rejects the common view that Christianity provides the unifying force in Gower's moral thought. He asserts that "Gower's ethics in the *Confessio* are not specifically Christian."[6] Rather, "Gower, in short, is what might be described as a liberal humanist" propounding "liberal humanism." The *Confessio Amantis* is a "humanist psychological allegory" which "might be described as liberal humanist."[7] What does such a devotedly historicizing scholar mean by attaching Gower to a term more intelligibly associated with John Stuart Mill and his heirs? By "humanism" he means to convey that Gower has "a profound confidence in the powers of human reason, and in the capacity of human reason to promote human perfection," a respectful engagement with "classical literature and philosophy" (especially Ovid and Aristotle) and a view of "politics as a pivotal, if not the supreme science." By "liberal" he means what he calls "constitutionalist," claiming that "Gower represents a constitutionalism,

---

[2] Minnis, "'Moral Gower,'" 71 and 69.

[3] Minnis, "John Gower, *Sapiens*," see n. 1.

[4] Yeager, *John Gower's Poetics*, quotations from 115, 201, 265, 241, but see *passim*; on the "pacifist" ethic see R. F. Yeager, "*Pax Poetica* and the Pacifism of Chaucer and Gower," *Studies in the Age of Chaucer* 9 (1987): 97–121; and Ben Lowe, *Imagining Peace: A History of Early English Pacificist Ideas, 1340–1560* (University Park: Pennsylvania State University Press, 1997), 82–87.

[5] Olsson, *John Gower*, here 1, 14; see also 24, 70–71, and chaps. 13 and 20; similarly, see Lynch, *High Medieval Dream Vision*, 168, 171, 186–88, 190–98, and Porter, "Gower's Ethical Microcosm."

[6] Simpson, *Science*, 196 n. 40, reiterated on 202 and argued for in chap. 7; contrast works by Olsson, Lynch, Minnis, and Yeager in n. 1.

[7] Simpson, *Science*, 19, 135, 229.

whose agreements are arrived at through dialogue and through the wisdom of an aged man in an aged world"; "at every point Gower's politics should be described as consensual and constitutionalist."[8] The relations between the allegedly total coherence of Gower's ethics and politics in the *Confessio* and the actual political struggles around the great popular uprising of 1381 or the actual political struggles which involved usurpation, regicide, and the violent maintenance of a usurping dynasty, are not investigated by Simpson, although Gower himself showed no reticence on these matters.[9] The final work I wish to recollect here is Larry Scanlon's study of Gower in *Narrative, Authority and Power*. In an often innovative reading of the *Confessio Amantis*, Scanlon seeks to show that Gower investigated ethics "as a rhetorical project." In doing so, "Gower is every bit as searching and self-conscious about poetic language as Chaucer," bringing this to fruit in a work which combines "anti-clerical critique with a more explicit celebration of lay political authority."[10] Gower is a coherent and "sophisticated political thinker" who understands all authority as the product of human fabrications but values kingship as the most effective form of order.[11] Justice itself is seen "as the king's gift," the product of his "voluntary restraint of his awesome, potentially absolute power."[12] So the *Confessio Amantis* discloses the foundationless nature of all authority. Simultaneously it constructs a coherent politics and ethics which belongs to the laicization of power in late medieval England. Here we encounter a very different version of Gower's ethics and politics to ones we find in Simpson or Yeager or Minnis, and yet one thing remains constant: Gower's poetry is a coherent, unified moral and political project.

Even the figure of Genius no longer presents difficulties in such versions of Gower. For example, Simpson sees him as "the increasingly rational imagination" moving the will (Amans) "towards its perfection."[13] Anything that might

[8] Ibid., see *seriatim* 18, 19, 273, 284; see also 294 and chaps. 7 and 9. On the allegedly unproblematic fusion of Aristotle's ethics and politics with Ovid, see 16, 275, and chaps. 5 and 7.

[9] I could find no consideration of the claims that Gower was a "constitutionalist" and a "liberal" in relation to the actual political struggles and options of the period, whether to the popular struggles embodied in the great rising of 1381 or to those around the Lancastrian usurpation. This is a rather peculiar, if revealing, absence in an argument that makes the claims it does about the nature of Gower's politics. In a Marxist vocabulary it might be described as an extraordinarily "idealist" version of politics. For an illuminating and informative study of constitutional thought in the Middle Ages, see James M. Blythe, *Ideal Government and the Mixed Constitution in the Middle Ages* (Princeton: Princeton University Press, 1992). Claims about Gower as a subtle "constitutionalist" thinker should engage with these contexts, among others.

[10] Scanlon, *Narrative, Authority and Power*, chap. 9: here quotations from 246 and 247; see similarly 250–52, 255–56, 258.

[11] Scanlon, *Narrative, Authority and Power*, 263.

[12] Scanlon, *Narrative, Authority and Power*, 286; see too 292.

[13] Simpson, *Science*, 194; see similarly 166, 172, 183, 185, 188, 196–97, 254, 258, 260–61; note the anticipations in Lynch, *High Medieval Dream Vision*, 19, 171, 182–85; the anticipation is noted by Simpson himself, *Science*, 186 n. 26.

seem contradictory in Genius's advice is to be read as a deliberately partial moment superseded in the final unities of Gower's theory and art. The sympathetic but nuanced account of Genius offered by Winthrop Wetherbee seems to have been assimilated to far more securely unifying and homogenizing readings.[14] However, in the view argued for below, it is time to return to a consideration of the kinds of "contradictory positions" that even as sympathetic a reader as Wetherbee found in the *Confessio*.[15] Here it will be argued that "contradictory positions" in the politics and ethics of Gower's writing cannot always or necessarily be read as carefully designed steps on a securely constructed pedagogic ladder belonging to a unified ethical and political system leading us to "perfection." Readers need not set out with assumptions that a work is coherent any more than they need set out with assumptions that it is incoherent.

My reflections on aspects of Gower's ethical thinking begin with *Vox Clamantis*. I have recently discussed the poem's responses to the English rising of 1381, and while I am not returning to that analysis here, it seems worth mentioning the relevance of Book I to any consideration of Gower's politics.[16] This is so because the current tendency is for scholars to set it aside and to derive accounts of Gower's ethics and politics exclusively from the *Confessio*. Yet the "vox" of the *Vox Clamantis*, its language, its prophetic role and many of its political assumptions, certainly survived the writing of *Confessio Amantis*.[17] Without determining the outcome of any ensuing enquiry, the acknowledgment of this fact might at least encourage us to ask some questions about continuities between works that certainly seem generically incommensurable. And if there are continuities, observing them might even be relevant to our understanding of the complex vernacular work.

I confine my comments on *Vox Clamantis* to aspects of Gower's treatment of violence, of war and peace, following in the steps of R. F. Yeager's "Pax Poetica and the Pacifism of Chaucer and Gower."[18] Yeager maintains that in the "*Vox Clamantis* and the *Confessio* there is an increasing certitude that all wars, including (or perhaps especially) England's with France, are more about

---

[14] Winthrop Wetherbee, "Genius and Interpretation in the *Confessio Amantis*," in *Magister Regis*, ed. A. Groos (New York: Fordham University Press, 1986), 241–60; see also, Wetherbee, "Latin Structure and Vernacular Space: Gower, Chaucer and the Boethian Tradition," in *Chaucer and Gower*, ed. R. F. Yeager (Victoria, B.C.: University of Victoria, 1991), 7–35, esp. 29–31.

[15] Wetherbee, "Latin Structure," 29.

[16] Aers, "'Vox Populi' and the literature of 1381," in the *Cambridge History of Medieval English Literatures*, ed. David Wallace (Cambridge: Cambridge University Press, 1998), chap. 16; see also Janet Coleman's comments on *Vox Clamantis* in her book, *English Literature in History, 1350–1400* (London: Hutchinson, 1981), 126–56, esp. 138–41.

[17] See, for example, the *Chronica Tripertita* and the *Carmen super multiplici viciorum pestilencia*: the former is trans. by Stockton in *Major Latin Works*; the latter is in Macaulay, *Latin Works*, 346–54.

[18] See n. 4.

money than justice." He argues that Gower sustained a coherent "pacifism" which is "both broad ranging and thoroughly developed," "a strengthening position" based on "legal and doctrinal authorities that war itself is contrary to most Christian positions."[19] But even if we set aside Gower's constant legitimization of killing on crusades, a legitimization Yeager of course noted, problems emerge which are not uncharacteristic of Gower's ethics, in whatever genres he chooses.

In Book III of *Vox Clamantis* Gower turns to the models of the good life offered by the founder of his religion. He tells readers that "Christ used to make peace," that "Christ was gentle [*mitis*]," that Christ suffered "humbly [*humilis*]," was "compassionate [*miserans*]" and did not seek "vengeance," unlike the modern ecclesiastics Gower is criticizing.[20] He reminds readers that "Christ taught us to follow his example of forgiveness" and traced the path of salvation through patience rather than through retaliation. Christian faith, he recalls, is disclosed in love that establishes peace and friendship, not even demanding, let alone defending, things that are one's own; it certainly does not "thirst for the possessions of others."[21] Here the *vox* of John Gower follows very closely the unequivocal and utterly demanding commitment to the practice of non-violence at the heart of Jesus's teaching in Luke 6:27–38.[22] The poet emphasizes that for a Christian a virtuous life entails following Christ's own "merciful" teaching.[23] Gower sets his outline of the ethics of the Kingdom of God proclaimed by Jesus against the current values and practices of Christians leading the Church, those especially obliged to follow "Christ's rule of peace" but now committed to violence and the killing of other Christians.[24]

Three books later the poet addresses the young King Richard directly. As one would expect in a poem that had propounded Christ's teaching on detachment and nonviolence as essential to the Kingdom of God, Christ is invoked as the decisive model for living well. Gower counsels the king in evangelical terms: "conduct yourself like a Christ," be like the "loving Christ" in self-discipline, generosity, and care of the poor.[25] Such are the demands of the founding texts invoked in Book III, and here Gower seems to be developing a consistent ethical counsel. Perhaps, the charitable interpreter may reflect, the first book's indulgence in revengeful violence against the men and women involved in the rising of 1381 was an aberration produced by fear and the deeply internalized

[19] *"Pax Poetica,"* 103–104, 108.
[20] III. I.116–17 (reference to book, chap., and page in Stockton's translation; cited in n. 1; I have also occasionally supplied the Latin text cited in n. 1 where I considered that helpful).
[21] *Seriatim*, III.3.122; III.7.126–27.
[22] An excellent introduction to the issues here is John H. Yoder, *The Politics of Jesus*, 2nd rev. ed. (Grand Rapids: Eerdmans, 1994), esp. chap. 2.
[23] III.8.128; the meditation continues in III.9.130–32.
[24] III.9.131; Gower displays a militaristic and worldly understanding of Christians' relationship to Christ's kingship, allegedly derived through his mother and to be gained by the carnal sword: III.9.131–32, III.5.124.
[25] VI.8.234 and VI.11.238–39.

norms of class contempt and dehumanization.[26] However, such a genial reading is not sustainable. For from advocacy of evangelical ethics the poet moves to an altogether different paradigm of the virtues. Having just exhorted Richard to conduct himself like the "loving Christ" he commends an altogether different kind of model, "that most illustrious prince, his father," the Black Prince.[27] Gower leaves us in no doubt about the entailments of such a model for the young man whom he has just exhorted to follow the way of Christ, the Christ whose practice and teaching of nonviolence his poem had made clear. The poet reminds Richard, in an unironic celebration of aristocratic violence that could have come from the Chandos Herald's adoration of the Black Prince, how the father:

> plundered [*depredat*] foreign lands . . . France felt the effects of him; and Spain, in contemplating the powers with which he stoutly subjected her, was fearful of him . . . .he hurled his troops into the midst of his enemies . . . He pursued and destroyed them, he cut them down and killed them just as a wolf driven by hunger. . . .his sword was often drunk with the blood of the enemy. Harshly assaulting his foes, he fought and overcame them. His sword point refused to go back into the sheath dry. His hostile blade was sated with enemy gore; a torrent of blood slaked the thirst of his weapons. . . . He attacked strongholds, annihilating the people [*Depopulans populos forcia castra ruit*]. In order to seize booty [*Ut predes raperet*], he boldly penetrated deep among his antagonists.[28]

Along with this transformation of the evangelical paradigm we should recall that while Gower had criticized the pursuit of war for material profits, here the self-aggrandizing economic motives of English invasions of France ("to seize booty") are made explicit and extolled as part of the Black Prince's glory.[29]

---

[26] On Book I see works cited in n. 16 together with Andrew Galloway, "Gower in his most learned role and the Peasants' Revolt of 1381," *Medievalia* 16 (1993): 329–47, and Steven Justice, *Writing and Rebellion* (Berkeley: University of California Press, 1994), 208–11. (I remain completely unpersuaded by Justice's account of Chaucer's "criticism" of Gower in the *Nun's Priest's Tale* and of his assumed response to the English rising, 208–27: for a far more careful account of Chaucer's political perspectives in this context, see Derek Pearsall, *The Life of Geoffrey Chaucer* [Oxford: Blackwell, 1992], 143–51.) On conventional contempt for the peasantry (the majority of European Christians) by the governing and writing classes, see the evidence and references in Lee Patterson, *Chaucer and the Subject of History* (Madison: University of Wisconsin Press, 1991), 262–74.

[27] Heading to VI.13.241.

[28] See VI.13.241–42. For the Chandos Herald, see *Life of the Black Prince* by the Herald of Sir John Chandos, ed. M. K. Pope and E. C. Lodge (Oxford: Clarendon Press, 1910), text and translation. For the relevant paradigms here see the following: M. Vale, *War and Chivalry* (Athens, Ga.: University of Georgia Press, 1981); M. James, *English Politics and the Concept of Honour* (Oxford: Past and Present Society, 1978); S. Knight, *Arthurian Literature and Society* (London: Macmillan, 1983); M. Keen, *Chivalry* (New Haven: Yale University Press, 1984); P. Coss, *The Knight in Medieval England* (Stroud: Sutton, 1993).

[29] On the criticism of economic motivations for war, see Yeager, "*Pax Poetica*," 103–104. Such motivations were pervasive, certainly not confined to those classified as "mercenaries": see

And this is now proposed as a model for Richard, *"in exemplum."*[30] In fact the poet calls on Richard to *surpass* the militaristic deeds of his father.[31] True enough, peace "excels," observes the poet; however, "when our tried and tested rights call for war it should be waged" and the king should seek honor and glory, the familiar goals of the ruling class and its chivalry.[32]

How does all this relate to the evangelical proclamations of Book III and the advice to Richard to follow the loving Christ in Book VI? How does it relate to Gower's understanding of the Church, the body of Christ into which all Christians are incorporated, including the French Christians whose slaughter Gower is celebrating? How does Gower's exaltation of violence in defence of "our rights" (that is, the dubious nationalist claims of the ruling English dynasty to the French crown) relate to his earlier insistence that Christian faith or love "does not thirst for possessions of others, nor does it ever demand things that are its own"?[33] Has the moralist forgotten what he had written about Christ and discipleship in Book III and within Book VI itself? Apparently not, for a little later in Book VI he again instructs Richard to recall "Christ's sacred writings."[34] But to what purpose would one who is exhorted to "surpass" the violence of the Black Prince disturb the dust upon a manuscript of the Gospels? Gower's answer displays no sense of any difficulty here: Christ's words simply warn the king to become a worthy pilgrim "resplendent with the light of virtues," one who remembers that he is made in the image of God and so should "follow Him, conforming to His law" – that is, to the evangelical doctrine the poet articulated clearly enough. So, he writes, "it is to your advantage that you love with all your might Him who fashioned and redeemed you."[35] The poet's moral counsel instructs the addressee to "withdraw" from the world while simul- taneously surpassing the military and chivalric triumphs of the Black Prince. Be like the Gospels' Christ; follow his unequivocal condemnation of violence and worldly attachment (Luke 6:27–38). Also be like and surpass the Black Prince; that is, plunder, destroy, cut down, kill; make sure your sword is drunk with blood; depopulate lands (i.e., perpetuate massacres and ethnic segregations); make war to seize booty; and through this win honor, glory, and peace, a peace unperturbed by the richly unfolded distinctions of different forms of peace in St. Augustine's *City of God*.

What are we to make of this? How could the poet, celebrated by scholars as

H. J. Hewitt, "The Organization of War," in *The Hundred Years War*, ed. K. Fowler (New York: St. Martin's Press, 1971), and Hewitt, *The Organization of War Under Edward III* (Manchester: Manchester University Press, 1966). See also Coss, *The Knight in Medieval England*.

[30] VI.13.241.

[31] VI.13.242.

[32] Ibid. It should be noted that such commitments entailed the unprecedentedly heavy levels of taxation that were the catalyst to the rising of 1381. See n. 16.

[33] III.1.127.

[34] VI.17.246.

[35] VI.17.246–47.

sapiens in ethics and politics, produce such contradictory admonitions on such a major moral issue without any signs of discomfort, let alone ironization? My answer involves two strands. They could very loosely be called "cultural" and "literary." The first term directs us to consider the constitution of Christian traditions (plural) in relation to forms of social power and class practices in late medieval Europe. The second strand directs us to consider the genres Gower develops together with the particularities of his own formal choices. In the present case these strands combine to produce the ethical contradictions identified above. This is not the place to provide even an historical sketch of the first strand; all that we need to remember here is that the unequivocal demands Jesus made in passages such as Luke 6:27–38 were mediated by a Church predominantly committed to the existing organizations of power, including military power. It is no chance matter that the targets of the insurgents of 1381 included the head of the English Church, Archbishop and Chancellor Simon Sudbury, or that one of their leaders was a radical priest anathematized and jailed by the ecclesiastical authorities, or that the rebellious peasants at North Walsham were slaughtered by forces under the personal command of the militaristic Bishop Despenser.[36] The shorthand term to designate the Church's immersion in the powers of ruling elites is the Constantinianization of Christianity. This has taken numerous forms since the emperor made Christianity the official religion of the Roman empire and its armies, but in all its modalities it entailed a systematic marginalization, or inversion, of Jesus's teachings of nonviolence – teachings at the heart of the proclamation of the Kingdom of God.[37] The contradictions within the first strand enabled the cross to become the symbol around which military power was organized, enabled the eucharist to become a bond among those making war or burning heretics, and enabled pulpits of Churches to be instruments of royal propaganda in the years of war against French Christians.[38] Yet it seems that the Church's management

[36] For a good introduction to the late-medieval Church, especially in the contexts under discussion see P. Heath, *Church and Realm: 1272–1461* (London: Fontana, 1988), chaps. 3, 7, and 8. On 1381 the best introduction remains R. Hilton, *Bond Men Made Free* (London: Temple, 1973), read with R. B. Dobson, *The Peasant's Revolt of 1381* (London: Macmillan, 1970); see also Justice, *Writing and Rebellion*, chap. 4.

[37] On the issues here see chapter six (below) and the following: Yoder, *Politics of Jesus*; R. H. Bainton, *Christian Attitudes Toward War and Peace* (New York: Abingdon, 1960); Yoder, *Christian Attitudes to War, Peace, and Revolution: A Companion to Bainton* (Elkhart, Ind.: Peace Resource Center, 1983; now distributed by Cokesbury Bookstore, Duke Divinity School); W. Klassen, *Love of Enemies* (Philadelphia: Fortress Press, 1984); on the theology of the just war see: F. H. Russell, *The Just War in the Middle Ages* (Cambridge: Cambridge University Press, 1975).

[38] On the eucharist and the cultural and political roles it played see Miri Rubin, *Corpus Christi* (Cambridge: Cambridge University Press, 1991), and the essays by Rubin and Beckwith in *Culture and History 1350–1600*, ed. Aers (London: Harvester, 1992). On the use of pulpits for war and nationalist propaganda, see A. K. McHardy, "Liturgy and Propaganda in the Diocese of Lincoln during the Hundred Years War," *Studies in Church History* 18 (1982): 215–27.

of the contradictions became normalized and internalized. So it is hardly surprising if they are simply and unironically reproduced by an orthodox Catholic whose estates satire was written from a social position and political assumptions definitively bound up with the governing classes.[39] Not surprising, indeed, but a necessary topic of reflection for those studying Gower's ethics and politics.

This brings me to the second strand, the "literary" or more formal. Gower developed a form which facilitated the simple reproduction of the contradictions I have outlined, a mode of literary organization which is markedly paratactic. By this I mean that the poem tends to be compiled in units that are paratactically sealed off from each other *rather than* brought into dialogue. I am certainly not suggesting that a poem whose chief mode of organization is episodic must necessarily generate unexaminedly contradictory positions. An episodic mode of composition can be, in the terms I use here, dialogic rather than paratactic. Episodes can be juxtaposed to produce a carefully organized, complex range of mirrorings, echoes, qualifications, elaborations, perhaps with little connecting narrative. Far from sealing units off from each other and from critical scrutiny, such an organization could encourage a dialogue between conflicting episodes through which the writer explores ethical problems. This is one of the ways in which *Piers Plowman* unfolds.[40] *Vox Clamantis*, however, works very differently. The examples I have considered show how its paratactic mode becomes a powerful impediment to moral inquiry, to sustained critical reflection on the difficulties that are raised. The mode protects the poet from having to confront sharp contradictions in his ethics, let alone from having to explore their sources in the traditions he inherits and the culture he inhabits. Yet the particular contradictions observed above should be extremely serious ones for any Christian moralist, and any study of Gower's ethics needs to identify the poet's failure to *articulate* them as contradictions together with the consequent failure to explore the sources of such contradictions. R. F. Yeager may be right in thinking that there was "a profound division in Gower's own heart" over the practice of war.[41] If so, the poet's paratactic mode enabled him to repress this important "division" from critical exploration. Such occlusion would not be without advantages. It would allow the poet to assert with equal vehemence morally and theologically incompatible positions in areas of real difficulty, asserting whichever position most accorded with contingent demands, including contingent literary demands, as the poet saw them. This might also facilitate the poet's self-presentation as a prophetic and impersonal *vox*, the contemporary figure of the apostle St. John, "the one whom the Isle of Patmos received in the Apocalypse, and whose name I bear," as well as that voice of the people in

[39] Coleman, *English Literature*, 140–41.
[40] On the "episodic" form of *Piers Plowman*, see Anne Middleton, "Narrative and the Invention of Experience: Episodic Form in *Piers Plowman*," in *The Wisdom of Poetry*, ed. L. D. Benson and S. Wenzel (Kalamazoo: Medieval Institute Publications, 1982), 91–92.
[41] Yeager, "*Pax Poetica*," 105.

which God is often disclosed.[42] These are no small claims and the self-representation they involve may be more self-gratifying than the figure of the poet in *Piers Plowman*, that irascible, divided, wandering, falling, criticized but tenaciously searching Will, one figure of what it might be to think critically as a Christian moralist in a time of trouble and major dislocations.

Is the analysis offered above of any relevance to *Confessio Amantis*, the vernacular work begun soon after Gower wrote the first book of *Vox Clamantis*?[43] The current scholarship from which this essay set out would lead us to expect that the answer here will be an obvious negative. This may turn out be correct, but I hope to begin a discussion of *Confessio Amantis* which might indicate how its ethical and political dimensions could at least be explored along lines similar to those followed in the preceding discussion of *Vox Clamantis*. Here I merely intend to initiate such an exploration, but if this encourages a rather more critically alert engagement with Gower's account of the virtues and "the common good" in the *Confessio* it will have served its purpose even if it is finally shown to be wide of the mark.

On the face of it, the *Confessio* seems to be a thoroughly dialogic poem quite alien to the *Vox Clamantis*. After all, its literary models include the works of Boethius, Jean de Meun, and Ovid. Its procedures include the invention of different voices and perspectives through which the errant Amans and, according to some accounts, the priest of Venus are educated in substantial ethical and political matters, and, finally, reformed. Despite these facts, the ethical reflections of the *Confessio* manifest examples of the traits I have identified in *Vox Clamantis*. I shall illustrate these by considering the poem's treatment of the contemporary Church and Lollardy. Gower's previous works had included sustained criticism of the Church which drew heavily on conventional estates satire, antimonastic and antimendicant satire.[44] The *Confessio* returns to these traditions in its consideration of the contemporary Church but it does so in ways which may go beyond received conventions for lamenting disparity between current practices and shared ideals. These have been recently analyzed by Larry Scanlon. He argues that Gower's conventional criticism of the clerical estate is combined with a "celebration of lay political authority" which belongs to the new configuration of forces in late medieval England examined in *Narrative, Authority and Power*.[45] Gower presents "the collapse of clerical authority" in his England and calls for an expansion of lay power, particularly

---

[42] Prologue to Book I, 50 and VII.25.288: Gower's actual words here are these: "Quod scripsi plebis vox est, set et ista videbis,/ Quo clamat populus, est ibi sepe deus" (VII.1469–70).

[43] On the date at which Gower began the *Confessio*, see discussion and references in Simpson, *Science*, 293–94, esp. nn. 21 and 22.

[44] For surveys of these traditions: Jill Mann, *Chaucer and Medieval Estates Satire* (Cambridge: Cambridge University Press, 1973); Penn Szittya, *The Antifraternal Tradition in Medieval Literature* (Princeton: Princeton University Press, 1986); J. A. Yunck, *The Lineage of Lady Meed: the Development of Medieval Venality Satire* (Notre Dame: Notre Dame University Press, 1963).

[45] Scanlon, *Narrative, Authority and Power*, chap. 9; quotation from 247.

monarchic power, with the lay poet devoted to legitimizing the prince's authority which "is always discursively constructed."[46] Here Gower's treatment of the struggle between Pope Boniface VIII and King Philip the Fair is especially illuminating (*Confessio*, II.2798–3071). Scanlon's commentary on this *exemplum*, "no fable" (II.2800), addresses the poet's fascination with "the Church's power to fabricate divine authority."[47] Papal claims to power and the authority of apostolic succession, together with its claims of supernatural authentication, are represented as inventive fictions produced to serve thoroughly material interests. The decisive voice of God turns out to be no more than the projection of an ambitious cardinal who employs a "clergyman of yong age" with a concealed trumpet.[48] In contrast, King Philip (the poem's "Lowyz") represents legitimate power, including military power. In the face of a Catholic hierarchy led and represented by Pope Boniface, the lay power, according to the narrator, is entitled to use the violence it commands to displace the duly elected pope (II.2980–3029). This is a very striking image of the lay sovereign's licit role in challenging abuse in the Catholic Church, even at its most elevated level. Scanlon maintains that the king and the poet disenfranchise clerical power "by making it entirely spiritual":[49]

> And seiden that the Papacie
> Thei wolde honoure and magnefie
> In al that evere is spirital;
> Bot thilke Pride temporal
> Of Boneface in his persone,
> Ayein that ilke wrong al one
> Thei wolde stonden in debat.   (II.2985–91)

The poem expands lay power while restricting clerical power "to a realm entirely separate from the structures of lay power," a move that involved "an anti-papalism and an anti-clericalism that would be difficult to overstate." However, Scanlon concludes that all this "is not finally anti-ecclesiastic."[50]

For Scanlon this conclusion apparently presents no problems. For him there seems to be no tension, let alone contradiction, in a poem that allegedly "disenfranchises clerical power," that undermines the foundational legitimations of ecclesiastical authority, that presents an "extreme" form of "anti-clericalism" and yet is "not finally anti-ecclesiastical."[51] But to maintain all the terms in this project without incoherence would demand an understanding of Church, of "ecclesiastical" power and authority, quite incompatible with Catholic ortho-

[46] Ibid., 248–56; quotations from 251 and 250. Genius, Scanlon argues, is a decidedly lay moralist, like his maker: 255–56, 283–84, 292–94. (Perhaps V.1799 may suggest a slightly less consistent identification of Genius than Scanlon, persuasively enough, argues.)
[47] Scanlon, *Narrative, Authority and Power*, 260.
[48] *Confessio*, II. 2847–2931; Scanlon, *Narrative, Authority and Power*, 258–60.
[49] Scanlon, *Narrative, Authority and Power*, 262; see also 259–62.
[50] Ibid., 260, 262; see also the discussion of the Donation of Constantine at 263–67.
[51] Ibid., 262.

REFLECTIONS ON GOWER AS "*SAPIENS* IN ETHICS AND POLITICS"

doxy, at least *as it was instituted, understood and enforced* in late fourteenth-century England. A position can only be antiecclesiastic or not antiecclesiastic in relation to an historically determinate Church, an historically specific structure of power, authority, and self-understanding. And here we need to recall certain facts. First, by the time Gower wrote *Confessio Amantis* Wyclif and his followers had developed a major attack on the current authority of the pope and clergy together with a radical program of disendowment enforced by the lay power, especially the king. (This will be addressed in the next chapter.) For them papal and clerical claims to divine authority were as counterfeit as Gower made them appear in Book II of the *Confessio*.[52] Second, by the time Gower was writing this poem the Church's authorities had made perfectly clear that such attacks on the Church's temporal possessions were unequivocally antiecclesiastic and to be resisted as such. This resistance had been plain enough since the later 1370s. The Church's task was to persuade the lay power, particularly the sovereign, that what was antiecclesiastic would also prove subversive of the foundations of lay power, and that the sovereign needed the wholehearted support of the Church.[53] This, in brief, is the specific context in which "I thenke make/ A bok for Engelondes sake,/ The yer sextenthe of Kyng Richard" (Prol. 23–25). The *auctor* of the Prologue and Genius in Book II develop a radical critique of the actually existing Church combined with a defence of the secular sovereign's role in challenging the ecclesiastical hierarchy when it is judged to be in serious error – judged, that is, by lay poet and secular lord. In Gower's historical context such a secular and vernacular critique of the sources and scope of ecclesiastical power and authority, not one confined to itemizing practical failures to meet demanding ideals, was distinctly antiecclesiastical. In Wendy Scase's terms, such writing belonged to a radical and "new" anticlericalism.[54]

Against this, however, one should set some of the confessor's instructions in Book V. Here he undertakes a comparative history of world religions in the course of which he comes to Christianity (V.726–1970; on the Christian faith, V.1737–90). Having given an account of orthodox Christian teaching on the Fall, the Incarnation and Redemption, Genius identifies himself with Christ's power bestowed through apostolic succession in the Catholic Church, a power that "now is falle / On ous that ben of holi cherche" (V.1797–99).[55] From this

[52] On Wycliffism, see Anne Hudson's *The Premature Reformation* (Oxford: Clarendon Press, 1988); for exemplification of vernacular Wycliffism at the end of the fourteenth century, see the *English Wycliffite Sermons*, ed. Pamela Gradon and Anne Hudson, 5 vols. (Oxford: Clarendon Press, 1983–1996); and William Swinderby's statements summarized in *Registrum Johannis Trefnant*, ed. W. W. Capes (London: Canterbury and York Society, 1916), 235–51.

[53] Pope Gregory XI first condemned Wyclif's teachings on dominion and temporalities in 1377; on the relevant history here see M. Aston, "Lollardy and Sedition 1381–1431," *Past and Present* 17 (1960): 1–44, reprinted in her *Lollards and Reformers* (London: Hambledon, 1984), and Heath, *Church and Realm*, chap. 6.

[54] Wendy Scase, *Piers Plowman and the New Anti-Clericalism* (Cambridge: Cambridge University Press, 1989).

[55] This seems one of the many places in the *Confessio* where the text goes against Simpson's

identification he (and his *auctor*)[56] warns Amans, an orthodox but morally confused Catholic, about a contemporary threat to his Church, that inspired guardian of orthodoxy and sole ark of salvation:

> Now were it good that thou forthi,
> Which through baptesme properely
> Art unto Cristes feith professed
> Be war that thou be noght oppressed
> With Anticristes lollardie   (V.1803–7).

This "newe" teaching, he then insists, is one that "goth aboute/ To sette Cristes feith in doute" (V.1810–12). How exactly could "lollardie" bring "Cristes feith in doute"? After all, Lollardy was a form of Christianity which involved a strong commitment to traditional Christology, to traditional Trinitarian doctrine, to the Gospel's account of Christ and its demands of Christian discipleship. The claim is, of course, perfectly intelligible within a model of "Cristes feith" where this is inseparable from the canon law, the Church's liturgy, offices, doctrinal determinations, and authority. The narrator continues:

> The seintz that weren ous tofore,
> Be whom the feith was ferst upbore,
> That holi cherche stod relieved,
> Thei oghten betre be believed
> Than these, whiche that men knowe
> Noght holy, thogh thei feigne and blowe
> Here lollardie in mennes ere.
> Bot if thou wolt live out of fere,
> Such newe lore, I rede eschuie
> And hold forth riht the weie and suie,
> As thine Ancestres dede er this:
> So schalt thou noght believe amis.   (V.1813–24)

Lollardy is identified with the "new" and counterfeit (ll. 1810–11, 1818–20) while the contemporary Church is identified with apostolic foundations, ancient tradition, and an unambiguous "weie" to follow. Yet the poet's defense of the Church against Lollardy may be less straightforward than the confidence of the passage might suggest. Any moderately well-informed contemporary reader would note that the appeal to the primitive Church was a basic Wycliffite move. From it there followed a wide range of substantial *contrasts* with the con-

---

unifying reading of Genius as the soul's rational imagination: here Venus's priest, still classified as such to the poem's end, is propounding a conventional version of orthodox Christian doctrine that would fit into any contemporary "lay folk's catechism."

[56] For an example of Gower's attacks on Wyclif and Wycliffism outside the *Confessio* see especially the first part of *Carmen super multiplici viciorum pestilencia* (*Latin Works*, 346 ff.); a passage such as *Vox*, III.9.130 represents the commitment of the poet to the pope's massive authority: "Whatever the Pope does is permissible, as his office indicates . . . He can open the heavens and shut the foul pit of hell."

temporary Church. How then should one distinguish between different versions of the early Church, different claims about continuity and discontinuity? Wyclif and his early followers took patristic sources as seriously as any orthodox exegete or theologian, while they attacked the contemporary Church for fabricating novelties in doctrine, discipline, and ecclesiastical institutions. Instead of seeing such "novelties" as guided by the Holy Spirit, they were presented as a disqualifying rupture with apostolic and patristic traditions, the authentic sources of Christian life to which Wycliffites sought to return.[57] Furthermore, Wycliffites agreed wholeheartedly with the poet's treatment of the donation of Constantine and its venomous significance for the Church (II.3473–96).[58] How precisely does the allegiance of "Anticristes lollardies" to the early Church and its hostility to all that the Donation of Constantine symbolized differ from the poet's appeal to those "Be whom the feith was ferst upbore"? In the Prologue to the *Confessio Amantis* the poet had *contrasted* the contemporary Church and its "clerkes" with those "of daies olde." In those days the Church was uncontaminated by the market, committed to non-violence, free from temporal goods, free from worldly honor, devoted to "the bok," preaching, and prayer (Prol. 193–239). "Bot now," the poet laments, the Church is dedicated to the carnal sword and rejects Christ's demands that his disciples should pursue nonviolent peacemaking, poverty, patience, and unity. Now "the flock" is "withoute guide" and made the prey of rapacious pseudoshepherds; now the gap between inherited "word" and current norms has become massive (Prol. 240–480). Given this, a reader should wonder how Book V can so *simply* defend the authority of the contemporary Church by an appeal to earlier traditions; and wonder too just how to distinguish this appeal and critique from the alleged novelty of Wycliffite arguments. One might almost suspect that the poet is developing some kind of ironic reflection about the utterly contingent and self-interested grounds of all appeals to tradition and authority, an irony directed against both orthodox and Wycliffite arguments, an irony to share with his friend Chaucer, perhaps. But such a response would ignore Gower's virulent attacks on Lollardy in the *Confessio* and elsewhere, ones that accompany defences of the actually existing Church and, it follows, of its current practices. It would also ignore his unequivocal admiration for Archbishop Arundel who led the Church toward the triumphant alliance with the lay power which enacted the

---

[57] These are basic commonplaces in Wycliffite ecclesiology and understanding of tradition and authority: see Hudson, *Premature Reformation*, chap. 7 and 377–78. For the full predestinarian contexts of Wyclif's own address to contemporary conflicts, see his *De Ecclesia*, ed. J. Loserth (London: Wyclif Society, 1886).

[58] On this see Scanlon, *Narrative, Authority and Power*, 257–58, 263–67. These matters are at the heart of chapter 6. For identification of related difficulties in Nicholas Love, see Sarah Beckwith, *Christ's Body* (London: Routledge, 1993); K. Ghosh, "'Authority' and 'Interpretation' in Wycliffite, Anti-Wycliffite, and Related Texts, c.1375–1430" (Ph.D. diss., Cambridge University, 1996; Cambridge University Press, forthcoming), chap. 5; and Katherine Little, "Reading for Christ: Interpretation and Instruction in Late Medieval England" (Ph.D. diss., Duke University, 1998), chap. 3.

115

statute enabling the burning of Lollards.[59] Having set aside this ironic, proto-Nietzschean reading, does one have any explanation of the conflicts in the poet's representations of the Church, her authority, and her relation to earlier traditions? Conflicts, it is clear, that the poet does not acknowledge as such, let alone explore. As in *Vox Clamantis*, the explanation is parataxis, a paratactic mode which seals off units from each other and facilitates the propagation of conflicting positions whose conflicts are left unattended, unnoticed.

Even within Book V itself this mode can be observed. Here it eases the poet's move from a vehement defense of the Church, against critics he classifies as Antichrist's followers, to a description of the same Church's catastrophic degeneration from its earlier forms of life (V.1848–1959). Today, Genius declares, "the feith discresceth" and the ark of salvation, Peter's ship, the Roman Church has almost sunk (V.1849–73). Whereas Wycliffites had just been attacked for allegedly undermining "Cristes feith" (V.1810–12), now it seems that the Church herself has done the undermining. Indeed this is made explicit as when we learn that the Church's own abandonment of earlier tradition has generated both "cokel"sowing heretics and an audience ready "to taken hiede" of these Lollards and their teaching (V.1874–87;[60] see also V.1904–49). The Church is vehemently defended and its own radical critics demonized; yet soon the Church is vehemently attacked as the cause both of these demons and a dissolution of Christian faith, an attack with radical implications. After all, *if* the contemporary Church has become an agent through whom "the feith discresceth," that is, an impediment to saving faith, *if* it has changed from being the invulnerable ark to a sinking ship, "welnyh dreynt" by worldly attachments, what authority does it have and why should radical reformers be called Antichrist's followers? How is the presence of the Holy Spirit in the Church to be discerned, and by whom? Undoubtedly the description of the Church I have just summarized converges with the one offered by radical critics and raises just the issues they raise. Namely, if the ark has become a sinking ship, actually undermining Christian faith, should disciples of Christ stay on board? Is that God's will? Perhaps. But perhaps not. (Think of that voice from heaven: "Come out, my people, away from her, so that you do not share in her crimes and have the same plagues to bear. Her sins have reached up to the sky, and God has her crimes in mind" [Apoc. 18:4–5].) Yet by what authority does one leave, and to where does one go? Outside of the Roman Church there was no salvation, as the Church maintained. At the end of *Piers Plowman*, Conscience makes the decision to search outside the actually existing Church for Piers, *Petrus id est Christus*.[61] But in that long poem, conflicting positions, arguments

---

[59] See the epistle to Arundel translated by Stockton in *Major Latin Works*, 47–48 and note Macaulay's commentary on 340.

[60] Here the Lollards are called "Pseudo": Macaulay's note refers to Rev. 19.20 and Matt. 7.15 as well as relevant passages in *Mirrour de l'Omme* and *Vox Clamantis*; in a context where the poet had already referred to "Anticristes Lollardie" (V.1807) the allusion to the apocalyptic "pseudo" refers again to Wycliffites; in *Carmen* Wyclif is thoroughly diabolized.

[61] See *Piers Plowman: The B Version*, ed. G. Kane and E. T. Donaldson, rev. ed. (London:

and emotions have been brought into a critical, often thoroughly vexed, dialogue. Where contraries meet it is not because the poet has not noticed that he may be drawn to conflicting positions but because he seeks to explore them through the juxtaposition. Some contradictions are certainly found to be irresolvable, including ones in Langland's ecclesiology. So at the poem's end we are shown how a contemporary orthodox Christian might have to make the terrifying move Conscience makes.[62] Gower's *Confessio Amantis* includes responses to the Church that are as conflicting as many in *Piers Plowman*. But the paratactic mode I have described enables the occlusion of fundamental problems that are ethical, political, and ecclesiological.

This paratactic mode is also displayed in another feature of the passage of Book V under discussion. Genius accuses Lollards of using a kind of ear-trumpet to propagate doctrine whose source is not authentic Christian tradition but their own fabrications: "thei feigne and blowe / Here lollardie in mennes ere" (V.1818–19).[63] We met this act and image in the story of Pope Boniface in Book II. There it disclosed the fabrication of ecclesiastical authority and the effectiveness of such counterfeiting (the cardinals, Pope Celestine, and the whole Church accept Boniface as St. Peter's due successor). What are readers to make of this reiteration? It certainly reveals a striking convergence between the Roman Church and "Anticristes lollardie." Are we being invited to cultivate ironic reflection on the grounds of *all* doctrine, on the grounds of *all* claims to unfeigned, uninvented authority in matters concerning the divine? Is the reiteration designed to show that Lollards merely reflect the practices of the Church they attack, while the Church merely reflects the desires of the Lollards it anathematizes? Are we being led into an antifoundationalism where modern Christians must accept that all they can have access to is self-interested human organizations locked in conflicts over carnal power and material resources? Once more we have to reject such proto-Nietzschean reading as incompatible with too many of Gower's commitments, including his favored self-representations.[64] Whatever contradictions emerge in his treatment of Lollardy, the Church, and the grounds of authority, they remain that, unresolved and unacknowledged. There is no intention to initiate a dialogue between contrary positions. It is just here that the paratactic mode helps the poet to escape the consequences of the

Athlone, 1988), XX.368–86, and XV.212. On the traditional affirmation of no salvation outside the Church, see chapter 2; it is clearly formulated in *Unam Sanctam* of 1302 in *Documents of the Christian Church*, trans. Henry Bettenson (London: Oxford University Press, 1963), 159–61.

62 On the ending of Piers Plowman, see Aers, *Chaucer, Langland and the Creative Imagination* (London: Routledge, 1980), 56–61 and *Community, Gender, and Individual Identity* (London: Routledge, 1988), 63–66; see also James Simpson, *Piers Plowman: An Introduction to the B-Text* (London: Longman, 1990), 243–45.

63 See also the first part of *Carmen*, esp. lines 30 ff.

64 On the kinds of intention and self-representation I have in mind see especially the following: Simpson, *Science*, chaps. 8–9; Wetherbee (cited in n. 4); Lynch, Yeager, and Minnis (all cited in n. 1).

contradictions he has composed, contradictions with far-reaching and profoundly disturbing consequences for his ethics, politics, and ecclesiological assumptions. The paratactic mode helps to conceal these difficulties, enabling the poet to maintain the stance that although the prophetic pose of the Latin *Vox* has been set aside in the *Confessio*, the vernacular Gower remains an auctor in control of his matter, one to whom prince, courtiers, clergy, and people should pay attention, one from whom they have much to learn: "John Gower, *sapiens* in ethics and politics," for sure. The paratactic mode facilitates a paratactic moralism occluding substantial problems. It staves off dialogic relations between units which might force poet, and readers, to address and explore the congruences between aspects of his work and aspects of "Antecristes lollardie." It might force him, and his readers, to suspect that if Lollards are Antichrist's in their reformist challenge to the Roman Church, then the poet may be one of the smaller horns of the beast. And to escape such acknowledgment who would not use any available rhetorical forms?

6

John Wyclif's Understanding of
Christian Discipleship

Et certum est ex fide, quod nemo potest venire ad patriam, nisi fuerit Christi discipulus.

(John Wyclif, *De Officio Pastorali*)[1]

This chapter explores a central area of Wyclif's reformation theology: the constitution of Christian discipleship. It picks up themes and problems we have seen Chaucer (chapter 1 and 2), Thorpe (chapter 1), and Langland (chapter 4) addressing. What is entailed by becoming a disciple of Christ ("Christi discipulus," in the words of the epigraph)? The very fact that Wyclif's writing during the last six years of his life foregrounded Christian discipleship as an issue is a mark of its critical relations to orthodox Catholicism in fourteenth-century England. Within this Catholicism there were a relatively small number of people whose profession elicited special attention to imitating or following Christ: friars, monastics, hermits, anchorites, some priests. These groups were sustained by the lands, commodities, and money given by lay Christians, the vast majority of European Christians. The laity also supported the secular clergy whose class affinities and styles of life ranged from the aristocratic Archbishop Courtenay or Arundel to parish priests and unbeneficed clergy who could be living in a mode shared by middling or lower strata of rural and urban people. Within the well endowed, politically powerful Catholic Church what should constitute Christian discipleship, unlike confession, was not made a topic for reflection in which all Christians (most of whom were lay people) should engage. Let the friars, enclosed orders, some women and some priests pursue the imitation of Christ, under the supervision of duly authorized ecclesiastic superiors, but let most people be content with their role in the traditional practices of the Church and the traditional social order. If they followed these customary roles, through the sacraments and intercessions of their Church, they could reasonably hope to reach their heavenly homeland. Wyclif, however, lost confidence in such a model of the Church and in the Church that sanctioned it.

[1] *Tractatus De Officio Pastorali*, ed. G. V. Lechler (Leipzig: Edelman, 1863), 39. Williel R. Thomson, *The Latin Writings of John Wyclif: An Annotated Catalog* (Toronto: Pontifical Institute of Medieval Studies, 1983), 96, dates as "spring of 1379." All dating of Wyclif's works below is Thomson's, referred to by his name, followed by date and page.

He came to identify the laity's endowment of the Church as the root of all current evils and a disastrous impediment to the practice of Christian discipleship. Constantine's donation was a remarkable poison ("venenum notabile") that disclosed the presence of Antichrist in the Church and was the root of most contemporary troubles.[2] Wyclif's diagnosis and cure, disendowment of the Church, has been described by a number of historians and is well known.[3] When one considers his ecclesiastic program in conjunction with his understanding of Christian discipleship, certain crucial problems emerge. I shall argue that while the problems identified in this chapter are actually disastrous for Wyclif's project of Christian reformation, he himself could not discern them, let alone address them. Although I will not pursue the inquiry beyond Wyclif in this chapter, the contradictions analyzed here are important both for understanding fundamental problems in the project of his English followers and for understanding the historical trajectory to which Wyclif's reformation belongs. This trajectory would take us into the magisterial reformation of sixteenth-century England, the emergence of the Protestant nation-state and the forms of secularization famously and controversially explored long ago by Max Weber and R. H. Tawney. It will become clear that many strands of this trajectory would have appalled Wyclif. But such it is to be human agents: what we describe as our own projects (collective and individual) habitually come from sources of often impenetrable opacity and merge with others in consequences that are very different from anything we might have foreseen, let alone intended. St. Augustine's *Confessions* and *City of God* would have reminded Wyclif himself of this. Whether he himself could take these reminders seriously is not the subject of this chapter.

In exploring Wyclif's account of Christian discipleship a logical place to begin is his representation of Jesus. Wyclif assures his readers, in *De Officio Pastorali*, that "no one can come to the homeland unless he has been the disciple of Christ."[4] This is a characteristic statement. In *De Ecclesia* Wyclif observes that all Christians should strive to follow Christ in all things, as far as they can, and should follow no one else except in so far as that person follows Christ.[5] *De*

---

[2] *Tractatus De Blasphemia*, ed. M. H. Dzieweicki (London: Wyclif Society, 1893), chap. 4, 55; see also 61–61. Thomson, "late summer or fall 1381," 66. This is a recurrent refrain in Wyclif. For example, *Tractatus De Ecclesia*, ed. Johann Loserth (London: Wyclif Society, 1886), chap. 16. Thomson, 1378–79, 58. Of course, until the hierarchy decided otherwise, one did not have to be a heretic to see the Donation of Constantine as anomalous. For example, William Langland, *Piers Plowman: the B-Version*, ed. George Kane and E. Talbot Donaldson, revised edition (London: Athlone, 1988), XV.557–67. All references to *Piers Plowman*, unless otherwise stated, in this chapter are to this edition. See W. A. Pantin, *The English Church in the Fourteenth Century* (Cambridge: Cambridge University Press, 1955), 126–29.

[3] On Wyclif's diagnosis and his proposed cure of the Church, see Gordon Leff, *Heresy in the Later Middle Ages*, 2 vols. (Manchester: Manchester University Press, 1967), 2:516–46.

[4] Latin text in the epigraph to this chapter, see n. 1.

[5] *De Ecclesia*, 195; see also 52.

Officio Regis instructs us to be moved by no teacher's instructions except in so far as they teach us to imitate Christ, the best teacher and the abbot of the whole Christian order.[6] In the *Trialogus*, a late and substantial survey of his views (late 1382 or early 1383), he declares that all the faithful must follow Christ's form of life ("in moribus").[7]

If our salvation entails being a disciple of Christ, and if this involves following Christ's way of life, we need to know his virtues, his ethical practices, his guidance on how we should live together in communities. But how does one discover this vital knowledge? The traditional answer was that one discovers it by living as a Christian in the Roman Church, the spouse and body of Christ. Here, and only here, were the narratives of Christ authoritatively constituted and appropriately understood. Here one encountered the lives of Christ with the sacraments and Scriptures, immersed in the liturgy and mediated by traditions of commentary approved by the Church in which they took place. As the Carmelite Thomas Netter argued in his monumental critique of Wyclif and Wycliffites, *Doctrinale Antiquitatum Fidei Catholicae Ecclesiae*, to Catholic Christianity any splitting apart of Scripture and Church would seem an unwarranted eccentricity: for Christ is in the Church's ministry of word and sacrament, the head giving life to his members. We do indeed find out about Christ in the Scriptures; Christ does indeed speak in the Scriptures. But he also speaks in the Catholic Church in which the sacred canon was determined. Netter opposes any splitting here as a monstrous rending apart of Bridegroom and Bride, of head and body. How, he asks, following Augustine, can we believe Christ, the head, if we disbelieve his Church, the body? How can we even approach Christ if we reject the Church of Christ? How could the people be persuaded of the authority of Scripture separated from the Church?[8] Here Netter draws on both Augustine's accounts of his own relations to Scripture and Augustine's hermeneutics: without the authority of the Church there would be no authoritative canon, and without being directed by the Church one would not know what texts are Scripture, not know how to read sacred texts and not have faith in the Gospel which became such within the Church. Indeed, if we abandon the authority of the Church, Netter maintains, we will not believe the Gospel, and we will come to renounce areas of Christian faith proclaimed in the Creeds.[9]

[6] *Tractatus De Officio Regis*, ed. A. W. Pollard and C. Sayle (London: Wyclif Society, 1887), 278; Thomson, mid-1379, 60.

[7] *Trialogus cum Supplemento Trialog*, ed. G. Lechler (Oxford: Clarendon Press, 1869), 302; the date of the work is taken from Thomson, 79. In his *Sermones*, ed. J. Loserth, 4 vols. (London: Wyclif Society, 1887), 1:358–59, the statement is applied to all Christians. Thomson, 1375–83, 96; on this sermon, 119 (item 108).

[8] Thomas Netter of Walden, *Doctrinale Antiquitatum Fidei Catholicae Ecclesiae*, ed. B. Blanciotti, 3 vols. (facsimile reprint, Farborough: Gregg, 1967). Here I paraphrase from II.25.1–4 (vol. 1, 370–72).

[9] *Doctrinale, seriatim*: II.19.5–6 (vol. 1, 339–40), II.20.3 (344–46), II.21.1 (349), II.23.2 (362). On Netter, see Kantik Ghosh, "'Authority' and 'Interpretation' in Wycliffite, Anti-Wycliffite,

Netter was articulating orthodox ecclesiology, hermeneutic theory, and hermeneutic practice against Wyclif's challenges to these. Given that no one can be saved without becoming the disciple of Christ, how is this crucial knowledge to be discovered? In trying to address this question, Wyclif habitually maintained the division that Netter ascribes to him, a sharp division between Church and Scripture. This ruptured the kind of dialectical and traditional unity that Netter defended.[10] Wyclif maintains that we discover the requisite knowledge from Scripture read in the light of the Holy Spirit and with a sound reason that grasps Scripture's special logic. Scripture read in this way discloses the law of Christ ("Christi lex") and signifies Jesus Christ, the book of life in whom all truth is written. Church, Church fathers, and hierarchy are only to be accepted insofar as they are founded in Scripture: all determinations of the Church that cannot be shown to be founded in Scripture should cease.[11] Here I need not discuss the ways in which the intractable difficulties of Wyclif's hermeneutic theories are bound up with his ecclesiology and ultra-realist metaphysics, nor do I need to address the relations between his theory and his exegetical practice. For present purposes the answer extracted from Wyclif's work is sufficient: you will discover the necessary knowledge about Christian discipleship from Scripture independent of its interpretation and articulation within the Church, articulation that includes liturgy, exegesis, and oral traditions.

What then does this Scripture tell us about Jesus Christ's form of life, the model for discipleship? The model Wyclif generates in text after text can be summarized as follows: Jesus lived as the most materially destitute of people; and although he enjoyed the universal dominion by grace bestowed on the predestinate, he utterly renounced civil dominion, temporal proprietorship, and worldly violence, violence inextricably bound up with the exercise of civil dominion. These propositions are reiterated. For example, in *De Blasphemia*,

and Related Texts, c. 1375–1430" (Ph.D. diss., Cambridge University, 1996), chapter 6. This thesis is due to be published by Cambridge University Press.

[10] Representative disagreements in the interpretation of Wyclif's exegetical theology are those between Paul de Vooght and Michael Hurley. De Vooght, *Les Sources de la doctrine chrétienne d'après les théologiens du XIVe siècle et du début du XVe siècle* (Paris and Bruges: Desclée, de Brouwer, 1954), 168–200. For Hurley, "'Scriptura Sola': Wyclif and his Critics," *Traditio* 16 (1960): 275–352. For the general contexts, see Heiko Oberman, *The Harvest of Medieval Theology* (Cambridge: Harvard University Press, 1963), chap. 11. Three essays by Beryl Smalley remain essential resources in approaching Wyclif's hermeneutics: "John Wyclif's *Postilla super totam Bibliam*," *Bodleian Library Record* 4 (1953): 186–205; "The Bible and Eternity: John Wyclif's Dilemma," *Journal of the Warburg and Courtauld Institute* 27 (1965): 73–89; "Wyclif's *Postilla* on the Old Testament and his *Principium*," in *Essays Presented to Daniel Callus* (Oxford: Oxford University Press, 1964), 253–96. Gordon Leff stresses the importance of Wyclif's metaphysics in his reading of the Bible, *Heresy in the Later Middle Ages*, 2:500–14. For a recent survey of relevant materials, Ghosh "'Authority' and 'Interpretation' in Wycliffite, Anti-Wycliffite, and Related Texts," chap. 1.

[11] These characteristic positions are illustrated in *Trialogus*, III.31 (238–43) and *De Blasphemia*, chapter 3, 44–46, 51. See also *Sermones* 3:390–92. *Trialogus* II.31 offers a nice example of Wyclif's ultra-realist metaphysics in his theology of Scripture.

Wyclif contrasts the life of Christ with that of cardinals and the current ecclesiastic hierarchy: Christ lived as the poorest, lacking all temporal proprietorship.[12] Indeed, if Christ lived and taught now as he once did, by visiting us as a "prelatus incognitus" and challenging contemporary priests with his doctrine and life, it is obvious that he would be excommunicated, and unless he recanted the truth, he would be condemned to the flames as a heretic and blasphemer. Despite this situation, Wyclif insists that Christians must imitate Christ by living similarly to him and to his apostles: this means living as pilgrims, content with little and with what one gets from one's own labor (citing Acts 20.33–34).[13] We should note that this model of discipleship is mandatory for all Christians, not only for a few who belong to special orders of friars or monastics. In the sermons he notes that Christ exercised universal dominion and true innocence in an earthly life utterly free from civil dominion, power, and wealth, a life of genuine destitution. Unlike modern prelates, he humbly tolerated injuries, not even cursing his persecutors (1 Peter 2.23) and espoused the state of destitution. His disciples grasped the model and showed us what imitation means: evangelical poverty, in every way.[14] Similarly, *De Officio Regis* recalls that Christ taught his disciples to live in poverty, utterly free from possessions. Wyclif approvingly quotes Grosseteste's association of the true religious life with Luke 14.33: "So likewise every one of you that doth not renounce all that he possesseth cannot be my disciple."[15] *De Ecclesia* includes the representation of Christ pursuing the path of evangelical poverty, renouncing civil dominion, sharing common goods, and living expropriately, as did the apostles in the early Church.[16] Not surprisingly, then, Wyclif begins *De Paupertate Christi* by emphasizing that Christ, our God, head of the universal Church, was, for the duration of this pilgrimage the poorest man. His fourth conclusion in this work recalls that the poor Christ taught his apostles to beware of dominion, quoting Luke 22.25–26: "The kings of the Gentiles lord it over them . . . but you not so." Since Christ came in the greatest poverty, he notes later, it is not surprising that evangelical poverty is seen as the head of the Christian religion ("caput religionis christiane"). One could easily compile a substantial anthology of such statements from Wyclif's writing, but I will take leave of them with an observation that comes at the end of the twenty-fourth conclusion of *De Paupertate Christi*. Because the exemplary life of Christ is necessary to clergy and laity, it is ordained that the Gospel is read daily in Church and, thus, some part of his life is declared: for all Christians are obliged to follow Christ ("Omnes enim christiani tenentur

---

[12] "Christus enim vixit vitam pauperimam, non habens temporaliter proprium" (*De Blasphemia*, chapter 5, 69).

[13] *De Blasphemia, seriatim*, chap. 4, 62 and chap. 1, 223–24.

[14] *Sermones, seriatim*, sermon 14 (109–12), sermon 19 (147–48, 151). See similarly, *De Ecclesia*, chap. 14, 303; and *Trialogus*, 191–92, 195.

[15] *De Officio Regis*, 63 and 86. The translation of the Latin vulgate is the Douai–Rheims one, *The Holy Bible* (London: Burns and Oates, 1964).

[16] *De Ecclesia*, chap. 8, 178; chap. 14, 303, 306–307.

sequi Christum").[17] Once again, it is important to note that *all* Christians are called to such discipleship, not just some priests and regulars.

The examples offered above have tended to focus on Christ's destitution, his extreme poverty. But they include illustrations of the concomitant emphasis on lack of civil dominion, the renunciation of civil power both in the life of Jesus Christ and in his teaching. As Langland observed in *Piers Plowman*, through the authoritative figure of the neo-Franciscan Patient Poverty:

> Selde sit pouerte þe soþe to declare,
> Or as Iustice to Iugge men enioyned is no poore,
> Ne to be Mair aboue men ne Mynystre vnder kynges;
> Selde is any poore yput to punysshen any peple.
> *Ergo* pouerte and poore men parfournen þe comaundement
> *Nolite iudicare quemquam.*[18]

Haukyn, the "Actif man," had asked whether patient poverty or wealth licitly won and reasonably spent is more pleasing to God.[19] The passage just quoted is part of the long answer he receives from Patient Poverty, an answer in which poverty is presented as a discipline which, when shaped by patience, cultivates specifically Christian virtues and facilitates the avoidance of powerful temptations to set aside the life and teachings of Christ. Here the renunciation of dominion over others is part of the general renunciation of control (over others and the world) which is voluntary poverty (XIV.102–335). The speaker remarks that wealth often impedes the way to heaven and invokes Matthew 19.23–24: "a rich man shall hardly enter into the kingdom of heaven . . . . It is easier for a camel to pass through the eye of a needle than for a rich man to enter the kingdom of heaven." But his own rendering of the Gospel text is even harder: "*Ita inpossible diviti* [Thus it is impossible for a rich man] etc." (XIV.212a: compare Mark 10.23–27 and Luke 18.24–27). Poverty, as Jesus's chosen form of life, is "sib to god hymself" (XIV.273), a form pointing to the freedom from solicitude taught by Jesus (Matthew 6.25–34, Luke 12.22–32).[20] All these responses to the Gospel, part of a neo-Franciscan heritage, were ones Wyclif shared with Langland.[21]

[17] *Conclusiones Triginta Tres Sive de Paupertate Christi* in *Opera Minora*, ed. J. Loserth (London: Wyclif Society, 1913); Thomson, early 1378, 257. My references in this paragraph are *seriatim* to pp. 19, 21, 52, 33, 54.

[18] *Piers Plowman*, XIV.288–93. For an attempt to present *Piers Plowman* as a "coterie" poem produced by a radical Franciscan for radical Franciscans, see Lawrence M. Clopper, *"Songes of Rechlessnesse": Langland and the Franciscans* (Ann Arbor: University of Michigan Press, 1997). On the "coterie" nature of the poem, for example, 320, 333, but the perspective is *passim*. Clopper is unable to produce any "coterie" of "spiritual Franciscans" in London.

[19] XIII.457, XIV.102–103.

[20] On the theme of freedom from solicitude in *Piers Plowman*, see especially M. W. Bloomfield, *Piers Plowman as a Fourteenth-Century Apocalypse* (New Brunswick: Rutgers University Press, 1963), 135 and R. W. Frank, *Piers Plowman and the Scheme of Salvation* (New Haven: Yale University Press, 1957), 29–33.

[21] Of course, Wyclif assumed that these responses cohered with his thoroughly un-

Wyclif's understanding of what is entailed by Christ's renunciation of wealth and civil dominion can be illustrated from *De Officio Regis*. This represents Jesus as the king of peace whose love and counsel moves his people not to make war. The school of Christ stands in patience, in suffering injuries, as Jesus did (1 Peter 2.21–23). Free from any ambiguity, Jesus taught this in word and deed, making it plain that those taking vengeance through the sword (without Christ's own authorization) act against his school. Jesus, after all, could easily have set his armies against his persecutors (Wyclif cites John 18.36), but chose to suffer. This enacted his teaching on non-violence and love of enemy in Matthew 5.38–48, teaching that draws together the virtues of voluntary poverty and non-violence, as Wyclif sees. Invoking Jesus's insistence that commitment to his way must be absolute and that whoever refuses to carry his cross and follow him cannot be his disciple (Luke 14.26–27), Wyclif notes the toughness of this precept. Once more he proclaims that *no one* can be saved without being the disciple of Christ: and, he stresses, *no one* can be a disciple of Christ without fulfilling his command.[22] Coming in a work that includes a political and ecclesiastic program for the king of England, this passage suggests that Christ's teaching and practice of non-violence, one that led to the Cross, was understood by Wyclif to have serious consequences for Christian discipleship, for everyone at all times and in all places.

Wyclif's rejection of the traditional distinction between Christ's counsels and his precepts reinforces this suggestion. It is a very striking move, as Thomas

Langlandian theories of predestination, dominion, and grace. I do not need to address this assumption here because I am concentrating on Wyclif's models of Christian discipleship and his understanding that Jesus renounced civil dominion. Commentators disagree about the political force of Wyclif's theory of dominion. Gordon Leff argued that its subversive potential was largely nullified by his views on the church, the bible, and royal authority (*Heresy in the Later Middle Ages*, 2:546; see also 549). Against this view others have claimed that Wyclif's theory of dominion was of more immediate impact than Leff maintains. See Anne Hudson, *The Premature Reformation: Wycliffite Texts and Lollard History* (Oxford: Clarendon Press, 1988), 359–62. See also H. Kaminsky, "Wycliffism and the Ideology of Revolution," *Church History* 32 (1963): 57–74; Michael Wilks, "Predestination, Property, and Power: Wyclif's Theory of Dominion and Grace," *Studies in Church History* 2 (1965): 220–36 (the force of this fine essay is untouched by Leff's observations in *Heresy in the Later Middle Ages*, 2:564 n. 2). My own view is that Leff's account of the political dimensions of Wyclif's theory of dominion is substantially correct: Wyclif's theory can cast *doubts* on the just entitlement of lords but it can do no more than this, for reasons that Leff has made sufficiently clear. Leff also rightly noted a lack of clarity as to whether the predestinates' lapses into sin excluded them from lordship while sinning (*Heresy in the Later Middle Ages*, 2:548). But given Wyclif's reiteration that one cannot tell whether oneself or anyone else is predestinate, the *theory* seems to me of no consequence in political practice.

[22] See *De Officio Regis*, 266–68; the conclusion of the passage is as follows: "Quod dictum videtur esse preceptum strictissimum, cum nemo potest salvari nisi fuerit Christi discipulus, et nemo potest esse Christi discipulus nisi hec fecerit, ergo nemo potest salvari nisi hec fecerit." See the similar statement in *Sermones*, 4:312, sermon 37. Here John 18.11 is joined with 1 Peter 2.23 in addressing Jesus's decision to be killed rather than to kill.

Netter's criticism makes clear.[23] Wyclif insisted that the conventional distinction between counsels and precepts had no foundations in Scripture. In *De Ecclesia* he treats it as the product of human traditions (habitually seen as antithetical to the binding law of Christ in Scripture) and hypocritical glossing. If you claim to love Christ, then you will be obliged to follow his mild counsels, abandoning the precepts of the world.[24] A similar line is pursued in *Opus Evangelicum*. Considering Christ's teaching on non-violence and love of enemy in Matthew 5.38–42, Wyclif notes his rejection of the law propounded in Exodus 21.24–25 ("Eye for eye, tooth for tooth, hand for hand, foot for foot,/ Burning for burning, wound for wound, stripe for stripe"). Christ commands the renunciation of retribution and the acceptance of injury, a practice which Wyclif presents as quite contrary to the habits of modern Christians. Here he turns to the conventional distinction between counsels for those pursuing perfection and commands which must be obeyed by all Christians. He unequivocally rejects this distinction. The counsel of so great a lord must be accepted by all his children as command. Wyclif invites his readers to think of the way earthly lords are served by their subordinates, how even the silent indications of their will are fulfilled, let alone their overt counsels and commands: how much more is such behavior required by the Lord of lords. Whoever sets aside the counsel of so great a patron violates the command of God and most ungratefully, and most stupidly, offends that Lord and patron. No one can excuse himself from Christ's counsels, he insists, and these call for the humble patience displayed by Christ himself in his Passion and practiced by the martyrs.[25]

This seems an unequivocal critique of the received distinction and its ethical consequences. It is certainly congruent with Wyclif's attack on the donation of Constantine as the poison that corrupts the Church, for Wyclif is challenging a distinction that emerged in the period when Christianity became the official religion of the Roman empire. It was part of the response to the mass admittance of people to the Church in a context (by the end of the fourth century) where public worship by anyone other than Christians had been banned, and open adherence to paganism had become a serious social disadvantage, part of the shifts that transformed the meaning of Christian discipline and discipleship. As John Yoder remarked in his study of "The Constantinian Sources of Western Social Ethics":

---

[23] For example, see Netter's criticism in *Doctrinale*, ed. Blanciotti, III.12 (especially vol. 1:738–41).

[24] *De Ecclesia*, chap. 3, 52: "Nec valet glosa ypocrite quod hec sunt consilia, non precepta. Si enim sunt Christi consilia et tu in habitu pretendis te super alios Christum diligere, adheres eius leni consilio, preceptis seculi pretermissis; aliter enim fores ypocrita, offendens in dilectione Dei super omnia." However, the continuation of this passage shows the constitutive split in his thinking even here as he says that the "officium" of administering temporalities belongs to the Christians classified as laity, while it is up to priests to pursue Christ's path (52–53).

[25] *Opus Evangelicum*, ed. J. Loserth, 2 vols. (London: Wyclif Society, 1895); Thomson, 1383– end of 1384, 220, 221. Here vol.1:191–93, chap. 52.

The "evangelical counsels" will be commended to the religious and highly motivated. The "precepts," less demanding, will suffice for catechesis and the confessional. Two levels, two kinds of motivations and sanctions will be discerned, entailing different specific duties (contradictory ones, in fact, at points such as power, property, marriage, bloodshed, which were morally proper for the laity but not for the religious).[26]

Wyclif, so it seems, is committed to undoing such "human tradition," to curing the Church of the poison it drank and reforming it to a community in which Christ's counsels were acknowledged as constituting a distinctively Christian discipleship. Such a cure would certainly have radical consequences in Wyclif's social world. This was, after all, a culture in which governing elites were not only wealthy and powerful but also shaped by a politics of honor in which retaliating force and the carnal sword were central.[27]

Did Wyclif's critique and cure include a vision of the priesthood of all Christians? One can see the reasons for answering in the affirmative: his dismissal of the conventional division between counsels and precepts, combined with his neo-Franciscan version of discipleship for all Christians; his rejections of the centrally sacramental role of priests in traditional Catholicism (not unrelated to his rejection of the doctrine of transubstantiation); his substitutions of preaching for the sacrament of the altar as the major task of the priest; his exceptionally sharp division between the invisible and visible Church. All these moves seem to encourage the claims about the priesthood of all believers made by some of his early followers.[28] And there are modern commentators who have

---

[26] The quotation is from J. H. Yoder, *The Priestly Kingdom: Social Ethics as Gospel* (Notre Dame: University of Notre Dame Press, 1984), 139; see also chap. 7. I also draw on Yoder, *Christian Attitudes to War, Peace, and Revolution* (Elkhart, IN: Peace Resources Center, 1983; distributed by Cokesbury Bookstore, Duke Divinity School, 1998), chaps. 1–3, chap. 18. For a modern theologian defending Constantinian Christianity, see Wolfhart Pannenberg, *Systematic Theology*, vol. 3, trans. G. W. Bromiley (Grand Rapids: Eerdmans, 1998), 509–11. See also the helpful survey by François Paschoud, "La doctrine chrétienne et l'idéologie imperiale romaine," in *L'Apocalypse de Jean*, ed. Y. Christe (Geneva: Droz, 1979), 31–72. For an example of early thirteenth-century uses of the donation that are orthodox, see R. E. Lerner, "Poverty, Preaching, and Eschatology in the Revelation Commentaries of 'Hugh of St. Cher,'" in *The Bible in the Medieval World*, ed. K. Walsh and D. Wood (Oxford: SCH, Blackwell, 1985), 157–89.

[27] For an excellent introduction to these issues see Mervyn James, *English Politics and the Concept of Honor, 1485–1642* (Oxford: Past and Present Society Monographs, 1979). Also relevant and helpful here: Maurice Keen, *Chivalry* (New Haven: Yale University Press, 1984); Peter Coss, *The Knight in Medieval England* (Stroud: Sutton, 1993); Richard Kaeuper, *War, Justice, and Public Order: England and France in the Later Middle Ages* (Oxford: Clarendon Press, 1988), chaps. 1–3. For a classic example of the chivalric and political honor at issue, see *The Life of the Black Prince* by the Herald of Sir John Chandos, ed. and trans. M. K. Pope and E. C. Lodge (Oxford: Clarendon Press, 1910). A far more ambivalent product of this class, riven by the pressures of a Christian account of virtues and vices, is Duke Henry of Lancaster's *Le Livre de Seyntz Medicines* (Oxford: Blackwell, 1940).

[28] For a lucid account of these issues in Wyclif and his followers, see Anne Hudson, *Premature Reformation*, 325–27, 351–58, 281–301 (on the sacraments). See also *English*

ascribed such claims to Wyclif himself. In 1996 Stephen Lahey wrote that according to the reformer, "all Christians are, in fact, priests," while seventy years earlier, in a more Wycliffite vocabulary, Herbert Workman maintained that "Wyclif's doctrine involves the universal priesthood of the predestinate."[29] Gordon Leff's nuanced account of these issues in his survey of late medieval heresy decided that Wyclif's position "was tantamount to a denial of the priesthood as an order."[30] Such readings certainly recall the line taken by John Purvey and some of the East Anglian Lollards persecuted in the late 1420s. For example, Hawisia Mone maintained "that every man and every woman beyng in good lyf oute of synne is as good prest and hath as muche poer of God in al thynges as ony prest ordred, be he pope or bisshop." This view was shared by her friend Margery Baxter and others recorded in the Bishop of Norwich's court-book.[31] Did Wyclif teach them this?

My own reading of Wyclif agrees with Anne Hudson's passing comment in *The Premature Reformation*: "Hints of such an idea are to be found in Wyclif, but Netter seems accurate in perceiving it to be more fully developed in his followers."[32] Furthermore, the "hints" are customarily in contexts that make their consequences for the future of the Church less than specific and perhaps less than specifiable. For instance, *De Potestate Pape* affirms that all holy men and women who are members of Christ are priests.[33] This sounds like Hawisia Mone. But the context reminds us of Wyclif's ultra-Augustinian predestinarianism and his distinctive understanding of "Church." He is talking about only the

Wycliffite Sermons [hereafter *EWS*], ed. Pamela Gradon and Anne Hudson, 5 vols. (Oxford: Clarendon Press, 1983–96), 4:111–20; Leff, *Heresy in the Later Middle Ages*, 2:520–27, 549–57, 579–80. For a clear statement of the priesthood of believers, see John Purvey in *Fasciculi Zizaniorum Magistri Johannis Wyclif* [hereafter *FZ*], ed. W. W. Shirley (London: Longman, 1858), 387, 390, 402. For the traditional account of priesthood of all believers through participation in the priesthood of Christ, see St. Thomas, *Summa Theologiae* III.63.3. The edition of the *Summa* I use is *Summa Theologica* [sic], 4 vols. in 6 (Rome: Forzanus, 1894). Also, see *De Regimine Principum*, I.15.9, "all the faithful of Christ, insofar as they are his members, are called Kings and priests," in *On the Government of Rulers: "De Regimine Principum": Ptolemy of Lucca with Portions Attributed to Thomas Aquinas*, trans. James M. Blythe (Philadelphia: University of Pennsylvania Press, 1997).
[29] Stephen Lahey, "Toleration in the Theology and Social Thought of John Wyclif," in *Difference and Dissent: Theories of Tolerance in Medieval and Early Modern Europe*, ed. Cary J. Nederman and John C. Laursen (New York: Rowman and Littlefield, 1996), 40; Herbert B. Workman, *John Wyclif: A Study of the Medieval Church*, 2 vols. (Oxford: Clarendon Press, 1926), 2:12–13.
[30] Leff, *Heresy in the Later Middle Ages*, 2:520; compare 2:527.
[31] *Heresy Trials in the Diocese of Norwich 1428–31*, ed. Norman P. Tanner (London: Royal Historical Society, Camden 4th series, vol. 20, 1977), 142; see also 42, 49, 52, 60–61, 67, 81, 147, 166, 179, 205. Contrast, however, *The Lanterne of Liȝt*, ed. L. M. Swinburn (EETS o.s. 151, 1917), 34–35, 59–60.
[32] *Premature Reformation*, 325; and *EWS*, 4:11–20.
[33] John Wyclif, *Tractatus de Potestate Pape*, ed. J. Loserth (London: Wyclif Society, 1907). Thomson, "Fall 1379," 62. "Omnes sancti viri et femine membra Christi sunt sacerdotes" (312).

predestinate for these only are members of Christ or part of holy mother Church and, properly speaking, Christians.[34] And these, as Wyclif so often reiterates, can now be known as such by no one, not even the predestined.[35] Given the complete hiddenness of these predestinate members of Christ, alone true priests, it becomes clear that claims such as those made by Hawisia Mone have set aside Wyclif's own theological framework and the qualifications demanded by its metaphysical convictions. It can make no sense in Wyclif's framework to claim the priesthood of all believers, if "believers" is understood in anything like its traditional sense (a baptized member of the Catholic Church who fulfills the basic demands of that Church, such as annual confession and reception of the eucharist). But taking "believers" in Wyclif's sense, what are the practical consequences for the Church? They are not at all obvious. True priests cannot be known by themselves or anyone else (except by the kind of guess-work from the appearance of works that Wyclif customarily practices). So how is the Church on earth to proceed? Are there to be priests who constitute a determinate order in the Church?

In *De Officio Regis* Wyclif asserts that a pope or a priest need not be a cleric ("clericus"), while *De Eucharistia* argues that God can give a layman ("layco") the power to consecrate and to fulfill the other offices of priesthood. Yet these laity, *De Eucharistia* makes clear, are the predestinate.[36] And, as we have noted, nobody knows who they are. But Wyclif does seem to envisage a distinct order of priesthood, however obscure its identity and warrants may be. In *De Quattuor Sectis Novellis* he states that any predestinate person is a priest in the homeland. However, this does not mean that a layperson should exercise all the rites and works of priests nor that the faithful should despise a bishop's consecration without a revelation.[37] The late summary of his views, *Trialogus*, addresses the sacrament of orders in the fourth book.[38] Phronesis, Wyclif's spokesman, summarizes received teaching on ordination. He maintains that in the early church ("in primitiva ecclesia"), there were two orders of clerics, priest ("sacerdos") and deacon ("diaconus"). In apostolic times, he says, there was no distinction between priest ("presbyter") and bishop ("episcopus"). He thus affirms that the distinct order of priesthood is founded in Scripture and therefore remains a legitimate part of the Church.[39] What kind of coherence,

---

[34] *De Potestate Pape*, 312–13: "solum predestinati sunt membra Christi vel pars sancte matria ecclesie et proprie christiani."

[35] For a typical example, *De Officio Regis*, 133: "licet abscondite." On this issue, Leff, *Heresy in the Later Middle Ages*, 2:518–19.

[36] John Wyclif, *De Officio Regis*, 149 and *De Eucharistia Tractatus Maior*, ed. J. Loserth (London: Wyclif Society, 1892), 98–99; Thomson, "mid to late 1380," 67.

[37] *De Quattuor Sectis Novellis* in Wyclif's *Polemical Works* (London: Wyclif Society, 1883), 259; Thomson, "mid 1383," 296.

[38] Thomson dates *Trialogus*, late 1382 or early 1383, 79. See *Trialogus* IV.15 (*De Sacramentis Ordinis*), IV.16 (*De Possessione Temporalium Clero Concessa*), and IV.18 (*Reges ac Dominos hac ipsa de Causa Reprehendos Esse*). With these, see also IV.1 (*De Signis et Sacramentis*).

[39] Here see *Trialogus*, IV.15, 297.

if any, does this distinction between priests and laity have in Wyclif's version of the Church and in his ecclesiology? Why did he, unlike some of his followers, retain the distinction? What were the consequences within his political theology? These questions are central ones in our exploration of Wyclif's understanding of Christian discipleship. In addressing them I am particularly interested in the fate of those Scriptural narratives we have seen Wyclif invoking as foundational, those that disclose Jesus Christ's commitment to the renunciation of dominion and violence. We will recollect his proclamation, reiterated in Book 4 of the *Trialogus*, that we must all follow Christ in our way of living ("omnes debemus sequi Christum in moribus . . . omnes fideles sequi Christum in moribus").[40]

After discussing the order of priesthood in the *Trialogus*, Wyclif considers priests' specific office. He argues that clerics ("clerici") are those Christians who are actually obliged to follow Christ's path. We must all follow Christ's path, he has stressed, but priests seem obligated in a different and more binding way. We will pursue the grounds of this distinction in due course, but it is worth noting how vehement Wyclif is in claiming that priestly failure to follow Christ's renunciation, to live like Christ ("more Christi"), is heresy, apostasy, and blasphemy.[41] In this context he proclaims one of his most reiterated formulations. The leading cleric, the pope (whose scriptural warrant, the only one that matters to Wyclif, he has just denied and whose office he has just advocated abolishing) is the vicar of Christ ("vicarius Christi") and he should certainly follow the form of life Christ chose in his humanity, a life of poverty and non-violence. The leading layman, the king should be the vicar of God ("vicarius Deitatis"). As such, this Christian *must use violence*. Why? To coerce, sternly, with compelling force, those who rebel against and disturb God's order (invoking Romans 13.4).[42] In *De Officio Regis* Wyclif states that it is necessary for mother Church to have secular lords ("seculares dominos") who can defend her forcefully.[43] So those Christians who participate in secular power do not, after all, have to follow the path of Jesus, do not have to embrace "the humanity of Christ" even as a model, let alone as a decisive model. On the contrary, such Christians can follow Christ in a manner that *sidelines* Jesus, "the humanity of God." Not only can, but must. The radical critic of Constantinianized Christianity has generated a story in which most Christians can, and some must, follow God's will by setting aside Jesus's own disclosure of what following God's will entails, of what constitutes the Kingdom of God. Neither here nor elsewhere, as he indefatigably repeats these moves, does

[40] *Trialogus*, IV.16, 302.
[41] *Trialogus*, IV.15, 298–99. For a similarly vehement definition of heresy, see the Wycliffite work printed under the title, *Remonstrance against Romish Corruptions in the Church*, ed. J. Forshall (London: Longman, 18–51), 4–7.
[42] *Trialogus*, IV.15, 297–98. For other examples of frequent statements that the lay power is the vicar of God, see *De Officio Regis*, 4–5, 13–14, 54–55, 121–22; *De Ecclesia*, 12, 254; *De Potestate Pape*, 12, 377–78. See Hudson, *Premature Reformation*, 362–67 and Leff, *Heresy in the Later Middle Ages*, 2:543–45, an excellent summary.
[43] *De Officio Regis*, 121 (line 32)–122.

Wyclif ask whether he might be reintroducing aspects of the Constantinian settlement he has condemned as poison. As he sets aside "the humanity of Christ" (elsewhere, as we have seen, the indispensable model for Christian discipleship), as he discovers a way of following God's will unaffected by the Incarnation, it seems not to cross his mind that he could be making the mistake Jesus corrects in John 14.7–10:

> If you had known me, you would without doubt have known my Father also
> . . . Philip saith to him: Lord, shew us the father; and it is enough for us.
> Jesus saith to him: Have I been so long a time with you and have you not
> known me? Philip, he that seeth me seeth the Father also . . .
> Do you not believe that I am in the Father and the Father in me? The words
> that I speak to you, I speak not of myself. But the Father who abideth in me,
> he doth the works.

Why would Wyclif, with his Scriptural foundationalism, fail to consider the relevance of this passage, and others propounding similar teachings in the New Testament, to the moves under consideration? The ensuing discussion provides one answer.

Building on the distinction between priests and laity, *Trialogus* IV.16 proceeds to attack clerical wealth. Wyclif takes up a text we have already encountered in his reflections on Christian discipleship: "every one of you that doth not renounce all that he possesseth cannot be my disciple" (Luke 14.33). He remarks that the practice of Christ and his disciples is the best interpretation of the precepts, and cites Matthew 10.21–25, "The disciple is not above the master, nor the servant above his lord. It is enough for the disciple that he be as his master." This is the kind of perspective from which our exploration of Wyclif's understanding of Christian discipleship set out, one represented in the chapter's epigraph. Jesus is without civil dominion (citing Matthew 8.20), and Wyclif quotes the powerful exchange between Jesus and his disciples in Luke 22.24–26:

> And there was also a strife amongst them, which of them should seem to be
> the greater.
> And he said to them: The kings of the Gentiles lord it over them; and they
> that have power over them are called beneficent. But you not so: but he that is
> the greater among you, let him become as the younger: and he that is the
> leader, as he that serveth.

None of these texts on Christian discipleship give any encouragement to the moves Wyclif has just made, ones that generate a form of Christianity in which the life and teaching of Jesus can be set aside. But that is no impediment to Wyclif's hermeneutics. He simply splits open "you" in "But you not so [vos autem non sic]." Without the slightest warrant from text or context, he glosses Jesus's words as propounding the split between priesthood and laity that Wyclif now desires. Only the former, apparently, need to renounce worldly greatness and all that composes it. Only a very tiny minority of Christians is, allegedly, addressed by Jesus's command, "But you not so." Only these Christians are to be vilified as "disciples of Antichrist" for involvement in the practices opposed by Christ's precepts in the texts just quoted. Somehow the vast majority of Christians, the laity, are not called to this obedience.[44] But even then Wyclif recollects Paul's statement that Christ "became poor for your sakes" (2 Corinthians 8.9), observing "all the faithful" should follow Christ's form of life. However, this statement is swiftly assimilated to the preceding exegesis: clerics are those who really are obliged to follow Christ's life and precepts, "specially [specialiter]." Wyclif does not acknowledge that the split his exegesis has introduced owes nothing to Jesus or Paul but a great deal to the Constantinian traditions he vilifies. Instead of pausing over this, he turns to his habitual attack on contemporary clergy for their involvement in secular affairs, that is, the affairs of lay Christians. Taking a text that warns Christians against becoming entangled with secular business (2 Timothy 2.3–5), Wyclif assimilates it to his own split between Christians who are laity and those who are clerics. He once more invokes Luke 14.33, turning it in the same way, and confidently reasserts his judgment that a cleric involved in secular affairs cannot be the disciple of Christ but is rather the disciple of Antichrist.[45] The moves I have been following are reiterated; they are a constituent part of his version of reformation. Only clergy are to be held to evangelical teaching on renunciation: those Christians classified as lay people can continue with business as usual (according to their social class, status, occupation, and gender). And if business is to continue as usual, it is clearly imperative that Wyclif maintain the distinction between the order of priesthood and the laity even as he had seemed to dissolve it. I will return to the consequences of Wyclif's procedures, but for the moment stay with book four of the *Trialogus*.

In chapter seventeen Wyclif defends his criticism of Constantine's donation.[46] In doing so he emphasizes that Christ's teaching calls disciples to renunciations that are illicitly negated by the donation (Matthew 10.9–10 is cited as the guide: "Do not possess gold, nor silver, nor money in your purses,/ Nor scrip for your journey, nor two coats, nor shoes, nor a staff"). Temporal lords should only donate, moderately, to the poor listed in Luke 14.13, while able-bodied beggars should be forced to work.[47] There are, he finds, no grounds for the endowment of the Church. Christ and his apostles rejected all the dominion and possession legitimated by earthly justice. For Christ's rule is that none of his disciples should contend for temporal goods. Here Wyclif quotes from Luke 6.30 (misascribed to Matthew 6): "of him that taketh away thy goods, ask them not again." He notes that civil laws and the custom of those with secular

[44] *Trialogus*, IV.16, 299–301.
[45] *Trialogus*, IV.16, 302.
[46] *Trialogus*, IV.17, 303–306.
[47] Such statements by Wyclif and his followers are obviously directed against religious mendicants, but they should be seen in the ethical, political, and social contexts explored in Aers, *Community, Gender, and Individual Identity in English Writing: 1360–1430* (London: Routledge, 1988), chap. 1.

dominion are very far removed from Christ's command. The stage seems set for Wyclif to reconsider the splitting of Christian discipleship that we have been tracing, to undertake some searching explorations of the relevant tensions, explorations such as Langland undertook in *Piers Plowman*.[48] But this does not happen; nor does anything remotely like it. For Wyclif seems impervious to any tensions in his treatment of the Gospels, simply concluding that the texts exclude *clerics* from worldly laws, the worldly management of temporalities, from the solicitude and conflict they involve. Once more, the vast majority of Christians are delivered from having to engage seriously with the evangelical ethics Wyclif had recounted and continued to quote. Not once does he comment on the fate of his unequivocal rejection of the traditional distinction between Christ's counsels and precepts. There seems to be no indication that he was aware of reintroducing the rejected move.

Chapter eighteen of *Trialogus* IV invites us to concentrate on aspects of Christian discipleship from which we set out: non-violence and the renunciation of dominion. The chapter begins with one of the interlocutors praising Wyclif for his customary invectives against priestly cupidity, the root of all evils (1 Timothy 6.10): priests, he says, should be the root of justice drawing lay people to heaven. The formulation reinforces the split we have been tracing between the mass of lay Christians and priests. On these foundations, he asks whether lay people should be rebuked for endowing the clergy.[49] Wyclif's own spokesman notes that he (*Phronesis, alias* John Wyclif) has often been charged with a failure to criticize the sins of lay lords. He claims that he wishes to remedy any omission here. One might expect that this would lead to some examination of the striking differences between Jesus's teaching and the forms of life that *constitute* secular lordship in Wyclif's culture. One might anticipate some concern with the latter's relation to the evangelical warnings Wyclif so frequently deployed (for example, Luke 6.24–25, Luke 18.24–30). Such concern was not unknown to contemporary lay lords.[50] But that is not the way Wyclif chooses. Instead, he names the lay elite's endowment of the Church as their grave sin. So displeasing is this to God that he has punished them. How? By making many of them poor, according to the theologian. Wyclif's thinking is so shaped by the split emerging in the Constantinian settlement, which he both opposes and reproduces, that he feels no pressure to mention his own insistence, reiterated elsewhere, that impoverishment is a privilege, a divine gift.[51] When he attacks the donation of Constantine he actually turns out to be attacking the erosion of the split between laity and priests, a split whose sources are, ironically enough, remote from the evangelical texts from which he claims his authority. Equally remote is his remedy for the possessing classes' sin: their forceful disendowment

[48] See, for example, X.23–111, XIII–XV, XIX.383–406, 465–79a.
[49] *Trialogus*, IV.18, 307.
[50] A particularly good example from Wyclif's England comes from the father-in-law of his most powerful protector, Henry of Lancaster's *Le Livre de Seyntz Medicines*, see n. 27.
[51] *Trialogus*, IV.18, 307. Compare *De Ecclesia*, chapter 7, 176–80.

of the Church. In a use of his letter that Paul may not have anticipated, Wyclif cites Romans 13.1–5 to show the lay powers their duty to strip the Roman Church of its possessions. Not to act thus is itself a sin. Furthermore he now represents Jesus as a model for precisely such organized coercive force, having, as we saw, frequently presented him as a model of renouncing dominion, violence, and wealth. This turn is attached to John 2.13–22, where Jesus drives from the temple those selling coinage and animals necessary for enacting traditional sacrifices. John places the episode at the beginning of the ministry, a prophetic sign in which Jesus proclaims his Sonship (John 2.16). Wyclif's gloss is that Christ is attacking the priests ("sacerdotes") and deploying his regal power.[52] From this reading he goes on to consider relations between Christ and the lay ruling classes.

They hold their power from Christ and, so Wyclif argues, should therefore revenge any injury done to him. Jesus becomes a feudal overlord. And yet Wyclif knew many New Testament texts in which Jesus is shown to practise the antithesis to a feudal ethic of revenge and honor. But these are not considered here. The basic split I have followed encourages him to set them aside: leave them to the tiny minority of Christians called "clerics" (a minority Wyclif wanted to diminish substantially) and let the lay elites force these texts down priests' throats. He recalls John 14.15: "If you love me, keep my command-ments." How else should secular lords show their love of Christ than by using worldly power to defend his order? Wyclif apparently thinks this so obvious that he does not find it necessary to discuss Jesus's rejection of all such "defense" in his life, death, and teaching. He models Christ as an offended lord whose wife has been violated and whose kingdom laid to waste: his faithful lieges will know the revenge due to his enemies.[53] Given this kind of exegesis Wyclif's account of Jesus Christ's special favor to the wealthy and powerful of the world is probably less surprising. But in the present context it is important that we take note of it.

According to the reformer, Christ's special favor to lords is shown in six ways. (1) Christ, the lord of time, chose to be born when secular dominion most flourished, a proposition grounded in Luke 2.1. Christ is allegedly blessing the secular power of the Roman empire, a view that would certainly have bemused the writer of the Apocalypse. (2) Jesus Christ could have ruled all worldly kingdoms had he wished, but he was unwilling to diminish secular power in the slightest. Wyclif wheels in Matthew 8.20 to support the assertion: "The foxes have holes and the birds of the air nests: but the son of man hath not where to lay his head." In Matthew, these words are directed to someone wanting to follow Jesus as a disciple. Interpreting them as words designed to safeguard contemporary secular dominion illustrates the exegetical licence Wyclif allowed himself even as he castigated others for glossing Scripture against the grain. (3) Christ was so committed to sustaining secular dominion that he arranged the

---

[52] *Trialogus*, IV.18, 308.
[53] *Trialogus*, IV.18, 308–309. A comparison with Chaucer's *Melibee* would be fruitful.

plundering of the priests of his temple in Jerusalem. Wyclif cites Luke 19 to support this assertion, presumably having in mind Jesus weeping over Jerusalem, foreseeing its destruction by the Romans (Luke 19.41–44). (4) Christ paid tribute to Caesar. (Oddly enough, Wyclif cites Matthew 17.23–27, a passage in which Jesus pays the *temple* tax.) (5) Christ determined that the goods of Caesar should be given to Caesar, "Render therefore to Caesar the things that are Caesar's" (see Matthew 22.15–22). (6) Christ has maintained the lay power's rule over their poor tenants, teaching them through the Gospels and apostolic writings how they should obey lords. Indeed, he made, redeemed, and rewarded secular lords.[54]

Despite these six manifestations of Christ's special favor to secular lords they have responded ungratefully. The donation of Constantine represents their rejection of Christ's order. Here Wyclif tells a famous story: when Constantine endowed the Church an angelic voice was heard pronouncing that poison had now been shed into the holy Church of God.[55] Wyclif sees this as a diminishment of the imperial power and secular lordship which, according to him, Christ had come to sustain. Elsewhere, as we have seen, he stressed Christ's own renunciation of everything connected with secular, civil power: dominion, jurisdiction, honor, possessions. Such renunciation constituted a model for Christian discipleship. But here a very different model is constructed. So we encounter a position like this: Constantinian endowment of the Church is a poison, purge it; Constantinian, imperialized Christianity is what Jesus Christ intended – except for the tiny minority of Christians who are "clerics." What then should the secular powers do to show their gratitude and obedient discipleship to the crucified and risen lord? They must use their secular power to take away all temporalities from the Church (understood only as clerics here, of course): Wyclif asserts not only that this is a licit action but that lay lords must do it if they are to avoid damnation.[56] Furthermore, the reformer sanctifies thoroughly worldly, secular motives. Lay elites must disendow clerics if they want to maintain their secular lordship in its full power and keep their tenants duly subordinate to them. Only thus will they deliver themselves from any of the threats they had experienced in June 1381.[57] Wonderful to relate, such

[54] The bizarre use of the "didrachma" in Matt. 17.23–27 is also found in *De Officio Pastorali*, I.3, 10. The sixth item is relevant to work by Steven Justice and Anne Hudson on Wyclif and the great rebellion of 1381. For the former, *Writing and Rebellion: England*, chap. 2. For the latter, "*Piers Plowman* and the Peasants' Revolt," *YLS* 8 (1995): 85–106. The relevant text from *Trialogus* IV.18 is as follows: "Christus tenentes pauperes dominorum secularium pavit, sanavit, et in obedientia facienda illis multipliciter instruxit, ut patet ex decursu evangeli et scriptis apostoli, quomodo servi debent dominis suis obedire, et . . . Christus dominos temporales fecit, redemit et finaliter praemiavit" (309).

[55] *Trialogus*, IV.18, 309–10. For Langland's use of the legend, see *Piers Plowman*, XV.557–69.

[56] *Trialogus*, IV.18, 311: "Nos autem dicimus illis, quod nedum possunt auferre temporalia ab ecclesia habitualiter delinquente, nec solum quod *licet* illis hoc facere sed quod *debent* sub poena damnationis gehennae, cum debent de sua stultitia poenitere et satisfacere pro peccato, quo Christi ecclesiam macularunt."

[57] *Trialogus*, IV.18, 310. The best introduction to the 1381 rising remains Rodney Hilton, *Bond*

a materially self-interested reformation of the Church will bring in a new golden age for Christians: clerical simony will disappear along with sloth and heresy among Christ's clergy; wars will cease, as will the "translatio" of kingdoms through conquests and the inequitable plunder of poor tenants.[58] All this will result from the expropriation of ecclesiastical dominion by the hand of the secular powers. On top of these joys more souls will fly to heaven. The blasphemy of papal indulgences, "a poena et culpa," will cease along with an unspecified infinity of other blasphemies.[59]

Wyclif elaborates his understanding of Christian discipleship in *De Officio Pastorali*.[60] In the third chapter he considers a command of Jesus that we have already seen him glossing: "The kings of the Gentiles lord it over them, and they that have power over them are called beneficent. / But you not so: but he that is greater among you, let him be as the younger: and he that is the leader, as he that serveth" (Luke 22.25–26). Here Wyclif invokes this text in a *defense* of the role of secular power in the Church. He does so by imposing a threefold division onto Jesus's statement. First, necessary to salvation is the renunciation of the immoderate love of worldly goods. In support of this gloss he quotes a saying of Jesus from Luke 14.33 (cited as Luke 13.33): "everyone of you that doth not renounce all that he possesseth cannot be my disciple [nisi quis renunciaverit omnibus que possidet, non potest meus esse discipulus]." The disparity between gloss and texts is very striking. The imperiousness of Wyclif's scheme imposes distinctions in degrees of renunciation, imposes criteria of what is necessary to salvation and turns renunciation of Jesus's "all" into the indeterminate renunciation of the immoderate love of temporalities. And it does so without comments on the exegetical decisions, without self-reflection. The second stage of renunciation, according to Wyclif, is renunciation of temporalities that exceed the needs of one's office. The third degree of renunciation is stricter and pertains to priests alone. They must abandon worldly goods that are not necessary to the divine office of priesthood, and this includes secular dominion and endowments.[61] Once more Wyclif glosses Jesus's statements about discipleship to fit his own version of the sharp division between laity and priests. He makes Jesus offer a model of discipleship that only

Men Made Free (London: Temple, 1973), part 2, with Kaeuper, *War, Justice, and Public Order*, chap. 4.

[58] *Trialogus*, IV.18, 310. On the plundering of poor tenants, the 1381 Rising, and his own characteristically uni-causal account of the rising's genesis, see *De Blasphemia*, chap. 13, 190–91, 196–98. As usual, the root of all problems and conflicts is the endowment of the clergy: were these people disendowed, the king would not have needed to tax the people in the way he did, and they would not have rebelled (190–91).

[59] *Trialogus*, IV.18, 310; see also IV.19, where Wyclif maintains the urgency of his insistence that secular powers act now to expropriate the Church. His spokesman declares that no scholastic issue is closer to his heart than this. King and kingdom risk damnation by not enacting Wyclif's version of reformation (311–13).

[60] *De Officio Pastorali*, see n. 1. For an English version, see *English Wycliffite Tracts 1–3*, ed. C. Lindberg (Oslo: Novus Forlag, 1991).

[61] *De Officio Pastorali*, I.3, 10–11.

pertains to the priesthood. As for the laity, their discipleship seems defined by the kind of inner moderation towards worldly goods that any stoic would aim to cultivate: to renounce the immoderate love of temporal goods ("renunciare immoderato amori eorum [temporalium]"). There seems nothing distinctively Christocentric about such temperance, nothing specifically Christian.[62] Whose account of the virtues and whose life are Wyclif's imagined laity actually being invited to follow? We began this chapter with Wyclif's statements on the decisive role of the Gospels' narratives of Jesus in any understanding of Christian discipleship. *De Officio Pastorali* itself opened with one of these statements.[63] However, the version of Christian discipleship now emerging is more complex, and far less cohesive, than the apparent clarity of such statements would lead one to expect. Furthermore, we have just seen how Wyclif's ways of reading the Gospels are in the service of cultural, political, and ethical convictions which will entertain no resistance, not even from texts he ascribes to Truth.[64]

This is nicely illustrated in his claim that God granted secular dominion for men to defend the law of Christ with secular power, to force subordinates to join the sect of the Lord.[65] Wyclif simply assumes that the gospel of the kingdom preached and embodied by Jesus (for example, Matthew 4.23–24, 5.38–48) *needs* secular power, *needs* the carnal sword. Despite his radical, passionate, endless assault on his Church and the donation of Constantine, he could not recognize his own internalization of certain fundamental arrangements and their legitimizing ideologies. This proved to be so even when he was reading texts that most sharply called these into question. What I find remarkable is his apparent lack of any anxiety or puzzlement as he turns texts such as Luke 22:25–26 (disciples must renounce dominion and choose the place of slave) into texts commanding disciples of Christ to wield carnal power with the aim of forcing people to follow Jesus. Of course, one would hardly be surprised to find orthodox members of Wyclif's Church propagating such exegesis and its ideology. The Church had long since cobbled together a theory of justifiable war, including crusades, and a theory sanctifying the flogging, imprisonment, and burning of Christians judged to be pertinacious heretics.[66] It is worth recalling how Augustine's *De Correctione Donatistarum* had

---

[62] *De Officio Pastorali*, I.3, 10. For the attempt to develop a strictly Christian view of temperance, one that comes between the theological virtues and the work of Christ, see St. Thomas, *ST*, II–II.141–70. For a recent consideration of these issues, see Stanley Hauerwas and Charles Pinches, *Christians Among the Virtues* (Notre Dame: University of Notre Dame Press, 1997).

[63] *De Officio Pastorali*, II.1, 7–8; see also II.4, 39.

[64] On Wyclif's hermeneutics, see n. 10.

[65] *De Officio Pastorali*, I.3, 11: "deus enim concessit seculare dominum, ut homo potestative defendat legem Christi et compellat inferiores intrare in sectam domini."

[66] This is, of course, a complex history. The following are basic works: Frederick Russell, *The Just War in the Middle Ages* (Cambridge: Cambridge University Press, 1975); Roland H. Bainton, *Christian Attitudes Toward War and Peace* (New York: Abingdon, 1960); R. I. Moore,

given the Church an exegetical passage that became a canonical part of its legitimization of the use of violence against Christians resisting its determinations. In Luke 14.15–24, Jesus tells one of the parables of the Kingdom. A certain man invited people to a great supper. Having difficulty filling his hall, he sent servants "into the highways and hedges" and ordered them to "compel" people to come in so that his house would be full ("compelle intrare ut impleatur domus mea"). Augustine had believed that the use of the empire's force to drive people into the Catholic Church was incompatible with the Gospels. But he changed his mind in his struggle with the Donatists. So his *De Correctione Donatistarum* takes Jesus's parable of the kingdom and allegorizes it to legitimize the use of secular power against heretical Christians. What else could Jesus mean by "highways and hedges" than "heresies and schisms?" And since God had now given the Church access to the secular power of the Roman empire it seemed that this force must be the providential instrument for building "the body of Christ," the Church, "not only in the sacrament of the altar but also in the bond of peace."[67] These Augustinian cultural norms did not constrain all Wyclif's followers. Hawisia Mone, for example, maintained that Christian discipleship makes it "not leful to slee a man for ony cause, ne by processe of lawe to dampne ony traytour or ony man for ony treson or felonie to deth, ne to putte ony man to deth for ony cause, but every man shuld remitte all vengeance oonly to the sentence of God."[68] This was not Wyclif's view any more than it was that of Archbishop Courtenay or Archbishop Arundel.

De Officio Pastorali certainly does maintain that no one will come to heaven without being a disciple of Christ.[69] But we can now see how evangelical discipleship is restricted to the priesthood. Lay people can be occupied licitly with temporal goods and grand buildings that Christian discipleship forbids to priests.[70] In fact those powerful and armed Christians composing the lay elites are to manage the tiny minority of priests who must renounce civil dominion, wealth, and violence. The latter are to be put to use in maintaining the power of the armed ruling classes. Priests, Wyclif says, are the peace and tranquillity of the secular kingdom; their duty is to teach the inhabitants how to obey their superiors.[71] We could call this Wyclif's confirmation of the bureaucratization

The Formation of a Persecuting Society (Oxford: Blackwell, 1987); Peter McNiven, *Heresy and Politics in the Reign of Henry IV: The Burning of John Badby* (Woodbridge: Boydell, 1987). For a recent study of late medieval and early modern counter-currents, Ben Lowe, *Imagining Peace: A History of Early English Pacifist Ideas, 1340–1560* (University Park, PA: Pennsylvania State University Press, 1998).

[67] St. Augustine, *The Correction of the Donatists*, 6.24 in *Writings in Connection with the Donatist Controversy*, trans. J. R. King (Edinburgh: T. & T. Clark, 1872).

[68] I quote Hawisia Mone from *Norwich Heresy Trials*, 142. For similar views among other East Anglian Christians, see pp. 42, 53, 58, 61, 71, 86, 96, 148, 153, 158, 160, 166. On this issue, see Hudson, *Premature Reformation*, 367–70 and *EWS*, 4:159–60.

[69] *De Officio Pastorali*, II.4, 39; see also I.1, 7–8.

[70] *De Officio Pastorali*, II.5–6.

[71] *De Officio Pastorali*, II.7, 44: "docentes quomodo incole debent superioribus obedire."

of priestly believers. Since these priests are servants of Christ, Wyclif finds it obvious that they ought to be especially obedient to the king, to the dukes, and to other secular lords.[72] In fact the social group least committed to following evangelical precepts are to be in control of providing priests to the people.[73]

It is thus clear that far from dissolving the traditional divisions between laity and priests Wyclif maintains it as a fundamental component of both his ecclesiology and his politics. However much he transformed the orthodox office of priesthood he needed it as part of a basic binary structure. The division pervades his writing. It contributed to occluding one crucial question from his often radical interrogations of the history and practices of the Church to which he belonged: how could the gospel enacted in Christ's teaching and life need, indeed demand, secular power for its defense?[74] To have asked this question and stayed patiently with its consequences would have cut him off from his institutional, cultural, and patronage affiliations even more thoroughly than did his rejection of the current understanding of transubstantiation. Hawisia Mone did not have these particular affiliations to constrain her reflections on Christ's life.

I turn now to *De Officio Regis*. Wyclif offers this as a contribution to the practice of Christian religion ("religionis cristiane") that concentrates on the knightly order, the king's office, and the relations between regal and priestly power ("potestas") as Wyclif thinks they should be.[75] My focus is on the relations between the treatment of legitimate violence in *De Officio Regis* and the model of Christian discipleship from which we set out with Wyclif.[76] It is worth noting that he claims his stance on the power of kings and knights ("potestas regum et militum") is founded on holy Scripture, on the work of holy doctors and on the life of Christ (1).

De Officio Regis maintains a position reiterated both in the work itself and in

[72] *De Officio Pastorali*, II.7, 44. See Netter on this issue, cited in note 85.
[73] *De Officio Pastorali*, II.7, 44: the English version writes that kings are "to ordeyne" prelates "bi goddis lawe," chapter 30, 76.
[74] This division can be seen throughout *De Ecclesia* and *De Blasphemia*. In the former all dominion and jurisdiction that offers any resistance to the secular power are dissolved, while in the latter Wyclif stresses his will for a disendowed, poor Church and powerful lay elites (for example, *De Blasphemia*, 35–36, 55–57, 63–64). As so often we are told that the king is "the vicar of God." This move splits off Jesus's teaching on non-violence to "the vicar of Christ" (110).
[75] *De Officio Regis*, 1. References hereafter to pages in this text.
[76] The work I have found most helpful and reliable here has been done by Michael Wilks. Besides "Predestination, Property, and Power" (cited n. 21), see the following: "*Reformatio Regni*: Wyclif and Hus as Leaders of Religious Protest Movements," *Studies in Church History* 9 (1972): 109–30; "Royal Patronage and Anti-Papalism from Ockham to Wyclif," *Studies in Church History Subsidia* 5 (1987): 135–63; "Wyclif and the Great Persecution," in *Prophecy and Eschatology*, ed. Wilks (Oxford: Blackwell, 1994), 39–64. Also relevant here, Hudson, *Premature Reformation*, 367–70.

other writings by Wyclif: the king is the vicar of God, the image of Christ's deity (4–6, 13).[77] The Christian who governs is to deploy the kind of harsh, carnal violence over those classified as rebels that Wyclif associates with God in the Old Testament ("sicut fecit deitas in veteri testamento," 12–13). What about the specifically evangelical forms of life practiced and taught by Jesus? Once more Wyclif's answer is to restrict these to priests. It is they who are to model their lives on the "humanity" of Christ (for example, 13–14, 45–46). They, as the vicars of Christ, are to be ruled by the secular power as vicar of God. Here Wyclif analogizes the husband's headship over his wife in 1 Corinthians 11.3 (13–14), a chain of reflections that might later have pleased Chaucer's Walter, Richard II, or Henry VIII. Such secular power over priests and spiritual leaders in Christian communities is to be seen as *evangelical dominion* over them (69).

This brings us to the relations between the exercise of violence and Christian discipleship in *De Officio Regis*. Wyclif once again assumes that Christ's gospel needs defending with secular force. Despite his distinctive and much vaunted emphasis on Scripture *over* ecclesiastical traditions he apparently discerns no difficulty in asserting that the office of secular lords and kings is to defend evangelical law with secular power ("potestative").[78] He does not register the fact that Jesus did not merely overlook this alleged need but denied it on numerous occasions (for example Luke 6.27–36, Luke 22.50–51, John 18.10–11). The split we have been tracing enables him to proclaim that Christ's gospel must be defended by the accumulation of material resources in the hands of elites, by the deployment of a secular authority trained to be a dominant, armed class, and by the use of force which was intrinsic to secular dominion. That is, it enables him to proclaim that Christian discipleship must be sustained by practices *against* which Jesus called his disciples, practices negated by his gospel. Wyclif has not simply forgotten his own account of Jesus's life and teaching. The splitting in question allows him to block out any sense of the sharp contradictions between the evangelical texts he knows so well and his own gospel for lay Christians. Soon after this passage on the necessary use of secular power in defending "evangelical law," he turns to his campaign for the disendowment of clerics by the lay elites. On this occasion the reasons include the fact that temporal possessions weigh down souls, an invocation of Christ's parable of the rich man and Lazarus (Luke 16.19–31), and Christ's warning in Luke 18:24: "How hardly shall they that have riches enter into the kingdom of God" (85). He also quotes Luke 14.33: "everyone one of you that doth not renounce all that he possesseth cannot be my disciple" (86). These stark statements are as unqualified as Luke 6.24, "woe to you that are rich." They give no encouragement to those who would confine them to a tiny minority of

[77] See also, in *De Officio Pastorali*, 17, 54–55, 80, 121–22, 137, 148, 196–97, 241, 245. See also references in n. 76 to Wilks and Hudson.
[78] Wyclif's text is as follows: "officium dominorum temporalium et regum precipue est legem evangelicum potestative et ipsam in sua conversione diligencius observare" (78–79).

disciples. Wyclif's own dismissal of the orthodox distinction between counsels and precepts seemed to recognize this when he castigated his Church for imposing such concession to human traditions onto the Gospels.

But his own secular, class, and nationalist politics demanded that he restrict the scope of such texts quite as much as medieval orthodoxy had done. His own solution construed the gospel of Jesus as needing precisely what Jesus rejected, a result it would be euphemistic to call "paradoxical." This contradiction is given the illusion of coherence by the dichotomy between priests and laity preserved in his system, however incoherently. Thomas Netter argues that by deploying this binary structure in his system Wyclif actually denies discipleship of Christ to virtually all the faithful, but without grasping what he has done. In fact, Netter maintains, Wyclif would have most Christians live a life that, according to Wyclif's own account, is simply nothing to do with the religion of Christ.[79] My own concluding reflections will show why I think Netter's criticisms here are well justified. While Wyclif continues to pronounce that "every Christian should be subject to Christ's law," and that Christ's law entails the renunciation of secular dominion, violence and wealth, he simultaneously and, as we have seen, wholeheartedly advocates a form of life for the laity, especially the governing elites, that systematically negates "Christ's law."[80]

Class interests and nationalistic politics direct this theologian's Christian reformation like a giant's hand.[81] As *De Ecclesia* seeks to sweep away all traces of ecclesiastical independence in the face of secular powers, and as *De Officio Pastorali* brings the priesthood directly under the supervision of king and council, a model of nationalization under lay control, so *De Officio Regis* has the king's jurisdiction swallow up all forms of ecclesiastical jurisdiction and autonomy.[82] Even the surveillance of sin, the traditional domain of priestly confessors, bishops, and ecclesiastical courts, is moved into secular jurisdiction. Sin disturbs the kingdom's peace, disturbs peace with God, and so harms the kingdom: therefore it must come under the lay ruler's authority. Through his ministers (which include the clergy) he can castigate any kind of sin (119–20). Indeed, Wyclif insists that priests should not be ashamed to be called the king's priests ("Nec verecundamur vocari sacerdotes regum," 197), a statement whose evangelical source is not given. It is hardly surprising that secular lords are to deal with *heretics*. What the king's priests cannot deal with in their evangelical ministry, secular power is to discipline in its own way (120–21). Such discipline involved coercion and violence. But Wyclif had already conveyed his views here

[79] See *Doctrinale* IV.36, 942 and III.30.2–3, 802–805.
[80] The quotation here is from *De Officio Regis*, 94: "omnis Christianus subicitur legi Christi."
[81] Once again I refer to Wilks's work (n. 76).
[82] *De Ecclesia* is shaped and pervaded by this project; the sanctuary case, over which Wyclif addressed Parliament on behalf of the secular power, is a particular example of the commitment: chapters 7–12; see also chapter 1, chapters 15–16; *De Officio Pastorali*, II.7, 44 (see also the English version, chap. 30); *De Officio Regis*, chapters 4 and 6, especially 119–20.

141

in some interesting remarks about the early Christian martyrs. He says that had these troublesome people erred in their faith the rulers could licitly and meritoriously have annihilated them. The problem was that these rulers did not have good theologians to advise them. Wyclif draws the conclusion that theological science is necessary to the stability of a kingdom and so the king should have theologians helping him. He is absolutely unequivocal in his judgment that the king must remove heretics from his kingdom. No one in the later Middle Ages would be in doubt as to just what such "removal" meant (72).[83] Even excommunication in Wyclif's Christian reformation is to involve

[83] On the "removal" of heretics, see the classic statement by St. Thomas in *ST* II–II.11.3 and 11.4, *resp*. The works by Moore and McNiven in n. 66 are relevant here too. Wyclif adds that if the king is to uproot heretics "prudently" he needs guidance from theologians. But, of course, not theologians such as those who opposed him: only true theologians ("veri theologi"). These will know that it is not the Church that should determine what constitutes heresy; they will only judge heresy as that which is contrary to sacred Scripture, the law of God. As usual, Wyclif ignores the hermeneutic abyss here – unlike Thomas Netter. See Ghosh, "'Authority' and 'Interpretation' in Wycliffite, Anti-Wycliffite, and Related Texts" (cited in n. 9). This was not Wyclif's last word on heresy. For a later discussion see *De Blasphemia*, 72–77. In the Old Law he notes that the punishment for blasphemy was death inflicted by the whole people (Lev. 24.16, although the printed text mistakenly cites Lev. 14), a law appealed to in John 19.7. But in the New Law death for heresy should only be by divine miracle (this is how he interprets the story of Ananias and Saphira in Acts 5) and according to civil law (76). However, Wyclif then notes the relevance of Luke 9.52–57 where Jesus rebukes James and John for offering to burn up the Samaritans who would not receive Jesus and his disciples: "The Son of man came not to destroy souls, but to save." Wyclif sees Christ as deferring reckoning until the Last Judgment (Matt. 25.31–45). From the other New Testament texts Wyclif constructs a model of what would be an evangelical punishment of heresy (Matt. 18.17; 2 John 1.10; Titus 3.10; 2 Thess. 3.14): all communication with heretics should be avoided. Who is to judge a heretic? Wyclif determines that all members of the Church are competent to do this, but he does not specify in what sense he is taking "Church [ecclesie]" (77). As for clerical heretics, they too should be ostracized but their rations will be reduced to subsistence levels; Rom. 12.20 is cited (feed your enemy and in doing this you shall "heap coals of fire upon his head"). There is a different inflection here to the earlier treatment in *De Officio Regis*, one perhaps prompted by the change in Wyclif's own situation. For an extended discussion of heresy see *De Veritate Sacrae Scripturae*, ed. R. Buddensieg, 3 vols. (London: Wyclif Society, 1907), 274–310 (Thomson, 55–57, dates this as being composed between late 1377 and the end of 1378). Here the emphasis is on Scripture as the rule by which heresy is to be determined and on insisting that all deadly sin is heresy. It turns out, predictably, that most modern clergy are heretics, since they are simoniacs (299–301, 305, 309). Bishops and lay lords living against the teaching of scripture should be avoided (293). Wyclif invokes canon law on digging out heretics for punishment (304–305). He does so apparently without irony, even when he relates canon law pertaining to the treatment of lay lords who are unwilling to purge their lands of those identified as heretics by the bishop (306–307). Ultimately, in this tract, Wyclif maintains that all Christians ought to obey the bishop of souls, Jesus Christ, more than the modern episcopacy. Guided by Christ's apostle they will separate from a heretical hierarchy (he uses 1 Cor. 5.6 with 2 Cor. 6.15–17): "exite de medio eorum, et separamini ab eis, dicit dominus [Go out from among them, and be ye separate, saith the Lord]" (2 Cor. 6.17). He follows Paul's words with Christ's words in Matt. 18.15–17, quoted in support of this position (307). Given that most clergy

the secular power, in parliament (228–29). There is a grisly irony in Wyclif's confident invocation of the secular arm to deal with "heretics" and in his wish to strengthen its direct involvement in the proceedings. Netter's comments on this part of Wyclif's reformation are worth remembering. He observes that Wyclif and his followers called for secular lords' agency in matters of faith. But when a king well educated in the faith criminalized Wycliffism these heretics attack the ruler. Netter, however, calling himself the servant of King Henry V (thus fulfilling a part of Wyclif's wishes that clerics be not ashamed to be known as the king's priests), praises the monarch for frequently burning heretics. This, Netter claims, shows Henry to be a new Moses or a new Gideon. The sword of the word of God (deployed by Netter, the friar) now acts with the carnal sword of the lay power, in the cause of Christ and the Church.[84] Wyclif's response would have had to recapitulate his line on the killing of Christians under the Roman empire: right apparatus and correct role for secular power; wrong theological advice yielding up wrong victims. A fascinating convergence emerges here between the Catholic Church in Lancastrian England and the heretical reformation program of John Wyclif. The convergence is over the necessary role of the national secular power in "defending" Christianity, whether this is imagined as the defense of "Christ and the Church" or the defense of "Scripture and the law of God." Netter notices the passage in *De Officio Pastorali* discussed above, where Wyclif determines that the king should oversee priests whose task is to teach inhabitants to obey the king and their other superiors. With some derision he remarks that he who raged against "Caesarean bishops" has conjured up a Caesarean priesthood.[85] This is true. It is also true that Netter's orthodox celebration of the "defense" of "Christ and the Church" (in which king and parliament used the carnal sword against Wycliffites) converges with Wyclif's own reformation project. This convergence was of great theological, ecclesiological, and political significance: its occlusion by recent "revisionist" historians of the sixteenth

---

are bound up with simony, which is heresy, the faithful will communicate with very few clergy: only from these few will the faithful receive the sacraments (309). In this discussion Wyclif sets aside the issues of kingship, lay power, and ecclesiastic reform under the leadership of the ruling lay elite. How will the lay power supporting Wyclif in 1377–78 respond to the kind of separations from the English Church that Wyclif apparently envisages here? Time would tell. Wyclif also sets aside issues about the mediation of Scripture in a divided community. Who will determine whether Scripture is being interpreted and applied according to the Holy Spirit who wrote it when theologians (whether clerical or lay) are divided (281, 274)?

[84] Netter, *Doctrinale*, II.4.6 (vol. 1:485–86) and V. Pr. 1–2 (vol. 2: 3–4). For an anti-Wycliffite precursor to Netter here, see Roger Dymmok, *Liber contra duodecim errores et hereses Lollardorum*, ed. H. S. Cronin (London: Wyclif Society, 1922), presented to Richard II, and the chapter on Dymmok in Fiona Somerset, *Clerical Discourse and Lay Audience in Late Medieval England* (Cambridge: Cambridge University Press, 1998), 103–34.

[85] Netter, *Doctrinale*, II.63.2–3 (567–68).

century furthers neither our understanding of late medieval Catholicism nor of its complex metamorphoses in the English reformation.[86]

De Officio Regis closes with a consideration of violence in its last two chapters. Wyclif argued that secular lords are only entitled to fight in order to force people into concord and love after the failure of charity's bond (247–48). They are also entitled to pursue a form of war they still enjoyed, crusades – to honor Christ, to benefit the Church, and to profit those being attacked (248).[87] To these reasons for Christians to make war Wyclif adds that a ruler may do so to secure as much secular dominion as allows him to reign in conformity "with the law of Christ" (261). Given that for Wyclif "the law of Christ" is Scripture, one wonders where the evangelical doctor finds Jesus offering guidelines on the quantities of temporal dominion appropriately fought for by his disciples. (Contrast Luke 12.13–14 and Luke 22.24–26.) Has he simply decided to ignore texts we have seen him addressing elsewhere, texts that give none of Jesus's disciples warrant to kill?

Certainly not. Wyclif rehearses numerous texts showing that Christ is the king of peace who blesses peacemakers and who makes clear that violence is against his "school" (266–69). He recalls that Jesus bore his passion freely when he could have revenged himself on his enemies (John 18.36), and he writes that each Christian is bound to obey Matthew 5.39: "But I say to you not to resist evil: but if one strike thee on thy right cheek, turn to him also the other" (268). Here we again encounter what seems like a rejection of the conventional division between counsels and precepts. Wyclif appears to confirm this reading by quoting Luke 14.26 to bring home the demand that discipleship of Jesus be free from reservations (268). Does the Old Testament offer an escape route to Christians seeking to legitimize their punitive killings and their wars? Is Wyclif taking a line Calvin will pursue?[88] No, he explicitly rejects this. Old Testament wars have no authority for Christians because the teaching and life of Jesus had not yet been disclosed in the Incarnation (270; also 276). Followers of Christ now have no warrant to use violence in defense of their country or people, and Wyclif states that to resist violently does not seem appropriate for more mature disciples of Christ (273). In this context he acknowledges that it is certainly safer for Christians to cease from war even at the cost of losing earthly dominion (276). The conventional assumption that it is lawful to repel force with force, and so to

---

[86] For remarks on the issues here, see Aers, "Altars of Power," *Literature and History* 3 (1994): 90–102 and "Preface," *Journal of Medieval and Early Modern Studies* 27 (1997): 139–43.

[87] Wyclif does not address the problems raised by his ecclesiology: the only true Church is *invisible*, the Church of the predestinate whom no one can know. The *visible* Church is now treated as the church of Antichrist, the synagogue of Satan. So which Church is the beneficiary of these thoroughly carnal wars and who is the licit judge of this?

[88] For example, Calvin, *Institutes of the Christian Religion*, ed. John T. McNeill, 2 vols. (Philadelphia: Westminster Press, 1965), IV.20.10–12. Note that Wyclif rejects the use of the Old Testament to justify war-making by Christians in *De Civili Dominio*, ed. J. Loserth, vol. 2 (London: Wyclif Society, 1900), 247–50, 250–57. Thomson, "1375–late 1376," 48. For an illuminating discussion of war in the Old Testament, see James Barr, *Biblical Faith and Natural Theology* (Oxford: Clarendon Press, 1993), chap. 10.

make defensive war, is judged as one of Antichrist's deceptions (277).[89] Christians are to imitate the king of peace described in Matthew 12.18–21, one who eschews all contention (277). Christ alone is the Christian's teacher, Christ alone the Christian's hope and way to salvation (278–79). In this final sequence (266–80) it seems that Wyclif is heading for the kind of position illustrated in Hawisia Mone's abjuration, one in which Christian discipleship calls for a renunciation of judicial killing and war. That would undermine central arguments in *De Officio Regis*, as we have seen, arguments that form a substantial part of his vision of Christian reformation under the secular powers. But if he is to maintain his earlier vindication of carnal wars he seems obliged to contradict, explicitly, texts and narratives stemming from the Gospels, ones he has invoked against all war, including those waged in self-defense. How does he hope to resolve this conflict?

He apparently expects the reader to work through the evangelically shaped sequence with a reservation lodged earlier and reappearing within it: the ministry of priests is alien to the office of making war (248; see also 276–77). Will this reservation resolve the conflict? It seems not, for three reasons. First, neither the texts invoked by Wyclif nor his own commentary in this sequence suggest that the virtues of Christian disciples who are lay people are to be substantially different from those practiced by priests. Second, the Scriptural texts cited by Wyclif simply do not make the distinction between laity and clerisy. While this is no objection for an orthodox Catholic exegete, like Netter, it comprises a serious problem in terms of Wyclif's hermeneutics and ecclesiology. Third, the fact that priests are excluded from making war does not mean that *only* priests are so excluded. But if this reservation about the ministry of priests fails to resolve the conflict, does Wyclif now address the problem directly? He does not.

Instead he relies on two familiar strategies, assuming that they will restrict the force and scope of the evangelical materials he has introduced. The chief strategy involves splitting apart Christian discipleship between priesthood and laity. This was an orthodox commonplace for ploughing through obstacles built in the path of Christians' pursuit of secular dominion, violence, and war by the life and teaching of Jesus. However strenuously Wyclif opposed his Church, however much he abused it as Antichrist's instrument, this customary part of its practice and teaching informed his perceptions quite as thoroughly as it did those of most contemporaries. It was also congruent with the common sense of the cultures of those on whom Wyclif was relying to enact his reformation, the culture celebrated in the Chandos Herald's life of the Black Prince, the culture of the theologian's own protectors, John of Gaunt and Princess Joan, widow of the Black Prince.[90] Whatever the evangelical texts quoted by Wyclif might say, it

---

[89] Contrast the earlier acceptance of "vim vi repellere" as a motive for justifiable war, *De Civili Dominio*, vol. 2, 260. Here he maintains that it is licit for the laity to make war "corporaliter" in the circumstances he sketches: 240–44, 252–55, 260–62, 267. He is clear that heretics are justly killed, 271.

[90] Chandos Herald, *Life of the Black Prince* (cited in n. 27). On Gaunt, see Anthony Goodman, *John of Gaunt* (London: Longman, 1992), especially chap. 11.

seemed obvious that only a very few Christians need actually practice their teaching on non-violent love of enemies, on radical detachment from secular power and dominion. The division between "counsels" and "precepts" rejected by Wyclif is smuggled back into his models of Christian living. With this he saves a traditional "duality in ethics."[91]

The second strategy involves scapegoating priests. This deflects attention (his own, as well as his readers) from serious theological and ethical difficulties in his position. It also has the advantage of deflecting attention from the cultural norms of the Christian laity that seemed incompatible with Wyclif's own account of the forms of discipleship Jesus demanded. He asks his readers to consider, once more, how the latter, in all his life, was the poorest of men, the most humble and the most patient in all suffering. He then asserts that Christ freely understood this life so that *priests* would lead the laity to imitate it (280). By imposing this split, Wyclif makes priests responsible for the ways in which Christian communities set aside what he represents as the teaching of Christ. This move also obscures the contribution Wyclif's own splitting makes to the processes he laments, ones in which the account of Jesus in the Gospels is made largely irrelevant to the ethical and political practices of most Christians. Priests, being the essential mediators of divine teaching are the source of the most undivine realities of contemporary Europe. They are thus fitted to the role of scapegoat.[92] Discipline them; disendow them; expropriate them; subject them more completely to lay leaders. Then the golden age of the primitive Church will return (210–11). As he wrote in *De Ecclesia*, such disendowment would lead to the ending of wars among Christians.[93] However, the laity can still make war on

---

[91] The term is J. H. Yoder's in *The Priestly Kingdom: Social Ethics as Gospel* (Notre Dame: University of Notre Dame Press, 1984), 139. See too Wyclif's later treatment of the great texts on non-violence and love of enemy (Matt. 5.38–40) in his *Opus Evangelicum*, ed. J. Loserth, 2 vols. (London: Wyclif Society, 1895–96), I. Chaps. 52–62; here see chap. 52, 191–92; Thomson, "1383–end of 1384," 220. Wyclif notes that Christ's teaching decisively supersedes the law of retribution in Exod. 21.23–25, and laments the failure of modern Christians to follow Christ. He insists that they are mistaken in this decision. For they cannot licitly claim that Christ is only giving counsels that pertain to those pursuing perfection, ones that are not necessary for final beatitude. On the contrary, Wyclif maintains, the counsels of Christ are commands (191–92). But having made this clear rejection of the traditional split, he turns to attack the clergy (*clerici*) rather than *all* Christians who turn to violence (191–92). He claims that it is priests who should follow Christ most closely and that *they*, the ones who should follow Christ most closely, are most far from Christ's teaching (192). This seems a wild claim which allows him to turn away from the class whose form of life is *structurally committed* to *organized violence*, to tournaments, battles, wars, and the forceful extraction of rents and services to enable this. Wyclif himself is soon introducing qualifications to Jesus's teaching, hardly surprisingly in the contexts I outline (chap. 55, 201–204; chap. 56, 205–206; chap. 57, 210–12).

[92] On the scapegoat and Christian traditions, see R. Girard, *Things Hidden Since the Foundation of the World* (London: Athlone, 1987) and *The Scapegoat* (Baltimore: Johns Hopkins University Press, 1986). For an integration of Girard's work in a theology of sin, see James Alison, *The Joy of Being Wrong* (New York: Crossroads Herder, 1998).

[93] *De Ecclesia*, chap. 13, 290–91.

"infidels," and in fact their habitual modes of life require very little change. That is one of the advantages of a scapegoat: severe problems rooted in a community's forms of life and structures of feeling can be projected onto the scapegoat while nothing need change once the victim has been punished. So the scapegoat mechanism reinforces a splitting of Christian discipleship that, in effect, keeps the specific teachings of Jesus on violence, dominion, and competition marginal to the practices of Christians.

It also seems worth noting that Wyclif's planned abolition of the religious orders would further diminish the number of Christians committed to lives in communities where Jesus's renunciation of secular dominion, wealth, and bloodshed was, in principle, to be followed.[94] These were also communities committed, in principle, to imitating Jesus's way of forgiveness, a practice whose demands are as political as they are ethical and spiritual.[95] Did Wyclif have good reasons to be as sure as he was that his commitment to abolishing the religious orders, by the forces of armed secular power, was not action in the service of "the world" (John 15.8; John 17.9)? I think not.

There should be no doubt that Wyclif's reformation foreshadowed the future nationalization of Christianity under lay power. Michael Wilks, in a series of essays published over thirty years, has shown how Wyclif envisaged a "theocratic monarchy and a proprietary church" where "lay supremacy in ecclesiastical matters" was secured and where priests had become "royal tenants."[96] The sixteenth century English reformers were not mistaken to acknowledge him as anticipating some major elements in their own ecclesiastical politics.[97] And, as we have observed, Netter was right to argue, with understandable derision, that the scourge of the donation of Constantine and its "Caesarian bishops" had produced an agenda that would create an unprecedentedly "Caesarian" priesthood.[98] Wyclif should hardly have objected to this description since it accurately describes what he explicitly designed. But this chapter on Wyclif's understanding of Christian discipleship has brought out contradictions whose consequences would surely have appalled the reformer. For the way in which he dichotomized

---

[94] Because monasteries had in so many ways become integrated within the political and economic organization of secular power (as great landlords, users of serfs, servers of the lay lords who endowed them) this potential was thoroughly compromised. The same could be said of the modern, post-John XXII Franciscans in relation to St. Francis (as Langland, Wyclif, and many others proclaimed). Despite this, I have great sympathy with the observations in David Martin, *Reflections on Sociology and Theology* (Oxford: Clarendon Press, 1997), 160–61.

[95] See the illuminating study on forgiveness by L. Gregory Jones, *Embodying Forgiveness: A Theological Analysis* (Grand Rapids: Eerdmans, 1995).

[96] See the essays by Wilks cited in n. 21 and n. 76. Here I quote from, *seriatim*, "Predestination, Property, and Power," 235; "Wyclif and the Great Persecution," 59; and "Royal Patronage," 163.

[97] See Margaret Aston, *Lollards and Reformers* (London: Hambledon Press, 1984), chap. 8.

[98] See Netter, *Doctrinale*, II.63.2–3 (vol. 1:576–78); II.74 (643–66); II.46.6 (vol. 1:485–86). Although I do not recall Wilks citing Netter anywhere, their views coincide; they are both exceptionally good readers of Wyclif.

Christian discipleship, in the contexts of his ecclesiology and politics, outlines a *de-Christianization of the laity*, that is, of virtually all women and men. Christian discipleship is simultaneously essential to salvation and of marginal relevance to most Christians. Following the "humanity" of Christ, following Jesus's teachings on the renunciation of violence, wealth, competitive rivalry, and secular dominion, trying to cultivate the practice of forgiveness, a practice demanding the formation of communities that will teach and enable it, all this can be left to a strikingly diminished number of Christians.

These few are the priests, now abstracted from any community, or communities, devoted, in principle, to sustaining such practices. Yet the Gospels and Acts of the Apostles are the story of the foundation of "a new kind of community" that unfolds the meaning of Jesus's life and teaching, one that makes a social body within which discipleship becomes possible, discipleship of one who rejected the temptations of violence, rivalry, and secular power.[99] Wyclif's theology and ecclesiology had no vision of such a community nor of the need for one. And whatever uses the visible church had to king and Christian subjects, it was not the mystical body, the Body of Christ.[100] It seems that the contradictions in Wyclif's understanding of Christian discipleship were pursued in such a way and with such conviction that he could not see how he was *ratifying* the move in Constantinian orthodoxy "from Golgotha to the battlefield".[101] Wyclif could not see that he was substituting a new secular regime under expanded secular power for the new form of life proclaimed as the good news of the kingdom of God in the Gospels he revered, a kingdom without the violence of the sword or the dominion that was underpinned by the sword it wielded. The irony of his move into the contradictions addressed here was lost on Wyclif and most, though not all, of his followers.

[99] Here I allude to John Milbank, "The Name of Jesus," in *The Word Made Strange: Theology, Language, Culture* (Oxford: Blackwell, 1997), chap. 6. The quotation comes from p. 150, but the whole essay is relevant to my reflections here. So too, are these works by Stanley Hauerwas: *The Peaceable Kingdom: A Primer in Christian Ethics* (Notre Dame: University of Notre Dame Press, 1983), and *In Good Company* (Notre Dame: University of Notre Dame Press, 1995).

[100] On this, see especially, Leff, *Heresy*, 2:518 and Wilks, "Royal Patronage," 161. For Leff's account of Wyclif's version of Church, *Heresy in the Later Middle Ages*, 2:497, 501, 516–46. Also Malcolm Lambert, *Medieval Heresy*, 2nd edn. (Oxford: Blackwell, 1992), 230–34. Leff's survey of Wyclif's line on the Church shows how "the church as a visible body ceased to exist" (2:518); nevertheless, this statement underestimates the vestigial functions of the king's priests – in preaching, in exemplifying Christ's form of life, in fostering obedience to the increasing hegemony of royal power. See *De Ecclesia*, chapters 1–2, 17–19, 21, and *De Officio Regis*, 18–22, 42–46, 58–65, 221–30. Of interest is the sympathetic account of Wyclif's ecclesiology by Joan L. O'Donovan in "Natural Law and Perfect Community: Contributions of Christian Platonism to Political Theory," *Modern Theology* 14 (1998): 19–42, especially 32–39. In my view this essays's force is diminished by its failure to grasp the relevance of Wyclif's understanding of "Church," predestination, and hermeneutics to its concerns.

[101] Yoder, *Priestly Kingdom*, 145.

Index